12 60

G. W. CHOUDHURY served in the Government of Pakistan from 1967 to 1971, including an assignment as a member of the cabinet of President Yahya Khan. During this time, and while serving under President Ayub Khan, he had free access to classified documents and records, close contacts with key leaders in Pakistan, and frequent associations with leaders of the United States, the Soviet Union, and China. He accompanied Ayub Khan to the Soviet Union and Yahya Khan to China, and was also a member of the Pakistan delegation to the United Nations on several occasions. He is currently a Professor of Political Science and Director of the Center for International Studies at North Carolina Central University, and an Adjunct Professor of Political Science at Duke University.

INDIA, PAKISTAN,

BANGLADESH, AND

THE MAJOR POWERS

This volume is part of the Institute Book Series of the Foreign Policy Research Institute, Philadelphia, Pennsylvania. The series is devoted to the publication of studies in international relations, including original scholarly research, policy analyses, and pioneering methodologies developed for application in this field. The Foreign Policy Research Institute is a nonprofit, publicly supported, tax exempt corporation. It is engaged in research on U.S. foreign policy and international trends and seeks through publications, fellowships and conferences to foster the exchange of ideas aimed at promoting a stable international order.

India, Pakistan, Bangladesh, and the Major Powers

Politics of a Divided Subcontinent

G. W. Choudhury

THE FREE PRESS
A Division of Macmillan Publishing Co., Inc.
NEW YORK

Collier Macmillan Publishers
LONDON

To my wife
Dilara
who endured me patiently and
encouraged me greatly in my
work

The Free Press
A Division of Macmillan Publishing Co., Inc.
866 Third Avenue, New York, N.Y. 10022

Collier Macmillan Canada, Ltd.

Library of Congress Catalog Card Number: 74–34553

Printed in the United States of America

printing number

1 2 3 4 5 6 7 8 9 10

Library of Congress Cataloging in Publication Data

Choudhury, Golam Wahed.
   India, Pakistan, Bangladesh, and the major powers.

   Bibliography: p.
   Includes index.
   1. South Asia--Foreign relations. I. Title.
DS341.C48   327.54   74-34553
ISBN 0-02-905390-0

CONTENTS

FOREWORD

FOR SEVERAL CENTURIES South Asia has been vulnerable to, and greatly affected by, external influences and pressures. Since the independence of the major countries of the region it has been an arena of clashing interests and economic, political, and diplomatic competition, but not of direct large-scale military confrontation, of the superpowers and China, with the dominant external power of the past, Britain, playing an important but declining role. Many Western and some South Asian scholars have contended that on the whole the contributions of external powers to the subcontinent have been more constructive than destructive, but the prevalent judgment in South Asia is a more negative one, and suspicion of great powers—all great powers—is still persistent and strong, with varying degrees of intensity at different times and under different circumstances.

Prevailing attitudes in Pakistan toward China, and in India and Bangladesh toward the Soviet Union, are more positive than negative; but even here underlying suspicions remain, and prevalent attitudes can and often do change markedly. South Asian attitudes toward the United States vary greatly. At present they seem to be quite ambivalent, although U.S. relations with all the countries of the region are officially good if not really close.

For all the countries of South Asia, large and small, relations with the United States, the Soviet Union, and China are extensive and of great significance, as well as often unsatisfactory and worrisome. For the major powers relations with the South Asian countries are of lesser significance, viewed in the light of their overall national interests and international concerns; but these relations are really of greater importance than most citizens of the major powers, and many of their leaders, seem to realize.

The role of the major powers in South Asia has been discussed in a number of books and articles, but few if any of the previous studies are as informative and as insightful as the present work. Professor G. W. Choudhury has unique qualifications for undertaking this kind of study. He is a well-known and highly productive South Asian scholar. He served in important positions in the government of Pakistan from 1967 to 1971, including an assignment as Communications Minister in the Cabinet of President Yahya Kahn. He had close contacts with key leaders in Pakistan and frequent associations with leaders of the United States, the Soviet Union, and China. He accompanied Ayub Khan to the Soviet Union and Yahya Khan to China. He had access to important classified documents and records. Since February 1971 he has been associated with such major research centers as the Royal Institute of International Affairs and the Institute for Commonwealth Studies in London, the Southern Asian Institute and the Research Institute on Communist Affairs at Columbia University, and the Foreign Policy Research Institute in Philadelphia. He has been devoting most of his time to research and writing on recent developments in South Asia and the role of the major powers in the region. He has, in short, been a close observer, a concerned participant, and an academic student of the traumatic events in the Indian subcontinent in the postwar period, culminating in the tragic events of 1971 and their troubled aftermath. Although occasionally his understandable biases show through, he has been able to preserve a remarkable degree of objectivity and balance in appraising a changing and troubled scene that he observed carefully at first hand, sometimes at great cost to himself and those closest to him, with special regard to the causes that he championed with great dedication, ability, and integrity.

This book may be recommended both to readers not too familiar with the subject and to those who have special knowledge of South Asia and of great power policies and activities in the region. It tells the overall story clearly and well, with a rich fare of detailed narration and interpretative analysis. Perhaps its main value, however, lies in the remarkable insights that it provides into behind-the-scenes negotiations and events. Some of the most revealing insights relate to such major themes as the Sino–Indian border war of 1962 and its implications and aftermath, the evolution of the special relationship between Pakistan and China after 1960, and the policies of the major powers during the Indo–Pakistani wars of 1965 and 1971 (including the differences in the position and policies of China during these two crises). Others relate to such specialized and rather murky subjects as Brezhnev's scheme for a collective security system in Asia, the Tashkent Conference of January 1966, and Yahya Khan's "courier role" between Washington and Peking.

Not all of Professor Choudhury's readers will agree with all his interpretations or be wholly satisfied with the evidence that he presents in support of some of his more controversial views; but all will be informed and stimulated by this major contribution to the study of South Asian developments and international affairs.

NORMAN D. PALMER

PREFACE

In 1967 I was asked by the President of Pakistan, Mohammed Ayub Khan, to head the Research Division of the Ministry of Foreign Affairs. In October 1969 I joined the Pakistani Federal Cabinet under President Yahya Khan. I was privileged to visit the U.S.S.R. and China with Presidents Ayub and Yahya Khan on official state visits, and I was also a member of the Pakistan delegation to the United Nations on several occasions. In these capacities I was uniquely situated to study Pakistan's external relations, particularly its relations with the major powers—the U.S.S.R., the United States, and the People's Republic of China.

In the preparation of this book, even more important than my positions with the government of Pakistan was my free access to official documents and data. I have tapped original sources on Pakistani leaders' dialogues and dealings with Kremlin leaders such as Leonid Brezhnev, General Secretary of the Communist Party, and Chairman of the Council of Ministers Aleksei Kosygin; with top American policy makers including Presidents John F. Kennedy, Lyndon B. Johnson, and Richard M. Nixon; and with Chairman Mao Tse-tung, Premier Chou En-lai, and other Chinese leaders. These exchanges, in which I sometimes took part, not only reflect upon Pakistan's bilateral relations with the U.S.S.R., the United States, and China but also indicate the three major powers' roles in, and perceptions of, international politics and the Indian subcontinent.

I left the Cabinet in February 1971 to join the Royal Institute of International Affairs in London as a visiting fellow, and I paid two visits to Pakistan (including what is now Bangladesh) during the civil war to continue my research. Recently I was invited by Professor Zbigniew Brzezinski to join the Research Institute on Communist Affairs at Columbia University as a fellow, and the Foreign Policy Research Institute in Philadelphia awarded me a generous grant for the continuation of my research.

I thank former Pakistani Presidents Ayub Khan and Yahya Khan, who not only permitted access to official documents and papers but also granted lengthy personal interviews.

In the academic world, I am most thankful to Professor Norman D. Palmer for his valuable comments and excellent suggestions after he made a careful and thorough study of the manuscript. Dr. Peter Lyon's reading of, and comments on, the manuscript were also quite helpful. My sincere thanks go to Dr. Robert L. Pfaltzgraff, Jr., Director of the Foreign Policy Research Institute, for his continued encouragement and interest and for his acceptance of this book for publication under the auspices of the Foreign Policy Research Institute. I also wish to thank Mr. Todd Collins, Staff Editor at the Foreign Policy Research Institute, for his excellent editing of my manuscript.

Some parts of my research have already been published in the form of articles in *World Today* (the journal of the Royal Institute of International Affairs), *Orbis* (the journal of the Foreign Policy Research Institute), *Pacific Community* (Tokyo), and *The Year Book of World Affairs, 1973* (London). More articles are expected to be published soon in other professional journals.

I hope my work on this subject will stimulate further studies on a region whose complicated tensions have produced three wars in the last twenty-five years and have indirectly involved and been affected by the great powers. The tragic events of 1971, culminating in the sad dismemberment of Pakistan and the emergence of a new but perhaps fatally unstable state in the subcontinent, have introduced new complications. The Sino–Soviet conflicts as well as the current era of détente diplomacy add to uncertainty. And the crucial question remains: what are the prospects for peace and stability in a subcontinent of more than 700 million people? I sincerely hope that my work will help to answer this question and contribute to understanding of what my friend Peter Lyon has called "a still very confusing and little understood subject."

G. W. Choudhury

Center for International Studies
North Carolina Central University
January 1975

INTRODUCTION

THIS WORK discusses the policies toward the South Asian subcontinent of the Soviet Union and the United States, the superpowers, and those of China, the emerging superpower. I examine the extent to which the policies and actions of the external powers under consideration have heightened or lessened regional tensions. This book deals with the question of whether the major powers, to further their national or global interests, have taken advantage of Indo–Pakistani conflict; similarly, it presents an analysis of how India and Pakistan have sought to take advantage of world tensions—the tensions of the two-sided Cold War as well as those of the emerging period of tripolarity—to advance their interests, both military and economic. The political shape of the subcontinent is determined by global trends, by regional trends, and by the way the one set of trends works upon the other; I discuss these trends and their interrelations in depth.

India–Pakistan–Bangladesh has been a relatively unimportant area to the world powers; it has not yet threatened direct confrontation among them. The subcontinent has been, however, an area of active diplomatic competition among the Soviet Union, the United States, and China. The Soviets, who have invested billions of dollars in the development of India and millions in the development of Pakistan, have been outspent by the Americans, and the Chinese have begun in recent years modest but strategically important assistance to Pakistan. In addition to heavy economic assistance, vast quantities of military supplies have flowed into the subcontinent. Pakistan received American military aid worth more than $1 billion from 1954 to 1965, and since 1965 China's contribution to Pakistan's armed forces has been substantial. India has received more Soviet

1

military aid than any other nation in South Asia. The arms race between India and Pakistan has helped lead to the three Indo–Pakistani wars (in 1948, 1965, and 1971) and to the major border war between India and China in 1962.

The area therefore is unstable, and the U.S.S.R., the United States, and China are at least partially responsible for this; the major powers have been unable to avoid indirect involvement in the regional conflicts. What is more, tensions exacerbated through the dealings of international (external) actors affect international politics in turn. Thus the roles of the three major powers in the subcontinent and the Indian and Pakistani perceptions of world politics are important even though the area is not of special importance to the security of either the United States or the U.S.S.R. China, of course, is the central strategic factor in the area; both India and Pakistan neighbor China, and Bangladesh is located in an area that China perceives as its natural cultural domain, an area in which it will eventually play a dominating role.

This work is divided into four parts. Part I deals with the Soviet policy and role in the subcontinent. How did the Soviet Union react to the success of the bourgeois national movements in India and Pakistan? What was the Kremlin's attitude toward India and Pakistan when they obtained independence in 1947? What factors led the Soviet Union to modify its policies in the mid-1950s? To what degree was the Soviet policy influenced by U.S. involvement in the subcontinent during the same era? What led the Soviet Union to play the peacemaker's role at the Tashkent Conference in 1966? What was the background of the Soviet support for Bangladesh? Answers to these and other questions are sought.

In Part II, a similar analysis is made of the U.S. policy and role. The United States, in contrast to the U.S.S.R., greeted the two new nations of South Asia in 1947, and later the Eisenhower–Dulles era propelled the United States—to considerable effect in New Delhi and Moscow—into a major commitment to Pakistan, smaller and less stable than India. What led Pakistan and the United States into alliance? Were Pakistani and American aims similar or divergent? How did alliance prove diplomatically unsuccessful, and what patterns of alignment developed in the subcontinent once strains began to appear in the U.S.–Pakistani special relationship in the early 1960s? And how did President Nixon's China policy in 1969 restore cordial relations between the United States and Pakistan and complicate the Americans' role during the Bangladesh crisis?

In Part III, I study China and the subcontinent, reviewing different phases of Sino–Indian relations: the period of romantic belief in the myth of a "thousand years of Sino–Indian friendship," the ensuing era of *panch sheel,* and, finally, the era of confrontation. The most spectacular recent diplomatic event in the area has been the growth of friendship between Pakistan—long "America's most allied ally in Asia," as the American press called it during the mid-1950s, and long a devoutly Islamic member of SEATO and CENTO —and the People's Republic of China, the most doctrinaire and revolutionary communist country. What is the basis of the Pakistani–Chinese ties? What linking role has Pakistan played between the United States and China?

In Part IV, I analyze the roles of the major participants in the Bangladesh crisis and offer some observations on patterns emerging in the South Asian Triangle. I conclude that the great changes of 1971–1972 are unlikely to bring peace and stability to the subcontinent. India has emerged stronger and more dominant, and Indo–Pakistani amity is no nearer; Pakistan is frustrated and bitter after national humiliation and dismemberment; Bangladesh might still fall into chaos and confusion. The United States is likely to maintain a low profile, but the two communist giants will sustain their diplomatic competition in the area. The area remains prone to internal instability, regional tensions, and external pressures.

Part One

The Soviet Union and the Subcontinent

Chapter One

EARLY POLICY, 1947–1960

THE DOCTRINAL BARRIER
TO CORDIAL RELATIONS

WHEN THE BRITISH RAJ in India was voluntarily dissolved on August 15, 1947, and the sovereign states of India and Pakistan emerged, the Kremlin leaders, unlike their czarist predecessors, hardly glanced toward the subcontinent. Stalin and his ruling elite were preoccupied with East European and Far Eastern affairs. Moreover, they harbored prejudice and misunderstanding about the great events during the liquidation of the British Empire in India. They dismissed the whole process of the peaceful transfer of power as a set of new imperialist devices to retain British political, economic, and strategic influence in South Asia; their dogmatic interpretation of major political events, in strict accord with Marxist–Leninist theory, blinded them to political realities and dynamics in Asia.

Through the early postwar period, the two major potential catalysts to revolutionary upheaval in Asia were agrarian discontent and, more important, demands for national independence from foreign rule. At the second meeting of the Communist International in June 1920, Lenin recommended close alliance of all national liberation movements with the Soviet Union and suggested that the nature of alliance should be determined by the level of development in each country.[1] Subsequently Stalin amplified Lenin's theory. Stalin contended that the national bourgeoisie in colonial countries would split into the revolutionary group and the compromising group. In a colonial country such as India where capitalism was

7

already more or less developed, the compromising bourgeoisie, according to Stalin, had come to an agreement with imperialist powers.[2] Thus, though not deeply involved in South Asia at the time of Indian independence, the Soviet Union, alone among the great powers, had a comprehensive theory to back up its policy toward the new countries of Asia.

During the era of Stalin the whole approach to India's struggle for freedom and the Muslim demand for a separate state based on religion—and to the two new nations that resulted—was one of utmost skepticism and prejudice. The Soviets, leaning hard on their Marxist–Leninist–Stalinist doctrine, took hardly any note of the great appeal of nationalism in both India and Pakistan; they distorted the dignified response of the British authorities to the legitimate aspirations of the people of the subcontinent. The Soviet press maligned the new governments and their leaders, including Mahatma Gandhi, Jawaharlal Nehru, and Mohammed Ali Jinnah. Nehru's government was described as "an Indian variant of bourgeois pseudo-democracy."[3] Nehru was described as the "Chiang Kai-shek of India"[4] and as a "running dog of imperialism."[5] Gandhi was treated with scarcely more gentleness. According to the Soviets, the reactionary, bourgeois landlords who came to power in India in 1947 exploited Gandhism, a "reactionary political doctrine"; the Indian authorities were alleged to have adopted a policy of terror on the widest scale against the masses fighting for national independence and social liberation.[6]

The harsh Soviet analysis of both the Indian National Congress movement and the Muslim nationalist movement provided the background for the indifferent, even hostile attitude to the two new South Asian states. The Soviet leaders were not inclined to embrace two new sovereignties in which the great political changes had not been brought about by a revolutionary proletariat or an armed peasantry. Despite the sanguine declaration of the Sixth Congress of the Comintern in 1928—"the vast colonial and semi-colonial world has become an unquenchable, blazing hearth of the revolutionary mass movement"[7]—the liquidation of the British raj in India was carried out peacefully; independence came as a result of agreement between the imperial power and those whom Marxist–Leninists labeled "the national bourgeoisie."[8] A Soviet specialist on Oriental affairs, E. Zhukov, claimed in *Izvestia* that the Indian leadership had capitulated to imperialism because the big industrialists feared the masses more than they feared the British.[9] A strong Soviet delegation attended the unofficial Asian Relations Conference in

India in February 1947—Nehru's first attempt to form a third, or Asian, bloc—and the Soviet skepticism persisted. Zhukov's report on the conference praised Egypt, Indonesia, Indochina, and Burma but severely attacked Nehru for his alleged pro-British sentiments.[10]

On Pakistan, Soviet comments were even more hostile. The Pakistani government was described as antipopular, tied up with the imperialists, dominated by feudal elements, and more reactionary than India's government. The Muslim League, Moscow charged, colluded with the British authorities to disrupt and thwart the struggle of the people for liberation. If India was villified during the era of Stalin, Pakistan was damned as "lost" to the "imperialist powers." (However, as we shall see, the Soviet Union made some overtures to Pakistan in 1949–1950 in its efforts to win Pakistan away from the "clutches" of the "imperialist powers.") Reactionary and suspect in Soviet eyes were the Muslim nationalist movement in India, the creation of Pakistan, and the Pakistani government's leaders and policies. The Soviets particularly scorned Pakistan's concept of "Islamic socialism" and "the Islamic state" as well as its calls for the creation of an "Islamic bloc" comprising the Muslim countries of the Middle East.[11]

EARLY DIPLOMATIC RELATIONS

The U.S.S.R. and India established diplomatic relations in April 1947, four months before Independence, and Pandit Nehru appointed as Ambassador his sister, Madame Vijayalakshmi Pandit. Earlier, prior to Independence, Nehru had noted in his first declaration as Minister of External Affairs of the interim government that the Soviet Union was a neighbor with whom "we shall have to undertake many common tasks and have much to do. . . ."[12] The U.S.S.R. exchanged ambassadors with Pakistan in 1950 and, although it opposed Ceylonese membership, did not object to Pakistan's entry into the United Nations. (Only Afghanistan voted against Pakistani membership.) Relations with what had made up the British raj were thus established, but they were minimal, cool, even indifferent. It is indicative that Stalin did not receive Madame Pandit until her farewell call.

Propaganda assaults from Soviet authors and media continued, and both India and Pakistan reacted with restraint and diplomatic reserve. Neither country wished to offend the Kremlin leaders. In fact, the image of the Soviet Union stood quite high in India. Nehru had great admiration for social welfare and economic development in the U.S.S.R., and in the 1920s and 1930s he had looked favorably upon revolution and the Marxian analysis of capitalism, imperialism, and war. Recognizing the harsher aspects of life in the Soviet Union, Nehru desired for independent India not a totalitarian but a liberal and democratic society; as he wrote in his autobiography, "I am very far from being a communist."[13] Yet, although he tried to maintain a position of neutrality in speeches and statements, the Prime Minister's general approach to the socialist countries was more understanding and sympathetic than his general approach to Western countries; the colonial period had anchored in his mind doubts about the West.

Although whenever it felt dissatisfaction with the Western powers' policy on India, Pakistan tended inevitably to counter by looking toward Moscow, the considerable enthusiasm for Islamic ideology in Pakistan precluded widespread admiration for the Soviet Union. And the making of Pakistan's foreign policy in the early days was in the hands of a small elite—Foreign Minister Sir Mohammed Zafrullah Khan, Foreign Secretary Sir Mohammed Ikramullah, Defense Secretary General Iskander Mirza, and a few others—who were thoroughly pro-Western; for them any admiration for, or closer link with, communist Russia was unthinkable.

Both India and Pakistan strongly supported the causes of people under Western colonial rule. In their anticolonialism both countries found themselves much closer to the Soviet Union, inside and outside the United Nations, than on other issues. The Soviet Union was regarded by newly independent countries of Asia as a great champion of the people struggling for freedom from Western colonialists. These countries overlooked the fact that the "imperialism which rules the largest [number] of Moslems in the world is the Soviet imperialism." As one commentator put it, the Islamic peoples of Central Asia and the Caucasus endure incredible "political terror, economic exploitation and cultural oppression."[14]

MOSCOW FROWNS ON NEHRU'S NONALIGNMENT

During the 1947–1953 period, both India and Pakistan followed a policy of noninvolvement. Pakistani policy, which gave way to a less neutral stance in the mid-1950s, was admittedly more a matter of *realpolitik* than of philosophy, but India under Nehru tried hard to convince the world of the lofty ideals behind its policy.[15] Nehru was regarded by friendly observers as the great Asian leader who gave a new philosophy and meaning to the foreign policies of the young countries, which were bewildered and alarmed by the growing tensions between the United States and the Soviet Union.[16]

Stalin and the Kremlin leaders, however, frowned on Nehru's policy of nonalignment. For the U.S.S.R. this was a period of ideological intransigence, of revolutionary militancy, of "the world of two camps." The Soviet Union sharply defined the battle lines, automatically excluding all middle-of-the-roaders.[17] The idea of a "third force," of nations free of both power blocs, was unambiguously castigated by the Soviets: Zhukov characterized nonalignment as an "imperialist device, the purpose of which was to slander the U.S.S.R. by placing it on the same level with American imperialism"; he added that the theory of the third bloc had special success and appeal among the "Indian bourgeoisie."[18] *New Times* (Moscow) wrote, "The 'third camp' is in fact nothing other than the aggressive Pacific pact which the American imperialists have so long been trying to engineer and which the British Labour leaders support."[19] When India organized a conference of Asian and Far Eastern countries to mobilize support for the Indonesian struggle for freedom, *Pravda*'s comment was critical.[20] Nehru's first trip to the United States in 1949 at the invitation of President Truman, as well as some of his speeches in North America, brought more harsh comments from the Soviet press; he was virtually dubbed an American stooge.[21]

THE KREMLIN'S UNEXPECTED OVERTURE TO PAKISTAN

Nehru's invitation to the United States prompted an unexpected and spectacular development in Soviet–Pakistani relations.

The Soviet Union had noted carefully Pakistani resentment over the Western countries' wooing of Nehru—the perennial tensions and conflicts between India and Pakistan had been (and continue to be) such that if any country or bloc made a friendly gesture to the one, the other became suspicious if not hostile. On the whole, as Geoffrey Hudson pointed out in 1955, "the Soviet Union appears to have perceived more clearly than the British or the Americans have done that antipathy to Pakistan is the pivot of India's foreign policy."[22] The Soviets have also recognized the pivot of Pakistani policy. When Pakistan felt frustrated over Truman's invitation to Nehru and over the special provision to keep India in the Commonwealth even as a "republic," the Soviet government, in spite of its consistently unfriendly attitude, asked Pakistan's first Prime Minister, Liaquat Ali Khan, to visit the Soviet Union. The news of the Soviet invitation, a countermeasure to Truman's invitation to Nehru, surprised Pakistan as much as the rest of the world. Pakistan had not yet exchanged ambassadors with the Soviet Union.

What led to this development?[23]

On May 15, 1949, while Liaquat was on a visit to Tehran, the Soviet chargé d'affaires there inquired of Mrs. Khan at a dinner party if she and her husband would visit the U.S.S.R.; she replied that they would be receptive to an invitation. Subsequently, on June 2, the Soviet chargé conveyed verbally through Pakistan's Ambassador in Tehran an official invitation to Liaquat and his wife to visit Moscow. Liaquat accepted on June 7.

The Prime Minister was hailed for his acceptance by two senior political advisers, Ambassadors Raja Ghazanfar Ali Khan in Tehran and M. A. H. Isphani in Washington. Isphani wrote Liaquat on September 7, 1949:

> Your acceptance of the invitation to visit Moscow was a masterpiece in strategy. . . . Until a few months ago, we were unable to obtain anything except a few sweet words from middling State Department officials. We were taken much for granted as good boys: boys who would not play ball with communism or flirt with the left; boys who would starve and die rather than even talk to communists; . . . we were treated as a country that did not seriously matter. On the other hand, the US Government paid much attention to India. It was out to appease and pamper India. . . . [With the Liaquat acceptance] overnight Pakistan began to receive the serious notice and consideration of the US Government. . . . Every effort [is] being made to rid us of the feeling that US is being partial to India. . . . Effort is now being made to rid us of our suspicions and to impress on us that we shall be accorded just treatment and the attention we deserve.

Isphani's letter reflected the mood of the group headed by the Prime Minister, who wished to use the Russian gesture to enhance

Pakistan's importance—one of the basic objectives of Pakistani foreign policy has always been to attain parity with India in politics and diplomacy if not in military might. Indeed, the public in Pakistan welcomed the Soviet invitation as a way to balance the setback of Nehru's invitation from Truman.

Some, however, were not so enthusiastic. Foreign Minister Zafrullah made the announcement of the invitation, but he added that though the Soviet Union and Pakistan had agreed to exchange diplomatic representatives, the exchange could not be achieved immediately. A "shortage of housing in Karachi" was the problem, he said. This flimsy explanation for the delay in the exchange of ambassadors betrayed the negative attitude of the Foreign Minister toward Liaquat's proposed trip in particular and toward the warming of Soviet–Pakistani relations in general. Zafrullah reflected the views of the powerful clique—which included Finance Minister Ghulam Mohammed, who subsequently became the Governor-General of Pakistan, Foreign Secretary Ikramullah, and some other senior bureaucrats—that was accustomed to making decisions on external relations. Apprehensive about the Kremlin's intentions and motives, this group sought to sabotage any move toward Moscow. Its members regretted that the partition of India had exposed Pakistan to Soviet attention, and they discerned clear links between present policy and the traditional Russian interest "in the general direction of the Persian Gulf."[24] Moreover, they argued, Pakistan was in dire need of both economic and military assistance, neither of which could be expected from the Soviet Union at that time.

To back up their arguments against the Prime Minister's trip, Zafrullah's group sought influential foreign support. The British government was contacted, and it responded with subtle pressure on Pakistan. On September 28, 1949, the Pakistani High Commissioner in London, Habib Rahimtulla, wrote to Liaquat that Lord Addison, the Undersecretary of State for Commonwealth Affairs, had given him a long list of things that Britain had done for Pakistan and had asked if Pakistan harbored any grievances against the British. This seemed to indicate that Britain looked upon Pakistani moves toward Moscow as a loosening of ties with London. Another indication of British displeasure was the October 27, 1949, letter of the British High Commissioner in Pakistan to Liaquat relaying the concern of the British Ambassador in Moscow that, in the event of a Liaquat visit, "he [the Ambassador] may be prevented from showing the Prime Minister the courtesy which he [the Prime Minister] deserves." (At that time, the British Ambassador was representing Pakistan in Moscow.)

Tehran Ambassador Ghazanfar claimed that he himself had greatly improved relations with the Soviet Union: "The same Russians who did not attend our Independence Day celebrations last year [1948] and did not offer condolence on the death of the Quaid-i-Azam [M. A. Jinnah] are now *eating out of our hands*." Zafrullah replied that "eating out of his [Ghazanfar's] hand would have to be taken with a pinch of salt; I would be careful if I were the Ambassador"; similarly, Ikramullah advised Ghazanfar, "If I were you, I would be extremely careful in dealing with the Russians." Ghazanfar retorted, "While fear of Russia is as yet a mere bogey, there are others [the Western powers] who have let us down so often."

The tussle between the two groups frustrated Liaquat's visit to the Soviet Union. At the Soviet Union's suggestion the date of the visit was first postponed from August 20 to November 7, 1949. Russia wanted the exchange of ambassadors before Liaquat's visit; Zafrullah did not consider this essential, but the Soviets were firm. By the time Pakistan finally appointed her first Ambassador to Moscow, the Soviets were starting to show coolness—they approved the Pakistani Ambassador's appointment, but they gave no indication regarding the appointment of their own envoy. By the middle of November Liaquat's visit to Moscow was becoming more and more unlikely.

In the meantime, President Truman and Liaquat agreed upon a May 1950 trip to the United States, and the Soviets' chargé d'affaires in Tehran, in discussion with Ghazanfar, expressed regret that the Moscow visit would not come up earlier. Thus, in April 1950, the visit was postponed indefinitely. Able and seasoned diplomats, the Soviets realized that a powerful group inside Pakistan was not interested in developing closer links with Moscow.

In this manner a great opportunity to cultivate better relations between Pakistan and the Soviet Union was lost. Now the Soviet attitude toward Pakistan, never friendly, began to turn harsh, and it was not until the mid-1960s that the two nations exchanged visits by heads of state or government. When Ayub Khan journeyed to the U.S.S.R. for his first state visit in April 1965, Soviet Premier Kosygin's greeting was apt: "At last the head of the Pakistan government could land in Moscow!"

INDIA TURNS LEFT; PAKISTAN TURNS RIGHT

By 1950–1951, India's policy of nonalignment, previously West-ern-oriented, began to favor the Soviet Union. India played its first major role in international affairs during the Korean War. India, like Pakistan and most other United Nations members, supported the initial resolution of the Security Council condemning the attack by North Korea as "a breach of peace" and calling for the immedi-ate cessation of hostilities and withdrawal of North Korean forces to the 38th parallel. In a press conference on July 7, 1950, Nehru denounced North Korean aggression. At the same time, however, the Indian leader argued:

> Admission of the People's Republic in the Security Council and the return of the USSR are necessary conditions to enable the Se-curity Council to discharge its functions adequately and to bring the Korean conflict to a prompt and peaceful conclusion.

Nehru pursued this theme in his letters of July 13 to Stalin[25] and Dean Acheson, the American Secretary of State. Stalin welcomed Nehru's "peaceful initiative," and, in response, favorable comments flowed from the Indian Parliament and press; Acheson replied that the question of China's seat at the UN should be considered apart from that of the North Korean aggression, and this exacerbated the already negative attitude toward America.[26] Subsequently India supported in the UN Security Council and General Assembly the Soviet–Chinese positions on the Korean crisis. Nehru's statements and speeches also indicated that India agreed more with the Soviet Union than with the United States on the Korean War.[27] India's policy was greatly influenced by the Indian Ambassador in Peking, K. M. Panikkar, who had close contact with Mao and the other Chinese leaders.[28]

The Japanese Peace Treaty sparked the second major interna-tional controversy on which the Indians sided with the Soviet bloc. India, like the Soviet Union, was firm in its opposition to the treaty. Despite the attendance of Pakistan and Ceylon, India did not par-ticipate in the treaty-signing conference, which opened in San Francisco on September 4, 1951; the Soviets sent a delegate only to oppose the document.[29]

On the other hand, Pakistan was coming closer to the Western bloc. Although Pakistan voted mostly with other Asian and Arab countries on the Korean crisis, Foreign Minister Zafrullah satisfied Washington and angered Moscow. Liaquat wanted to maintain a neutral position, but Zafrullah's speeches at the UN were contrary to his Prime Minister's policy, and Zafrullah's address at the San Francisco Conference on the Japanese Peace Treaty was a clear sign of Pakistan's growing tilt toward the United States. Zafrullah's friendship with John Foster Dulles, who became Secretary of State in 1953, helped lead Pakistan to military alliances in the mid-1950s, but already by 1952 one could discern the new trends in Pakistani policy. Although Pakistan did not send any troops to fight in Korea, it seriously considered doing so.[30] Indeed, having interviewed a number of top decision-makers, I believe that at one stage Pakistan actually agreed to send troops. Recently, a former American Ambassador in Pakistan, Benjamin H. Oehlert, Jr., corroborated this in an unpublished paper.[31]

Thus as the Stalin era closed, relations between Moscow and New Delhi began to improve. India's independent role in the Korean crisis, together with Nehru's open criticism of the West's policies on the Japanese treaty and other Far Eastern questions, made Stalin appreciate both the genuineness of India's nonalignment and the advantages to the U.S.S.R. of the "third bloc" concept. The Kremlin began to look afresh at New Delhi's image among the Asian countries and independent role in international affairs. On the other hand, Moscow's softer policy toward Pakistan (manifested by the invitation to Liaquat) withered away.

THE U.S.S.R. CHANGES ITS MIND

Stalin's successors thoroughly reassessed Soviet policies in the East. G. M. Malenkov, Chairman of the Council of Ministers, declared in a speech to the Supreme Soviet on August 8, 1953:

> The position of so large a state as India is of great importance for strengthening peace in the East. India has made a considerable contribution to the efforts of peace-loving countries aimed at ending the war in Korea, and relations with India are growing stronger; cultural and economic ties are developing. We hope that relations between India and the Soviet Union will continue to develop and grow, with friendly co-operation as the key-note.[32]

Two and one-half years later, in the spring of 1956, the shift in Soviet attitude toward the newly independent countries of Asia and Africa was highlighted at the Twentieth Congress of the Communist Party of the Soviet Union. According to a lengthy article reprinted from *Sovetskoye Vostokovedeniye* (No. 1, 1956), which analyzed the congress, the study of Eastern affairs had previously been "gravely prejudiced by failure to understand the character and depth of the contradictions existing in the non-socialist countries of the East between the forces of imperialism and internal reaction on the one hand and the forces of national progress on the other." The author argued that Soviet Oriental economists, stressing the activity of foreign capital, had not fully appreciated "independent capitalist development which has undermined the dominant position of imperialism." The author further contended that the new countries no longer needed to rely on "their former oppressors" for aid and modern equipment; the socialist countries could now supply them "without any conditions or military direction." Thus, in a sharp break with earlier Soviet opinion, it was held that "the dominant position of foreign capital in the economy of some countries of the East is no longer such that imperialism irresistibly dominates their political life."

The author went on to cite the Marxist–Leninist proposition that in colonial and dependent countries where capitalism is comparatively developed, the proletariat may supply the leaders of a national liberation and antifeudal revolution; this occurred, he said, in China. While embracing this "unquestionable, correct proposition," the author attacked "the incorrect deduction that *only* the leadership of the proletariat can ensure victory in a struggle for national independence" [italics added]. India, Burma, Indonesia, Egypt, and other countries won actual sovereignty with the formal end of colonialism; "independence" was not merely a ruse of the imperialists to preserve their old control in new forms. But because the independence movements were "under the leadership of the national bourgeoisie, many Eastern experts were unable to appreciate objectively enough the great importance of this occurrence in the history of the East." The author showed that the Soviets no longer regarded this great development as a "final deal of the grande bourgeoisie with imperialism."[33]

Why did the successors of Stalin make such a *volte-face* in the assessment of so-called national movements of the bourgeoisie in countries such as India? There were a number of reasons. First, Stalin's rigid attitude had not served the Soviet global strategy of winning the support of a large number of Afro–Asian countries. On the contrary, the Western powers, particularly the United States during the Eisenhower–Dulles era, had made serious efforts to draw closer the new nations of the Middle East, South Asia, and Southeast Asia through various forms of alliance and economic assistance. Moreover, China, which shaped its strategy and policy independently of Moscow even before severe Sino–Soviet conflict erupted, had begun to woo India through recognition of the Nehru-led "progressive elements" in Indian bourgeois society. As early as July 9, 1950, during a period when the Soviet press was full of hostile comment for India's policies, the *People's Daily* (Peking) discussed India without criticizing Nehru. On July 13 the newspaper described India as an important member of the "peace camp." Finally, on January 1, 1951, *People's Daily* recognized "the Indian national liberation as part of the great tide of liberalism sweeping over Asia." China, like the United States and the West, threatened to undercut the inflexible Soviets.

Second, as already indicated, the Kremlin leaders began to appreciate the genuineness of the independent foreign policies of countries such as India. Neither India's goal to have a "Third World of nonaligned countries" nor India's importance in the world could any longer be ignored or discounted.

Third, as noted in the *Sovetskoye Vostokovedeniye* article, by the mid-1950s the Soviet Union was in a position to give assistance, both economic and military, to the countries of the Third World. The Soviets could now compete for the affections of the national bourgeoisie, and foreign aid began to enter into the political rivalry of the two superpowers.

Finally and perhaps most important, Pakistan, as we shall note, became a Western ally in the mid-1950s, and Moscow—quickest among the major powers to exacerbate Indo–Pakistani tensions for its own ends—immediately turned its attention to New Delhi. In complete reversal of its official attitude, the U.S.S.R. began to cultivate the friendship of Nehru's India.[34]

AN EXCHANGE OF VISITS

Nehru and India happily responded to the Soviet gestures, which they regarded as recognition of the success of India's foreign policy and the importance of the country in Asia. An

Indian interpreter of the new Soviet policy, M. S. Rajan, pointed out that another reason for establishing closer relations with the Soviet Union and the communist bloc was dissatisfaction with the West, dissatisfaction that flowed from Western annoyance at India; since the Korean War, he noted, the Western powers, particularly the United States, had been sharply critical of Nehru's policies.[35]

As his ever-growing involvement in Asian affairs increased India's differences with the West, Nehru began to emerge as the greatest contemporary Asian leader, particularly through his role at the conferences of the Colombo powers—Burma, Ceylon, Indonesia, India, and Pakistan. At the second conference of the Colombo power prime ministers, held in December 1954, Nehru argued that although the countries of Asia had secured political independence, they continued to be economically dependent—a theme that the Soviet Union stressed again and again. Nehru severely attacked the U.S.-sponsored Southeast Asia Treaty Organization (SEATO), which, according to him, had added "tensions in Southeast Asia."[36] At the 1955 Bandung Conference, despite the more pro-West stands of Pakistan, Turkey, Ceylon, and other countries, Nehru again condemned Western military pacts in the Third World.[37] The Soviet press was full of praises for India's "contribution to peace" and "independent foreign policy," and Nehru was the hero.[38]

It was in this highly favorable climate that on June 7, 1955, the Indian leader began his first Soviet state visit as Prime Minister. During his two weeks' stay he was accorded what was described as an unprecedented welcome from the Russian crowds. And he pleased the crowds. In an address to an audience of 80,000 in the Dynamo Stadium in Moscow he stated:

> Almost contemporaneously with your October Revolution under the leadership of the great Lenin, we in India started a new phase of our struggle for freedom. . . . Even though we pursued a different path in our struggle under the leadership of Mahatma Gandhi we admired Lenin and were influenced by his example. . . . there was at no time an unfriendly feeling among our people towards the people of the Soviet Union. . . . Wherever I have gone in the Soviet Union I have found a passion for peace . . . in India we have been devoted to the cause of peace.[39]

Premier Nikolai A. Bulganin had introduced Nehru to the stadium audience as "one of the outstanding leaders of the struggle of the Indian people for national independence." He had added that "the Soviet people are following with great interest and sympathy the efforts which the great Indian people are making to establish in their country a society on socialist lines."[40]

In the joint communiqué issued upon the Indian's departure, Nehru and Bulganin reiterated their belief in the principles of co-existence (*panch sheel*), acclaimed the results of the Bandung Conference, and described the construction of a steel plant in India with Russian help as a notable example of economic cooperation between the two countries; such cooperation, they noted, they intended to strengthen.[41]

Particularly at a time when the United States had developed special links with Pakistan, Nehru was no doubt pleased with the friendship of the Soviet Union. But he also seemed to be cautious about the Soviet Union; he told his people after his return from Moscow about the "differences" between the Soviet and Indian sociopolitical systems.[42] He did not become a "fellow traveler," as some elements of the U.S. press contended[43] in comments that represented a narrow approach and did harm to relations between India and the United States. India continued to receive much more aid from the United States than from the U.S.S.R., and Nehru paid a visit to Britain for talks with Foreign Secretary Sir Anthony Eden on his return journey from Russia. Nehru's policy leaned toward Moscow, but Nehru himself was keen to observe the spirit and meaning of nonalignment.

The Soviet leaders promptly paid return visits in response to Nehru's invitation. Bulganin and First Secretary of the Communist Party Nikita S. Khrushchev made a number of friendly gestures and speeches during their November–December Indian visit. They sought public approval through enunciation of several well-worn themes, including devotion to the principles of Gandhi and loyalty to *panch sheel*, a concept that was India's contribution to world peace. Even more important, they openly and unequivocally de-clared support of India's vital interests in relation to Pakistan.[44] This declaration of support served twin purposes: (1) it pleased the Indians to see their principal adversary condemned (even the creation of Pakistan on the basis of Muslim nationalism was chal-lenged, and Kashmir was declared an integral part of India), and (2) it penalized Pakistan for its alliance with the Western countries.

The significance of the Soviet leaders' visit was considerable. It was an effective psychological weapon from the standpoint of the Soviet policy makers, who, as we have seen, were beginning to seek closer relations with the uncommitted world. If the Soviet objectives in India were to create a favorable image among policy makers and public and to spread Soviet influence in the "third bloc," the visit was clearly a success. It laid the foundation for a closer, if not special, relationship between India and the Soviet Union, and India moved farther from its initial Western orientation in attitudes. India was already critical of the United States for, among other things, its arms deal with Pakistan and its sponsorship of defense pacts. On Goa, Dulles's support of Portugal and the U.S.S.R.'s open support of India contributed to India's edging toward Moscow.

In their report to the Supreme Soviet immediately after their return, Bulganin and Khrushchev spoke in highly optimistic terms for both home and international consumption:

> The visit has great significance primarily because the correctness of the basic Leninist principle of Soviet foreign policy—the principle of peaceful coexistence among states with different social and political systems—was confirmed again and again. . . . Asian countries which comprise over half the world's population are assuming growing independence in contemporary international life. . . . The identity of views between the Soviet Union and India on important international problems is explained, not by reasons or considerations of the passing moment. It stems from the deep-rooted interests of the policies of the two states who desire peace and security.[45]

But the Kremlin leaders were disappointed if they thought that India would completely break relations with the West, forsake the Western liberal system, and become a member of the "Socialist Commonwealth." The Indians enthusiastically applauded many of the Soviet leaders' speeches in India—such as those condemning SEATO and CENTO (the Central Treaty Organization), those endorsing the Indian case on Kashmir and Goa, and those promising more Soviet economic aid, particularly for the ensuing second five-year plan. On the other hand, the Indians, particularly Nehru, appeared embarrassed by the Soviet leaders' seemingly inflammatory speeches on several occasions. In a speech at Bombay, as well as in his speech in the Indian Parliament, Khrushchev used his platform for a propaganda drive against the Western countries.[46]

NEW CULTURAL TIES WITH INDIA

The warming of Indo–Soviet relations initiated a new era of cultural, economic, military, and diplomatic cooperation.

The Soviet Union always emphasizes the importance of cultural understanding in achieving closer relations with another country, and India in the mid-1950s was no exception. Since 1955 there has been a regular, annual exchange of delegations of scientists, artists, writers, and others. Between 1955 and 1958 the Soviet Union bought twenty-three Indian films for showing in the U.S.S.R. Indian dances and music became popular with the Russians, and more than 200 works by Indian writers were translated and published in twenty-six languages read in the Soviet Union. On the other end, almost 5 million copies of works by Soviet authors on political, economic, social, and cultural problems were distributed in India. In 1958 a society for Soviet–Indian cultural relations was formed in the U.S.S.R.[47]

NEW ECONOMIC AND MILITARY TIES WITH INDIA

The effects of good relations were especially apparent in the economic sector. In an article entitled "India's Economic Relations with Socialist Countries," Soviet author V. Kondrat'yev noted that during the early postcolonial period India looked to Western countries, particularly the United States, for aid for economic development. But, according to the author, the industrialization of underdeveloped countries was not advantageous to "imperialist monopolies," and in consequence India embarked on trade and economic relations with countries of the socialist system. The first significant manifestation of this new trend was the conclusion in 1953 of a five-year trade agreement with the Soviet Union. A new agreement, signed in Moscow on November 16, 1958, provided for further expansion of trade between India and the U.S.S.R. in the ensuing five years. From 1953 to 1959 India also reached trade accords with other socialist countries, and the volume of trade between India and the socialist countries as a whole increased twelve times. (Figures of this sort, though impressive, should be interpreted with the originally very low volume of trade in mind.) In 1959 the Soviet Union occupied fifth place in India's general trade turnover, fourth in exports and tenth in imports.[48]

Until the mid-1950s India's economic relations with the Soviet Union were confined to trade, but this changed with the improvement of relations. Now much emphasis was laid on Soviet help in capital construction and development of heavy industry. In September 1954 the U.S.S.R. indicated its willingness to assist India in constructing a steel mill, and in February 1955 an agreement was signed for the much-publicized steel mill in Bhilai. India had received outside help during its first five-year plan, launched in 1951, from the West. During the second five-year plan Western aid continued to be much higher, but Soviet assistance was significant: between November 1957 and February 1961 the U.S.S.R. extended credit to India totaling $670 million. Soviet aid in India's industrialization program was even more extensive in the third five-year plan. Most of the Soviet aid was utilized for industrial development.[49]

India obtained large amounts of economic assistance from both the U.S.S.R. and the Western countries during the height of the Cold War in the 1950s because of its special role as the leader of the "third bloc." Through the 1960s India and Egypt received more Soviet arms and military equipment than any other noncommunist countries. We shall note in the next chapter that major Soviet military commitments to India began in the 1960s, but the Soviet Union began to offer arms to India in the 1954–1960 period. In the mid-1950s, when Pakistan began to receive U.S. arms through various military pacts, a powerful section of the Indian public started to campaign in favor of soliciting Soviet military assistance. Nehru, however, was cautious in relying solely upon one superpower for military assistance, and—although Soviet arms assistance has increased enormously—his policy in this respect is still followed. Nehru's and India's caution was demonstrated by the four-year delay in accepting the U.S.S.R. offer, first made in 1956, to sell MIG 17s "on good terms."[50]

NEW DIPLOMATIC TIES WITH INDIA

We now turn to the success of the Soviet Union in winning India's aid on important international issues, aid that was balanced by Soviet support of India's position on such issues as Kashmir and Goa.

In 1956, Nehru and his government's attitude toward Soviet atrocities in Hungary was mild compared to their severe condemnation of Anglo–French–Israeli action in Egypt. "The Hungarian crisis," as one commentator put it, "produced a much discussed illustration of the Indian leader's kindly treatment of Soviet misdeeds."[51] In the UN General Assembly India, alone among the noncommunist countries, voted with the Soviet bloc against a resolution calling for free elections in Hungary. Nehru, whose foreign policy was for the first time criticized inside his country for its apparent dual standard of morality, tried to justify the Indian vote at the UN on the grounds that a UN-supervised election in Hungary might create a bad precedent elsewhere. Kashmir was obviously his concern. He eventually responded to the criticism at home and abroad by modifying his stand: later he told the Indian Parliament that the great majority of the Hungarian people wanted a change of government and that the Soviet forces which had suppressed their revolt should be withdrawn. In response, the Soviet government "pointedly reminded Nehru of India's many pressing domestic problems," particularly Kashmir, problems for which Soviet help was desired.[52]

Similarly, when Nehru expressed concern in May 1958 over worsening Soviet–Yugoslav relations, Premier Khrushchev was reported to have told the Indian Ambassador that India should not interfere; the Soviet government also resented Nehru's late 1958 article "The Basic Approach," which criticized all dogmatic ideologies including communism.[53] Nehru's actions regarding the Suez crisis were less ambiguous. The Israeli drive across the Sinai Peninsula and the British and French landings at the canal were labeled by the Prime Minister "a flagrant violation of the UN Charter" and "clear and naked aggression." But when Bulganin wrote to Nehru suggesting joint military action against Britain, France, and Israel, Nehru demurred, saying that any step that might lead to world war would be a "crime against humanity."[54]

Thus India's policies generally favored Moscow during 1954–1962, and the Soviets dropped their neutrality on the Kashmir dispute and openly and unequivocally supported India. In 1957, after a lapse of five years, the Kashmir issue was brought back to the Security Council. Pakistan complained of India's plan to annex the state with the help of the Kashmiri "constituent assembly." In response, the Security Council passed a resolution reaffirming its earlier resolutions for a plebiscite. On February 14 a draft resolution, moved by Australia, Cuba, Britain, and the United States, called for use of a temporary United Nations force to assist in demilitarization and the holding of a plebiscite. The Soviet delegate denounced the plebiscite suggestion and declared that the introduction of a UN force in Kashmir would be completely at variance with principles of the UN Charter and would frustrate the national sentiments of the people of Kashmir. When the Soviet amendments were rejected by the Council, the U.S.S.R. exercised its seventy-ninth veto—the first veto used by any permanent member in respect to Kashmir. The Soviet veto not only killed the four-nation resolution but also extended the ominous shadow of the Cold War over the dispute, thus further reducing the chances for a peaceful solution of the Kashmir issue through the United Nations.[55]

In 1960 India and the U.S.S.R. again exchanged summit visits. Khrushchev visited India for the second time in February, and Indian President Dr. Rajendra Prasad went to the U.S.S.R. in June. Gestures and speeches stressed Indo–Soviet friendship and both countries' contributions to world peace and adherence to peaceful coexistence. Khrushchev told the Indian Parliament:

> The growing prestige of the Republic of India and of its leaders, the prestige of Mr. Nehru, the Prime Minister is based on the policy of neutrality pursued by the Indian Government, on the policy of non-alignment with military blocs. Herein is wisdom and power.[56]

The platitudes of the 1960 state visits fit into what had now become the routine for relations. Indicative of this routine was the 1960 yearbook of *Bol'shaya sovetskaya entsiklopediya* (*Great Soviet Encyclopedia*). India's foreign policy, according to the approving yearbook, "continued to be one of non-alignment with large blocs as well as advocating a solution to the problem of disarmament and ending of atomic weapon testing." The article pointed out that at the UN the Indian government often "agreed with the Soviet Government's position on international affairs."[57]

STRAINED RELATIONS WITH PAKISTAN

During the August 8, 1953, speech in which he praised India, Malenkov noted that the Soviet Union "attaches great importance to the successful development of relations with Pakistan."[58] Within the next few years, however, Soviet relations with Pakistan worsened considerably. Pakistan's adhesion to a number of bilateral and multilateral defense agreements sponsored by the Western powers infuriated the Kremlin, and not a single opportunity was missed by

Soviet publicists to vilify Pakistan as "the stooge of the imperialist powers." Four strongly worded protest notes were delivered at Rawalpindi between 1953 and 1955[59] as Pakistan concluded military agreements with the West. The Soviet Union bristled at American bases, such as the communications center at Badabar near Peshawar and the nearby airfield from which U-2 spy aircraft—including that of the luckless Francis Gary Powers—took off for missions over Soviet territory. At that time Khrushchev was reported to have encircled Peshawar with a red pencil as one of the targets of annihilation by rocket.[60] In its replies to the Soviet protest notes, the Pakistani government, which considered the Soviet notes interference in internal matters, denied that American bases existed on Pakistan territory. A senior Pakistani diplomat told me that during this period his whole task was to receive Soviet protest notes and threats and give suitable but polite replies.

All this not only worsened Soviet–Pakistan relations but also strengthened Soviet ties with other nations and aggravated regional tensions. As India and some of the Arab states, particularly Nasser's Egypt, were equally opposed to the Baghdad Pact and SEATO, the Soviet protests to Pakistan improved Soviet relations with these countries; Nehru and the Kremlin leaders denounced Pakistan's participation in military pacts in almost identical terms.[61] Thus Indo–Pakistani tensions were exacerbated, as the Kremlin leaders grabbed a wonderful opportunity to serve their own interests at the cost of peace and harmony in the subcontinent.

The Soviet Union, however, did not abandon all hope of good relations with Pakistan. It sometimes employed the carrot as well as the stick—now it would threaten with rockets, now it would entice with the possibility of aid. The Soviet leaders must have recognized inherent contradictions in Pakistan's membership in Western-sponsored alliances; during the early 1960s they set to work exploiting the gap between the regional interests of the small power and the global interests of the American superpower.

NOTES

1. V. I. Lenin, *The Communist International* (London: Lawrence & Wishart, Ltd., 1938), p. 241.
2. See Hugh Seton-Watson, "Five Years of Cold War," in George W. Keeton and Georg Schwarzenberger, eds., *The Year Book of World*

Affairs (London: Stevens & Sons, Ltd., under the auspices of the London Institute of World Affairs, 1953).

3. *New Times* (Moscow), no. 22, 1950, pp. 30 f., cited in Peter Sager, *Moscow's Hand in India* (Berne: Swiss Eastern Institute, 1966), p. 30.

4. Chester Bowles, "America and Russia in India," *Foreign Affairs*, July 1971, p. 637.

5. Harish Kapur, "India and the Soviet Union," *Survey*, Winter 1971, p. 195.

6. *Bol'shaya sovetskaya entsiklopediya* (*Great Soviet Encyclopedia*), 2d ed. (Moscow: 1952), Vol. 10, p. 203, cited in *Central Asian Review*, no. 2, 1957.

7. See G. F. Hudson, "Communism in Asia," *India Quarterly*, January–March 1949.

8. *Ibid.* See also "Upsurge of the National Liberation Movement," *Soviet Encyclopedia*, 2d ed., cited in *Central Asian Review*, no. 1, 1957, pp. 55–56.

9. *Izvestia* (Moscow), July 5, 1947.

10. *Pravda* (Moscow), May 12 and 16, 1947.

11. "Borderlands of South Central Asia—India and Pakistan," *Central Asian Review*, no. 2, 1957, pp. 163–209 (hereafter cited as "Borderlands," with number and year of issue).

12. *Jawaharlal Nehru's Speeches—Vol. I: 1946–1949* (New Delhi: Ministry of Information and Broadcasting, Government of India), pp. 200–224.

13. Jawaharlal Nehru, *Autobiography* (London: John Lane, The Bodley Head, Ltd., 1936), p. 591.

14. Seton-Watson, *op. cit.*, p. 36.

15. See *Nehru's Speeches—Vol. II: 1949–1953, op. cit.*, pp. 141–249.

16. Cecil V. Crabb, *The Elephants and the Grass: A Study of Nonalignment* (New York: Frederick A. Praeger, Inc., 1965), pp. 9, 33; F. Parkinson, "Bandung and the Underdeveloped Countries," in *Year Book of World Affairs* (1956), *op. cit.*, pp. 65–84.

17. George Ginsburgs, "Neutrality and Neutralism in the Tactics of Soviet Diplomacy," *American Slavic and East European Review*, December 1960, p. 533.

18. Kapur, *op. cit.*

19. *New Times*, no. 29, 1949.

20. *Pravda*, Jan. 30, 1949.

21. *Ibid.*, Oct. 23, 1949. See also B. Sen Gupta, *Fulcrum of Asia* (New York: Pegasus, 1970), p. 63.

22. G. F. Hudson, "Soviet Policy in Asia," *Soviet Survey,* July 1955, pp. 1–4.

23. Except where otherwise indicated, all the foregoing comments on the Soviet invitation and what followed are based on my research and personal interviews in Pakistan, 1967–1971.

24. J. C. Hurewitz, *Diplomacy in the Near and Middle East* (Princeton, N.J.: P. Van Nostrand Company, Inc., 1956), Vol. II, pp. 229–230.

25. *The Statesman* (New Delhi), July 14, 1950.

26. See K. P. Karunakaran, *India in World Affairs: A Review of India's Foreign Relations* (Bombay: Oxford House, 1958).

27. *Nehru's Speeches—Vol. III: 1953–1957, op. cit.,* pp. 240–342.

28. K. M. Panikkar, *In Two Chinas* (London: George Allen and Unwin, Ltd., 1955), pp. 171–175.

29. *Survey of International Affairs, 1951* (London: Royal Institute of International Affairs, 1952), pp. 412–420.

30. Based on my research and personal interviews in Pakistan, 1967–1971.

31. Benjamin H. Oehlert, Jr., "How to Lose Allies," unpublished paper, May 9, 1970.

32. *Pravda,* Aug. 9, 1953.

33. "Political and Cultural Affairs: Revaluation of Bourgeois Nationalism," *Central Asian Review,* no. 4, 1956, pp. 343–345.

34. See Arthur Stein, "India's Relations with the USSR: 1953–1963," *Orbis,* Summer 1964, pp. 357–373.

35. M. S. Rajan, *India in World Affairs: 1954–1956* (New York: Asia Publishing House, under the auspices of the Indian Council of World Affairs, 1964), p. 301.

36. Based on my research and personal interviews in Pakistan, 1967–1971.

37. Ivison Macadam, ed., *Annual Register of World Events, 1955* (London: Longmans, Green and Co., Ltd.), pp. 107–108.

38. See Molotov's speech before the Supreme Soviet on Feb. 8, 1955, in *Pravda,* Feb. 9, 1955.

39. *Nehru's Speeches—Vol. III: 1953–1957, op. cit.,* pp. 301–306.

40. *Pravda,* June 22, 1955.

41. *Ibid.*

42. See *Nehru's Speeches—Vol. III: 1953–1957, op. cit.,* pp. 313–319.

43. "India: Mr. Nehru's Travels," *Round Table,* September 1955, pp. 382–383.

44. *Pravda,* Nov. 20–22, 1955; see also Khrushchev's speech at Srinagar, Kashmir, in *Pravda,* Dec. 11, 1955.

45. *Pravda,* Dec. 30, 1955.

46. *Eastern Economist* and *The Statesman,* Dec. 16, 1955.

47. For a fuller account, see "Indian–Soviet Cultural Relations," *Central Asian Review,* no. 3, 1961, pp. 307–313.

48. See "India's Economic Relations with the Socialist Countries," *ibid.,* no. 4, 1961, pp. 413–416.

49. *Ibid;* "Borderlands," no. 1, 1960, pp. 87–89; Leo Tansky, *U.S. and USSR Aid to Devloping Countries* (New York: Frederick A. Praeger, Inc., 1966), pp. 7, 101–102, 106–107, 109.

50. See Lorne J. Kavic, *India's Quest for Security* (Los Angeles: University of California Press, 1967); Norman D. Palmer, *Recent Soviet and Chinese Penetration in India and Pakistan: Guidelines for Political-Military Policy* (McLean, Va.: Research Analysis Corporation, 1970).

51. See Paul F. Power, "Indian Foreign Policy: The Age of Nehru," *Review of Politics,* April 1964, p. 274.

52. See Stein, *op. cit.,* p. 362.

53. *Ibid.*

54. Macadam, *Register of World Events, 1956–1957, op. cit.*

55. G. W. Choudhury, *Pakistan's Relations with India* (London: Pall Mall Press, Ltd., 1968), pp. 127–129. A senior Pakistani diplomat told me of an interesting aspect of this first Soviet veto on Kashmir. Before agreeing to support the Feb. 14 resolution, representatives of the United States and the United Kingdom told Pakistani Foreign Minister Malik Feroz Khan Noon that their support would be futile because the Soviet Union would veto the proposal. Noon contacted the Soviet delegate and received categorical assurances that the Soviet stand in favor of a plebiscite in Kashmir was unchanged; the U.S.S.R. would abstain from voting on the issue, the delegate said. Noon reported the Soviet pledge to the Western powers, and with this they agreed to proceed with the proposal. Subsequently it became clear that the Soviet Union had wanted an opportunity to demonstrate its new friendship with India and also to penalize Western-leaning Pakistan.

56. *Pravda,* Feb. 12, 1960.

57. Cited in "Borderlands," no. 1, 1962, pp. 68–69.

58. *Pravda,* Aug. 9, 1953.

59. *Ibid.,* Apr. 7 and Dec. 3, 1953.

60. *Ibid.,* May 14 and June 22, 1960.

61. For Egypt's opposition to military pacts, see the text of the Indo-Egyptian treaty of friendship and Nasser's speech on the occasion of the treaty signing, Apr. 6, 1955, in *Hindu,* Apr. 7, 1955. Also see "Baghdad Pact," *Round Table,* June 1957, pp. 215–224. As regards Nehru's opposition to military pacts, see *Nehru's Speeches—Vol. III: 1953–1957, op. cit.,* pp. 319–321, 344–346.

Chapter Two

NEW SOVIET DIPLOMATIC MOVES, 1960–1965

ESPECIALLY after the peaceful resolution of the Cuban missile crisis in 1962 and the signing of the Nuclear Test Ban Treaty on August 5, 1963, East–West tensions began to ease. In South Asia, however, tension persisted or even increased: serious armed conflict erupted in 1962 along the Sino–Indian border and again in 1965 between India and Pakistan. China's emergence as a major power in Asia, more significant involvement by the U.S.S.R. as well as China in the affairs of the subcontinent, Sino–Soviet disputes, and a new Soviet–American attitude toward neutralism changed and complicated the South Asian Triangle. In the new environment of the early 1960s the Soviets continued their special relationship with India and at the same time skillfully exploited Pakistan's growing dissatisfaction with the United States; they began to emulate the Western policy of maintaining neutrality in Indo–Pakistani disputes —a posture that, after the seventeen-day war in 1965, enabled them to play the role of peacemaker at the Tashkent Conference in January 1966.

SINO–INDIAN WAR

War between India, the befriending of which had enabled the U.S.S.R. to gain much influence in the Third World, and China, a fraternal member of the communist bloc, initially strained the

Indo–Soviet relations that had developed so well during the preceding eight years (though it eventually solidified them). Khrushchev described the border fighting as "an outright godsend" for "the imperialists,"[1] and he had good reason to despair about a conflict in which he did not want to have to favor one side over the other.

Prior to the war, India had hoped that the U.S.S.R. would restrain China and, in the event of major armed conflict, remain neutral. This hope was not entirely without foundation: the Soviet Union did not want to lose the close friendship of India and make it look to the West for help. The U.S.S.R. made its position clear on September 9, 1959, three years before the outbreak of war, declaring for the first time that it took a neutral position in a conflict between a communist and a noncommunist country.[2] But when the war erupted in the midst of the Cuban crisis, unity within the communist bloc against the Western countries was vital, and the Soviet Union felt compelled to show some fraternal leaning toward Peking. On October 25, 1962, *Pravda* and *Izvestia* praised as "constructive" China's three-point peace proposal of October 24, a proposal already rejected by India, and implicitly blamed India. The Soviet press did not condemn what the Indians regarded as Chinese aggression, and it endorsed Chinese views on the McMahon line, India's eastern boundary with China.[3]

As the Cuban crisis ebbed, however, the Soviet Union began to revert to its original neutrality, as evidenced by a leading article in *Pravda* on November 5. More tangible evidence of the shift away from a pro-China position, and of worsening Sino–Soviet relations, was the delivery at the height of the crisis of MIG fighter aircraft to India. The deal for the sale of MIG 17s, pending since 1956, was finalized in August 1962, before the Sino–Indian war. There were delays in the delivery of the MIGs and in the building of a factory in India to manufacture the aircraft.[4] This created concern in India and gave rise to speculation abroad.[5] But on December 4 Nehru said, "There has been no question of the Soviet Union backing out of this commitment," adding that the delay had "nothing to do with China."[6] Events proved his optimism justified. In January the Indian press reported that the first shipment of MIG fighters had left Odessa for India.[7] Within a few months the Soviets matched such anti-China actions with harsh anti-China rhetoric. On September 19, 1963, *Pravda* declared that in disputes with India the Chinese government was even going to the length of making the monstrous assertion that the Soviet Union was "pushing" India into a clash with China. China had negotiated frontier settlements with others such as Burma and even with Pakistan, a member of SEATO and CENTO; now why was she refusing to do the same in this case? Could it be that the rulers of China wanted to settle their dispute with India by force of arms and—receive support from the Soviet Union in so doing?

Thus neutrality, or at least the facade of it, gave way to support for India.[8] Precipitating this development were the growing dispute with China and fears in Moscow that India might enter into some form of military alliance with the West. The Soviet Union was concerned over the prompt and generous military aid—aid that might have won favors or constituted pressure in New Delhi— given by the Western countries as soon as the India–China war started. In a November 9, 1963, report to his government, the Pakistani Ambassador in Moscow quoted "some reliable diplomatic sources" as confirming that the Soviet government was worried over the effects of this military help, particularly from the United States.[9] The Soviet concern was expressed in a series of articles in the Soviet press,[10] which heavily criticized such Indian political parties as the Swatantra party for demands that India revise its foreign policy along pro-Western lines. As the Soviet press continued to extol the virtues of nonalignment, the Soviets watched vigilantly for any changes in India's policy.

The Soviet concern over India's dealings with the West, however, was less than it might have been. Both superpowers were changing their attitudes toward allies and neutrals, and India's or Pakistan's acceptance of aid, including military aid, from the other bloc was no longer as alarming to either bloc as it had been in the 1950s. This new superpower tolerance was partly a function of the cooling of tensions between the United States and the U.S.S.R. and partly a reflection of a common objective, the containment of China. India was a big factor in both superpowers' policies of containment in Asia, and in this light its policy of nonalignment was applauded, or at least accepted, in Washington and Moscow. Not so in Rawalpindi and Peking: critics here termed the policy "double alignment" or "bialignment."[11]

When President Sarvapali Radhakrishnan visited the U.S.S.R. in September 1964, he was given the same grand welcome that his Indian predecessors on state visits had received since Nehru's visit in 1955—another "brilliant demonstration of the friendship of

Soviet and Indian people." Talks during Radhakrishnan's visit confirmed that the Soviet Union and India had similar positions on many important problems facing the world. Both nations reaffirmed their adherence to the "principles of peaceful coexistence"; both welcomed the growing understanding of the policy of nonalignment. India endorsed Khrushchev's proposal of December 31, 1963, for an international treaty under which states would agree to refrain from the use of force in settling territorial and border disputes and to respect historically established frontiers. The Soviet government voiced appreciation for the continuation of Nehru's "policy of non-alignment and friendship with the Soviet Union," and India acknowledged the Soviet Union's help and cooperation in economic and other matters.[12]

Thus periodic and routine assurances of Soviet–India friendship were made. But four months before, in May 1964 with the death of Nehru, the emotionalism of Indo–Soviet *Bhai Bhai* (brother) ties began to erode. Ideological or philosophical aspects now gave way to a more pragmatic basis for the relationship. This change was effected mostly by India. "In promoting the same objectives by the same means, post-Nehru India has abandoned the idealist characteristics of Nehru's India," noted M. S. Rajan.[13]

THE THIRD PHASE OF SOVIET POLICY

In Pakistan, Soviet moves in the early 1960s were more striking: the Kremlin's links with India were already well established from the mid-1950s, and now—seeking to impede Pakistan's growing friendship with China and to weaken its pro-Western policy—the Soviets smiled at Pakistan. Thus began the third phase of Soviet policy toward the subcontinent, a phase of some gestures toward Pakistan, warm friendship with India, and neutrality in the two nations' quarrels. During this phase, lasting until the 1971 Bangladesh crisis, the Soviet Union took no step in the direction of Pakistan that might jeopardize its good relations with New Delhi, which it considered far more important than those with Rawalpindi. About Pakistan, still a member of SEATO and CENTO and a close friend of China, the U.S.S.R. always had doubts and misgivings. Despite their limitations, however, the U.S.S.R.'s new bonds with Pakistan offered some advantages and no liabilities; the Soviets acquired new leverage on India. As one commentator put it, "If

New Delhi shows signs of wavering on issues affecting major [Soviet] interests, Moscow need only cast a nod in the direction of Rawalpindi to induce clear thinking."[14]

Soviet press comments indicated some, but not all, of the change in feelings toward Pakistan. On April 15, 1962, *Pravda* published Ayub's message of thanks for President Brezhnev's greetings on Pakistan's National Day, March 23; Ayub expressed his hope that "good relations will develop in the future in a spirit of durable peace and friendship between our two countries." On May 1, 1962, *Izvestia* and several other newspapers reported on the award of the Lenin prize to Pakistani poet Faiz Ahmad Faiz (now Prime Minister Bhutto's cultural adviser). The Soviet press also briefly reported the ending of the martial law in Pakistan in June 1962.

An even more significant indication of the new Soviet attitude toward Pakistan was the signing of an oil agreement in February 1961, an agreement that represented the first Soviet economic and technical assistance to Pakistan.[15] Ayub, his close advisers, and the Cabinet discussed for months the Soviet oil offer. Bhutto, who was then Minister for National Resources but participated regularly in foreign policy matters, was strongly in favor of accepting; Finance Minister Mohammed Shoaib, who was noted for his pro-Western views (he is now vice-president of the International Bank for Reconstruction and Development in Washington), vigorously opposed acceptance. Finally, Ayub decided to go ahead. Uncertainties and misgivings on the part of both nations, however, delayed finalization of the agreement from August 1960 until March 1961.[16]

The agreement was signed soon after the stern Soviet warnings to Pakistan on the U-2 incident. The Soviet notes of May 14 and June 22, 1960, accused the Pakistani government of "complicity" in the flight of the U.S. reconnaissance aircraft over Soviet territory. The first note mentioned ominously that the Soviets had means to destroy military bases used for aggressive acts against them; the second note threatened that in the event of further "provocative flights" the Soviet government would be compelled to undertake appropriate measures, not excluding strikes at the bases used to conduct such flights.[17]

When asked by journalists if he was worried over the Soviet notes, Ayub was cocky: "Do I look shaky?" he asked sarcastically.[18] But Ayub *was* shaken, and the U-2 era had great impact on his subsequent moves to improve relations with the Soviet Union. Ayub had already begun a thorough reassessment of foreign policy. The

U-2 incident demonstrated Pakistan's dangerous exposure as a result of total commitment to the West, and Ayub now questioned whether that commitment was worth the risk. The U.S.S.R. had helped to initiate the questioning. Just as it had tried in the past to exploit dissatisfaction with the West—Pakistani dissatisfaction in the late 1940s and Indian dissatisfaction in the mid-1950s—the Soviet Union capitalized in the early 1960s upon Pakistan's frustration, which stemmed from its American ally's new, increased deference toward neutral India during the Kennedy era. "We support India and Afghanistan against you because they are our friends, even when they are in the wrong," Mihail Kapitsa, the Soviet Ambassador in Rawalpindi, told the Pakistanis. "But your friends do not support you, even when they know you are in the right."[19] It was a shrewd comment, part of a clever strategy, and it scored heavily. Among other factors leading to the Pakistani foreign policy reassessment were India's rebuff of Ayub's proposal for joint defense[20] and, most importantly, the emergence of China as a major power.

On their part, the Soviets had waxed conciliatory by December 1962 for several reasons, among them those discussed by Pakistan's Moscow Ambassador in the following note home:

> Recently an expectation has grown in the Soviet Union that Pakistan may follow a more neutralist policy in her foreign relations. This is partly due to the recent debate in the Pakistan National Assembly [over the U.S. decision to give arms to India after the Sino–Indian border war of 1962] and the trends in some sections of the [Pakistani] press.

The Ambassador pointed out also that the Soviets would welcome withdrawal from CENTO and SEATO and a declaration of non-aggression toward the Soviet Union along the lines of that adopted by Iran (that no national territories might be used for aggressive purposes against the U.S.S.R. or any other power).[21]

A dialogue was conducted throughout 1963 and 1964 between the Pakistanis—including President Ayub and Bhutto, the new Foreign Minister—and Soviet officials—among them Deputy Foreign Minister Sergey Lapin, who made a goodwill visit in November 1964, and the Soviet Ambassador.[22] An analysis of the minutes of the important discussions reveals that it was not correct to say, as such American interpreters as Professor Werner Levi had predicted,[23] that the initiative for improvement in the relationship would come mainly from Pakistan (because of its dissatisfaction with American policy and action). In fact, the Soviets' moves and overtures in 1963–1964 showed that like Pakistan they wanted to improve the relationship; as we have seen, improved relations with Pakistan were an integral part of the third phase of Soviet strategy toward the subcontinent.

When Bhutto and India's Swaran Singh, Minister for Railways, met in 1962–1963 for talks on the Kashmir dispute, the Soviet Union was not as disinterested as India would have wished. In the past, the Soviets had shied away from the issue; Pakistan's Ambassadors in Moscow and at the United Nations had almost always been rebuffed when they had sought to discuss Kashmir. But the Soviet Union could not continue to witness passively developments in Kashmir, particularly after March 2, 1963, when China signed a boundary agreement with Pakistan that gave it direct access to the strategically important areas in Kashmir.[24] During President Radhakrishnan's 1964 visit the Kremlin leaders reportedly advised India to adopt a "flexible attitude" on Kashmir and stressed the "risks" of continued tension, risks arising from "China's entry into the area."[25]

But serious problems persisted in the Soviet–Pakistani relationship. In January 1964 the Soviet Ambassador in Pakistan told Foreign Secretary Aziz Ahmad that the Soviet Union did not favor referring the Kashmir matter to the Security Council, which indicated that the Soviet hands-off policy on the Kashmir dispute remained basically intact. The Ambassador pointed out that the Soviet Union could not be expected to worsen its relations with other countries, e.g., Afghanistan or India, in its quest for better relations with Pakistan.[26]

In dealings with Pakistan, the Soviet Union was interested mainly in what it termed "non-political matters": "The Soviet Union will discuss subjects like trade and economic collaboration, expansion of cultural and scientific exchanges," the Soviet Ambassador told Bhutto on April 4, 1964. "Political and international problems that concern the U.S.S.R. and Pakistan will be taken up later on." Pakistan felt it imperative to discuss first vital issues, which included (in addition to Kashmir) Soviet arms supplies to India and links with Afghanistan. Under an agreement concluded in September 1964, the U.S.S.R. agreed to extend to India $400 million of additional military aid, consisting of three squadrons of MIG 21 supersonic fighters, missiles, and other weapons;[27] on October 16, 1963, the Soviets reaffirmed in a joint communiqué with Afghanistan their support of Kabul's demand for Pakhtoonistan, a claim involving a substantial part of Pakistan's territory.[28] Pakistan had no alternative but to accept the Soviet procedure of stressing the nonpolitical in bilateral discussions, but the dialogue bogged down in mutual distrust. On June 5, 1964, the Soviet Ambassador complained to Bhutto that about twenty proposals were pending to which the Pakistani government had not satisfactorily responded. Without a favorable political climate, the Foreign Minister replied, repeating his government's position, the process of normalization was likely to be delayed.[29]

A complicating factor that arose rather unexpectedly was the Indian move to invite the Soviet Union to the Second Afro–Asian Conference, scheduled for 1965 in Algeria. At a meeting of the preparatory committee, held at Djakarta in April 1964, the Indian delegate was apparently trying, very shrewdly, to create a split between Pakistan and the U.S.S.R. by proposing that the latter be invited to the conference. Pakistan was caught in a dilemma because China was totally opposed—"as a matter of principle," said its delegation—to Russian participation.[30] Bhutto hedged on the issue, saying that because "the matter was of considerable importance," he had to consult with his government. Ambassador Kapitsa called on the Foreign Minister on April 30, expressed disappointment that Pakistan was not supporting the Indian proposal, and read aloud a lengthy statement refuting the argument advanced by the Chinese Foreign Minister that the Soviet Union was not an Asian country. Bhutto replied that the Soviet Union should have started preparing ground several years before if it was going to seek, on the grounds that it was an Asian country, to join the conference, which had been under discussion for three or four years. He added, "To an average person the U.S.S.R. is a European power and the present claim of the U.S.S.R. was a new concept."[31] Subsequently, the Soviet Union decided not to press the matter.

Indicative of the atmosphere in this period was President Ayub's response to an April 6, 1963, suggestion by the Pakistani Embassy in Moscow that he visit the U.S.S.R. to expedite the process of normalization. Noting Bhutto's prompt approval of the suggestion, Ayub, who always acted cautiously and with statesmanship, vetoed the idea: "I believe that he [Bhutto] is overoptimistic and dragging me into a futile venture. If the Soviets wish to improve relations with us, they could have done it in many ways. At present they wish to play with us."[32]

Yet the game continued throughout 1963–1964 and resulted in

a series of agreements between the U.S.S.R. and Pakistan: the aviation agreement (October 7, 1963), the barter trade agreement (April 30, 1963), and the cultural agreement (June 11, 1964). These agreements opened new avenues of cooperation and, more important, of understanding that finally led to discussion on political and international issues.

THE POLITICAL DIALOGUE

As the political dialogue started, the Soviet Union wanted to discuss Pakistan's membership in CENTO and SEATO; U.S. bases in Pakistan, including the communications center at Badabar near Peshawar; and the possibility of issuing a Pakistani "Iranian type" declaration, which would prevent the establishment on Pakistani territory of rocket or nuclear bases poised against the Soviet Union. Pakistan wanted to talk about the U.S.S.R.'s continued support, which included vetoes in the UN Security Council, for India on the Kashmir issue; the Soviets' Pakhtoonistan stand, in favor of Afghan irredentist claims on Pakistani territories; and the Soviets' massive Indian arms supply program, particularly heavy since 1963, that had upset the balance of power in the subcontinent.[33]

Both sides realized that these important political issues should be discussed at a higher level than the ambassadorial level that had been used since 1962; indeed, both sides believed that one of the main reasons why the Soviet–Pakistani relationship remained strained was the lack of contact between the leaderships. Even Ayub, who until 1963 did not favor any summit-level discussion with the Soviets, now seemed to have changed his mind. Since the abortive invitation to Liaquat Ali Khan in 1949, no Pakistani head of state or government had gone to the U.S.S.R. nor had any top-ranking Soviet leaders visited Pakistan—despite their regular trips to Afghanistan and India. In November 1963 Pakistan informally invited Premier Khrushchev to visit in conjunction with his expected trip to Nepal and Ceylon. Although he could not accept the invitation because of the cancellation of his visit to Nepal and Ceylon, Khrushchev's reply to Pakistan in December 1963 sounded friendly and encouraging. In expressing thanks for the invitation, he referred to the Soviet principle of coexistence among countries of different social systems and claimed that the Soviet Union would always seek friendly relations with all its neighbors, including Pakistan; he added that good relations could be promoted by personal visits and by the development of economic, cultural, and commercial ties. The reply indicated the changed atmosphere.

In the next important development, Khrushchev invited President Ayub to visit the U.S.S.R. The invitation, which came through the Soviet Ambassador on June 22, 1964, was promptly accepted. Before the summit meeting, political dialogues were to be held at the ministerial level. With the changes in the Soviet government after the fall of Khrushchev in October 1964, the Soviet Ambassador promptly called on Ayub and explained the new government's desire to promote better relations with Pakistan, assuring the President that the invitation extended to him by Khrushchev was still valid and that the Soviet government attached great importance to his visit.

In the meantime, Deputy Foreign Minister Sergey G. Lapin went to Pakistan on November 21, 1964. During the visit, Bhutto gave a full account of Pakistan's "independent" foreign policy so as to dispel the notion that Pakistan was still "aligned." He told Lapin how Pakistan, although a member of SEATO, was not in agreement with U.S. policy in Vietnam; he pointed out that while Pakistan opposed the presence of the U.S. Seventh Fleet in the Indian Ocean, "India had gone along with the U.S." Bhutto also tried to justify his opposition to the Indian call for Soviet participation at the proposed Second Afro–Asian Conference. Lapin did not comment on Bhutto's claim that Pakistan should no longer be considered an aligned country, and he could not agree that India "is now tied to the U.S." Lapin noted, however, that "in all sincerity, the Soviet Union wants to cultivate better relations with Pakistan." The new leaders in the Soviet Union, he added, had "reinforced their foreign policy on principles laid down by Lenin of peaceful coexistence between different states. There is no real problem," he concluded, "that stands in the way of improvement in the relationship between the Soviet Union and Pakistan."

Lapin had also a cordial meeting with Ayub. "The Soviet Union is looking forward to receiving their dear guest," he said, referring to the President. In reply, Ayub told the Soviet Minister that the people of Pakistan trace their origin to Central Asia and that it was his desire to reestablish the traditional links. Lapin then brought up the "U.S.'s intention to use Article 19 of the UN Charter to suspend the Soviet Union's right to vote." According to Lapin, the

UN financial debts in question, which the U.S.S.R. refused to help cover, stemmed from "Western aggression" in the Congo and the Near East. Lapin told Ayub that the Soviet Union might be compelled to leave the UN if the United States did not change its position, and Ayub expressed his concern.

Ayub then began the discussion on Soviet–Pakistani affairs by stating that Pakistan wanted "the best of relations with the Soviet Union." He complained about the continued Soviet support for India on Kashmir and with military supplies, and he said that Pakistan had exercised a moderating influence in SEATO and CENTO on such issues as Vietnam. The Chinese, Ayub added, now appreciated Pakistan's role in these defense organizations. As with Bhutto, Lapin was noncommital on most of the issues raised. Again Lapin simply expressed "the sincere Soviet wish to improve relations with Pakistan."

Candid in discussing with Bhutto and Ayub the general international situation, the Soviet Deputy Foreign Minister was reticent on issues that were of vital interest to Pakistan. It seems that Lapin's visit was one of mere good will and exploration; the crucial discussions were left for Ayub's visit to the U.S.S.R.

Less than two months later, on January 12, 1965, Bhutto journeyed to Moscow for more talks. Bhutto was now at his zenith as Ayub's Foreign Minister; he had already made visits to Peking and had led the Pakistan delegation at the UN. Advocating a policy of "confrontation with India," he was in favor of closer links with Peking and claimed to be a great champion of Afro–Asian solidarity. At this point Ayub had full confidence in his Foreign Minister, and in consultation with Bhutto he was formulating Pakistan's new "policy of bilateralism"—the essence of which was to maintain simultaneously good relations with the U.S.S.R., the United States, and China.

Bhutto met with his Soviet counterpart, Foreign Minister Andrei A. Gromyko, and subsequently with Premier Kosygin and President Anastas I. Mikoyan. This was the first time a Pakistani Foreign Minister engaged in a political dialogue with the Kremlin leaders, and although they were a prelude to Ayub's, Bhutto's talks in Moscow were significant in themselves. The Soviet leaders were more willing to commit themselves than Lapin had been in Rawalpindi, and they gave some significant hints and indications of their current thinking on the affairs of the subcontinent. Shrewdly beginning his discussion with Gromyko with a reference to the

American threat to use Article 19 of the UN Charter against the U.S.S.R., Bhutto moved on to an analysis of the recent trends in Pakistan's foreign policy. He argued, as he had with Lapin, that although Pakistan still belonged to SEATO and CENTO, it was in practice nonaligned. Bhutto pointed out that Pakistan had refused to make any contribution, substantial or token, to America's Vietnam efforts; he claimed that on the contrary Pakistan was playing a moderating role inside SEATO in preventing escalation of the war. Pakistan, Bhutto disclosed, played the same role at the Commonwealth prime ministers' conference in 1964, when it had advocated reconvening the Fourteen Powers Conference that originally sought to bring about a settlement in Southeast Asia. Gromyko apparently expressed appreciation for Bhutto's exposition of Pakistan's stand on such international issues as the Vietnam War, nuclear free zones, and the presence of the U.S. Seventh Fleet in the Indian Ocean. Bhutto claimed that on all these issues the Soviet and Pakistani views were identical. (In this light, it is ironic that the Seventh Fleet's presence in the Bay of Bengal during the 1971 war raised great hopes in Pakistan.)

Bhutto then gave Gromyko an account of Pakistan's growing links with China—a factor that, as pointed out earlier, was largely responsible for the Soviet interest in Pakistan in the 1960s. "We have had political, economic and commercial relations with China for a long time," Bhutto noted; "in recent years these have grown considerably." He gave an account of the Pakistan–China boundary pact, which had aroused great interest in Moscow, and he vehemently denied an allegation voiced in Moscow and Washington as well as New Delhi that "Pakistan–China relations are based on common hostility towards India," that "there is some collusion, some secret understanding between Pakistan and China against India." Having listened carefully and without comment to Bhutto's analysis of the China–Pakistan relationship, Gromyko said simply, "The Soviet government welcomes the improvement of our relationship with all our neighbors including the People's Republic of China." The Kremlin leaders were not now openly expressing displeasure over Pakistan's friendship with China; that was to come later.

The next day, meeting with Kosygin, Bhutto again depicted Pakistan's foreign policy as more "independent" than that of India. When the question of Pakistan's adherence to military pacts arose, Bhutto asked why this should hinder improvements in relations in the light of the Soviet Union's comparatively harmonious dealings

with Iran and Turkey. Kosygin, like Gromyko, expressed "satisfaction" with Pakistan's recent trends in external relations. But he
also said, rather bluntly, that he did not share Bhutto's opinions on
the relative independence of Pakistan's and India's foreign policies.
What is more, in assuring Bhutto that the Soviet Union "under-
stands the complexity and delicacy of relations between India and
Pakistan," Kosygin embraced a view that was advocated by India
and opposed by Pakistan: "it is a question which according to the
Soviet Union should be resolved between the two countries." The
most significant remark made by Kosygin to Bhutto on the eve of
Ayub's visit summed up—and repeated—the Soviet attitude: "I
want to tell you, in all sincerity, that we do not want our friendship
with Pakistan at the cost of our friendship with other countries."
Pakistan could not take exception to this avowed policy because
its bilateralism was based on the same principles of not favoring
one nation over another. The rationale of such an approach by
both sides was understandable, but that approach made the
prospect of any big change in relations between the U.S.S.R. and
Pakistan remote; it was clear that the response to Pakistan from
the Kremlin would be less encouraging than that from Peking.

Despite this, the long-expected Ayub Khan state visit to the
U.S.S.R. took place in April 1965.[34] Ayub was received at the
Moscow airport by Kosygin and other top Soviet leaders, and he
was given a correct diplomatic reception. But compared to the
President's reception in Peking less than a month before, the Soviet
performance was rather cool. Banners across the deserted streets
through which Ayub rode read "Welcome President Ayub Khan,"
"May Friendship and Cooperation Develop between Peoples of the
Soviet Union and Pakistan," and so forth. Observers held that this
kind of purely formal welcome—with far more protocol than
warmth—for a visiting head of state had not been seen in Moscow
for several years.[35] "The talk began at Kosygin's office on a bitterly
cold and gloomy afternoon . . . the atmosphere inside the room
was no less cold in spite of central heating," wrote Ayub, in his
autobiography, on the Moscow discussions that began April 3, 1965.
"The Soviet delegation looked stolid and sullen."[36]

Thanks to Ayub's honest, patient, and straightforward efforts the
atmosphere relaxed, but Bhutto represented a great liability for
Ayub and a hurdle to any meaningful talks. Bhutto's irrational harp-
ing on India's "warlike" actions and policies toward Pakistan
irritated the Soviet leaders—particularly Brezhnev, who appeared
to be most rigid. Ayub later told me that on several occasions he

had to stop Bhutto's speaking to him in Urdu so as to avoid embarrassment. Fortunately, the most meaningful talks were held, not at the conference table, but by Ayub on his own, in informal exchanges with the Soviet chiefs—particularly with Kosygin, who was friendly on such occasions as when with the President in an automobile or at a ballet.

There were several formal meetings between the Soviet leaders and Ayub and his team between April 3 and April 8. After a general review of the international situation—in which the leaders of the two countries agreed on a number of important issues—the two sides considered their bilateral relations, touching particularly upon such matters as the Soviet stand on Kashmir, Soviet supplies to India, Pakistan's membership in Western pacts, American bases in Pakistan, and Pakistan's request for Soviet arms.

Ayub tried to convince the Soviet leaders of the threat to Pakistan's security and territorial integrity as a result of India's huge military buildup—to which the U.S.S.R. was the biggest contributor. The Soviets replied that they had sold some "small quantity of arms" only since 1964, only after "the Chinese had inflicted a humiliating defeat on India," only after rightist elements in India had started a campaign to make India ally with the United States and Britain and join the West's military pacts. According to the Soviet leaders, "if the Soviet Union had refused to supply arms to India, it would have crippled liberal elements in India who wanted India to remain non-aligned." Defending the military aid to India, Kosygin pointed out that "the Soviet Union provides arms to those countries who were fighting colonialism and imperialism . . . India is in this struggle." Ayub was skeptical. "Which imperialism is India suffering from?" he asked. Brezhnev went further and dismissed Pakistan's fears of India's military buildup. "India is a neutralist country," he said, "and non-aligned countries do not participate in war." Ayub replied, "Pakistan is one-fifth of India in terms of resources, military strength, etc., and if India were to fear Pakistan, it would be like the Soviet Union fearing Poland." Imperialism's legacy, not U.S.S.R. arms to India, seemed to be what the Soviet leaders thought was the cause of Indo–Pakistani tension. (One might ask how the Soviet policy led any more surely to lessening of that tension than the so-called imperialist policy.)

Countering Pakistan's objections to Indian arms supplies, the Soviet leaders questioned Pakistani membership in CENTO and SEATO. Pakistan was forced to join the pacts "owing to constant Indian threats," Ayub said, adding that Pakistan had begun a process of disengagement from them. Besides, Ayub claimed, Pakistan's membership in SEATO had prevented American reliance upon the treaty organization in the Vietnam War. As for CENTO, according to Ayub, "there is no life in it." Ayub claimed that by initiating the Regional Corporation for Development (RCD) with Iran and Turkey, Pakistan had virtually put CENTO "in cold storage."

At one stage Brezhnev said that the Soviet Union would not insist upon Pakistani withdrawal from the defense pacts as a condition for the improvement of relations, but Pakistan should consider three steps: (1) prohibition of foreign military bases on its territory, (2) prohibition of foreign nuclear weapons on its territory, and (3) limitation or termination of military cooperation with military blocs. Initially the Pakistani leaders got the impression that if they were willing to accede to these demands, the Soviet Union might reconsider its stand on Kashmir, on military assistance to India, or on military supplies for Pakistan. But subsequently it became clear that the Soviet Union was not willing to make any important departures from its policy regardless of Pakistani actions.

The Soviets did not accept fully, or publicly, Pakistan's analysis of the situation in the subcontinent as a result of Ayub's April 1965 visit. They did not substantively change policy. Ayub effectively presented his country's case, however, and the Soviet leaders certainly gained understanding of Pakistan's difficulties; developments would show that they seemed to have realized that Pakistan's concern over the Indian arms buildup was not altogether unjustified. The Soviet leaders also came to realize that Pakistan truly wanted to follow an independent foreign policy and to reduce its commitments to the Western allies. Thus Soviet–Pakistani relations were no longer bogged down in suspicion and distrust, and Ayub's visit can be labeled an event of momentous importance in the changing pattern of the politics of South Asia. Pakistan, an ally of the United States and later a close friend of China, had begun a new era of understanding, if not friendship, with the U.S.S.R.

NOTES

1. *Pravda*, Dec. 13 and 25, 1963.
2. For the text of the Soviet announcement, see *ibid.*, Sept. 10, 1959.
3. See special issue of *International Studies* (New Delhi), July–October 1963.

4. Kavic, *op. cit.;* Palmer, *op. cit.*

5. Reference was made in Lok Sabha to the Dec. 3, 1962, statement of Duncan Sandys, the British Secretary for Commonwealth Affairs, speaking before the House of Commons, that expressed doubts about delivery of the promised Soviet MIGs. See *Times of India* (New Delhi), Dec. 4–5, 1962.

6. *The Statesman,* Dec. 5, 1962.

7. *Times of India,* Jan. 16, 1963. See also the statement of Y. B. Chavan, Indian Defense Minister, in Lok Sabha on Jan. 21, 1963, in *The Statesman,* Jan. 22, 1963.

8. "Borderlands," no. 3, 1963, p. 323.

9. Based on my research and personal interviews in Pakistan, 1967–1971.

10. See, for example, *Pravda,* Apr. 24, 1963.

11. For Pakistani criticism of "bialignment," see Mohammed Ayub Khan, "Pakistan–American Alliances: Stresses and Strains," *Foreign Affairs,* January 1964, pp. 195–209; for Chinese criticism, see Selig S. Harrison, "Troubled India and Her Neighbors," *Foreign Affairs,* January 1965, pp. 312–330.

12. *Pravda,* Sept. 19 and 20, 1964.

13. M. S. Rajan, "India and World Politics in the Post-Nehru Era," *International Journal,* Winter 1968–1969, p. 146.

14. Harrison, *op. cit.*

15. *The Times* (London), Feb. 14, 1961.

16. Based on my research and personal interviews in Pakistan, 1967–1971.

17. "Borderlands—The U-2 Incident," no. 3, 1960, p. 334.

18. *Morning News* (Dacca), June 29, 1960.

19. *Daily Telegraph* (London), July 11, 1960.

20. See Chapters 8 and 9.

21. Based on my research and personal interviews in Pakistan, 1967–1971.

22. *Ibid.*

23. Werner Levi, "Pakistan, the Soviet Union and China," *Pacific Affairs,* Fall 1962, p. 216.

24. See Chapter 8.

25. Based on my research and personal interviews in Pakistan, 1967–1971.

26. *Ibid.* Also, see Kavic, *op. cit.*

27. Based on my research and personal interviews in Pakistan, 1967–1971.

28. *Pravda,* Oct. 17, 1963.

29. Based on my research and personal interviews in Pakistan, 1967–1971.

30. The Indian proposal on the Soviet Union, which had not participated in the First Afro–Asian Conference at Bandung in 1955, had the support of two delegations; five or six delegations, including China's, insisted that the Soviet Union was a European power and, as such, not eligible for participation. The preparatory committee made no decision for lack of consensus.

31. Based on my research and personal interviews in Pakistan, 1967–1971.

32. *Ibid.*

33. Except where otherwise indicated, all the information in this section is based on my research and personal interviews in Pakistan, 1967–1971.

34. I was a member of the President's entourage for the visit, and after his retirement in early 1969 Ayub gave me a comprehensive account of negotiations.

35. *Times of India,* Apr. 4, 1965.

36. Mohammad Ayub Khan, *Friends Not Masters: A Political Autobiography* (London: Oxford University Press, 1967), p. 169.

Chapter Three

THE U.S.S.R. PREDOMINANT, 1965–1970

AYUB'S VISIT to the U.S.S.R. initiated a new era for the Soviet Union in subcontinent affairs. Now both India and Pakistan seemed to pay greater attention to Moscow; both were eager to have Moscow's good will. India was anxious that its long-standing friendship with Moscow—which provided the most valuable diplomatic, economic, and military assistance in areas of vital national importance—not suffer as a result of the Soviet Union's new ties with Pakistan. Pakistan, on the other hand, was desperately trying to reduce the unqualified Soviet support to India. Thus the Soviet Union acquired considerable leverage with both countries. The Chinese viewed the new links between Moscow and Islamabad with concern, but Washington was little perturbed. Instead, like the U.S.S.R., the United States was worried about Pakistan's growing friendship with China; if the Soviet Union were successful in creating a rift between China and Pakistan, Washington would welcome the development. The global competition between the two superpowers persisted, of course, and an enormous increase in the Soviet influence in the subcontinent certainly would not have been looked upon favorably by the United States; but the United States seemed to have correctly assessed that Moscow's friendship with Pakistan could develop only so far. As I have implied, the Soviet attempts to have simultaneously good relations with India and Pakistan proved—in the end —no more successful than the American attempts to achieve the same objective.

Nehru's successor, Lal Bahadur Shastri, dashed to Moscow in

47

May 1965. Soon after Ayub's first state visit, Shastri was given the now familiar general reception for Indian leaders in Moscow, and the familiar theme of Indian–Soviet understanding on international issues was repeated. For the Indians the visit was intended to uncover any substantive changes in Soviet policy toward India, particularly in Indo–Pakistani affairs; for the Soviets the objective was to determine if India was shifting internal or external policies in the post-Nehru era. The Soviet Union was deeply interested in limiting, if not eliminating, the influence of the right wing in the ruling Congress party in India. This was evidenced in January 1965, when there was speculation that Morarji Desai might join the Indian Cabinet. The weekly *New Times* (Moscow) advised Shastri to keep Desai out, saying that as Finance Minister he was one "who had done everything he could to defeat Nehru's socialist policies."[1]

During their consultations with Shastri, the Soviet leaders may have assured the Indian Prime Minister of a special and continuing relationship, but they did not publicly support India or condemn Pakistan. With no mention of Kashmir or any other controversial Indo–Pakistani problem, the communiqué issued at the end of Shastri's visit contained nothing to which Pakistan could take exception. The Pakistani Ambassador in Moscow was gleeful. Quoting from diplomatic sources and drawing from his talks with officials at the Soviet Ministry of Foreign Affairs, the Ambassador reported on "changed thinking in Moscow on Indo–Pakistan problems."[2]

This changed thinking became more evident during the unfortunate and ruinous armed conflict of 1965. The war between India and Pakistan erupted in April in the marshy lands of the Rann of Kutch, spread in August to the mountains of Kashmir, and finally, on September 6, 1965, hit the plains of Punjab when India crossed the international border and attacked Pakistan in what President Ayub called "the biggest tank battle since the Second World War began,"[3] not surpassed until the Arab–Israel wars of 1967 and 1973.

The Soviet reporting of the war was unsensational in style and scrupulously impartial in content. The Indian and Pakistani versions of actions and events were published either in sequence or, more commonly, in parallel columns with the laconic headings "Delhi" and "Karachi."[4] When fighting began in the disputed territories of Kashmir, an August 24, 1965, *Pravda* article entitled "Urgent Necessity" noted the contradictory press reports put forth by the two sides "between which we are not going to adjudicate." No bias was betrayed in the Soviet press in respect to the competing claims, and no guilt was imputed to either side. The Soviets reported with satisfaction the April cease-fire in the Rann of Kutch, achieved through the mediation of Britain, in a terse message from Karachi. This contrasted markedly with previous Soviet attitude and practice. Even two years earlier, Indo–Pakistani fighting would have been condemned without qualification in the Soviet press as the work of the "Western stooge" Pakistan against "peace-loving, non-aligned" India. When full-scale war started on September 6, Brezhnev blamed the organizers of "aggressive military pacts" who, according to him, objected to the notion that India should be non-aligned; "lately," he added, "they have been displeased by Pakistan's determination to pursue an untutored policy."[5]

Subsequently Kosygin appealed to both Ayub and Shastri to stop fighting. On September 17 the second message from Kosygin suggested the talks between the two countries that ultimately took place at Tashkent in January 1966.[6] (At the Security Council in New York, the United States and the U.S.S.R. worked together to bring about a cease-fire; there was near identity of action and purpose between the two superpowers, particularly following China's ultimatum to India.)[7] When the cease-fire was signed, Kosygin again addressed the leaders of the two countries and expressed his government's satisfaction.

THE TASHKENT CONFERENCE

Although the September 20 cease-fire resolution of the Security Council had been accepted by India and Pakistan and the actual fighting ended on September 23, troops of both countries remained in positions occupied at the end of the fighting; tensions were still high; complaints of cease-fire violations were constant. Mediation was urgently needed to restore the prewar status quo, if not to resolve the causes that had led to the war. The United States could not play the role of peacemaker because of President Lyndon B. Johnson's abrupt, even discourteous cancellation of his invitations to Shastri and Ayub to visit the United States in early 1965.[8] The Commonwealth could not play the role because British Prime Minister Harold Wilson had denounced India's September 6 attack across the international frontier.[9] China could not mediate because it had openly favored Pakistan and even threatened to intervene.[10]

Only the Soviet Union, thanks to its new posture of neutrality in Indo–Pakistani disputes, could command the confidence of both India and Pakistan. And in sponsoring the Tashkent Conference, the peacemaking U.S.S.R. achieved what was regarded by large segments of the Western press as one of its greatest diplomatic feats since the Second World War.[11]

I had opportunities to read the minutes of the conference, and I also conducted interviews with Ayub, his principal secretary, and other senior Pakistani participants in the conference. The following account is the fruit of this research.

Ayub and Shastri met separately with Premier Kosygin on January 3, the day before the conference started; throughout the discussions, which culminated with the issue of the famous declaration at the end of the conference on January 10, Kosygin was the chief actor, holding long, separate consultations with Ayub and Shastri and also bringing the two together at the conference table for direct talks. At the first Kosygin–Ayub meeting on January 3, the Premier suggested that a "good way to deal with Indo–Pakistan differences would be to take up the relatively small problems and then go to the more complicated issues." As listed by Kosygin, the "small problems" were restoration of diplomatic relations, troop withdrawals, reestablishment of the frontier, and exchange of prisoners. Ayub termed Kosygin's suggestion "one possible approach" and added that "the first thing needed was an agreement on the disengagement of the armies by withdrawing them to the previous position." Ayub emphasized, however, that "there must be a settlement of Kashmir." Kosygin replied, "As soon as the Kashmir question would be taken up, all sorts of complications would arise." The first essential, Kosygin repeated, "was to create mutual trust and confidence in order to create a better atmosphere for the discussion of more difficult questions." (India also favored what it called a "step by step" approach—tackling the minor issues first and then proceeding to more complicated issues.) Pushing on, Ayub proposed that the question of reducing the respective armed forces to reasonable levels be discussed. Here Kosygin referred to India's "no-war declaration" offer that had been pending since 1950 and had long been debated in Indo–Pakistani dialogue.[12] Ayub told Kosygin that in his speech at the UN General Assembly in December 1965 he had offered to conclude such a pact with India, provided India agreed to a procedure for solving the Kashmir dispute; but a "no war" pact without such a procedure, the President said, would be totally unacceptable.

Kosygin's role as intermediary was crucial. Ayub made it clear that there would be no direct meetings between India and Pakistan without the Soviet participation, and Kosygin relayed Ayub's views to Shastri and Shastri's to Ayub. Speaking of himself, Kosygin told Ayub: "The question is not whether he agrees or disagrees with what Ayub thinks desirable or fair. It is for India and Pakistan to agree between themselves." Kosygin stressed the hope that "although the discussion will be very complex, some solution will be found."

Kosygin began the conference proceedings by welcoming the visiting parties and expressing the wish that fruitful results would emerge from the conference. Shastri and Ayub, avoiding polemics and bitterness, set a similar tone. The Prime Minister said he hoped that the conference would lead to a change in the political climate prevailing between the two countries. Shastri indicated that the discussion might be pursued on two levels—at the summit level among Ayub, Kosygin, and Shastri "to discuss the broad and complicated issues," and at the ministerial level to deal with "the other matters." This suggestion represented a compromise between, on one hand, India's earlier stand that secondary issues should be settled before talks began on such complicated issues as Kashmir and, on the other hand, Pakistan's demand that fundamental causes of the war be settled first. Ayub termed the conference historic and a possible turning point in the affairs of the two countries. So conciliatory was Ayub that in his opening speech he did not even mention the word "Kashmir"—an omission that was appreciated by the Indian press and criticized by the President's political opponents in Pakistan.[13]

Held in Gromyko's presence, a ministerial meeting on January 5 was marked by sharp and polemical exchanges between Bhutto and Foreign Minister Swaran Singh. Singh argued that Kashmir "is an integral part of India," that Pakistan realized that this was India's conviction, and that there was no need to discuss the issue; Kashmir, he stressed, "roused . . . even stronger emotions in India" than in Pakistan. Bhutto, on the other hand, repeated the gist of Ayub's remarks: "we must address ourselves," contended the Foreign Minister, "to finalizing a solution of the Kashmir problem." But it was clear that Bhutto's effectiveness was limited: setting aside his exchanges with Swaran Singh, his talks with Gromyko were far from friendly. The significant dialogues were those at the summit level, where Kosygin worked vigorously to bring about a rapprochement between Ayub and Shastri, both of whom were sincere in trying to find a solution. A reading of the minutes of the conference discussions indicates that the Kashmir issue could have figured more prominently in the Tashkent Declaration—as the Pakistanis would have liked—had Bhutto and his Foreign Secretary Aziz Ahmad been more realistic: their insistence upon referring to UN resolutions calling for a plebiscite in Kashmir was anathema to India and hardened the Indians' stand against any meaningful reference to Kashmir in the Tashkent Declaration.

With the Kashmir issue effectively buried, the crucial point at Tashkent was the withdrawal of troops by both sides to prewar positions. India would not agree to any withdrawal of troops unless Pakistan agreed to a "no war" pact, but it was impossible for Ayub or any other Pakistani leader to sign such a pact without some progress on the Kashmir issue. The result was deadlock, and the conference tottered on the verge of failure. India not only wanted to link the withdrawal of the troops with the signing of a "no war" agreement but also sought both nations' promise of "respect for each other's territorial integrity"—and Kashmir was to be counted as part of India's territory. This was totally unacceptable to Pakistan. Pakistan's draft stated that "all disputes should be settled through peaceful means"; Pakistan did not want the phrase "not resorting to force" included in the declaration.

Subsequently Kosygin offered a compromise: Pakistan and India "agree that disputes and differences between the two countries shall not be settled by recourse to means other than peaceful." Kosygin suggested this wording to Ayub during their meeting on January 9, and the President, complaining that Kosygin's formula was not an "improvement" over the Indian draft, presented Pakistan's own compromise formula: India and Pakistan "reaffirm their obligations under the UN charter not to have recourse to force and to settle disputes through peaceful means." Kosygin approved of Ayub's wording and promised to seek India's acceptance. At the same meeting Kosygin also reported to Ayub that India insisted upon an understanding that the cease-fire line in Kashmir would not be violated. Ayub fumed, perceiving that India wanted a subtle de facto recognition of the cease-fire line as an international border between India and Pakistan. "India always wants from Pakistan the last pound of flesh and the last drop of blood," he sneered. Kosygin suggested careful wording—"both sides will observe the cease-fire terms on the cease-fire lines"—and Ayub approved. The President made it clear, however, that he accepted Kosygin's suggestion only to avoid "embarrassing the Soviet Union"; he could compromise "no further." Thus Pakistan compromised, but it also gained at the January 9 meeting as Kosygin made his most significant remark on the Kashmir issue: "The Soviet Union appreciates that a dispute exists in Kashmir . . . of course there is a dispute," he said. Ayub thanked Kosygin for this major change in the Soviet attitude. Since the mid-1950s and the Khrushchev–Bulganin trip to India the Soviet Union had persistently supported the Indian claim that the Kashmir dispute had been settled and that Kashmir was an integral part of India. The change represented a great success for Ayub's personal diplomacy.

After his meeting with Ayub, Kosygin immediately called on Shastri to get India's approval on the compromise wording worked out with Ayub. With the fate of the Tashkent Conference depending on Shastri's acceptance, Kosygin applied all his tact and skill and finally achieved success.

The Tashkent Declaration was signed by India and Pakistan on January 10, 1966. In lieu of the "no war" declaration sought by India, there was a "no force" commitment proposed by Ayub. On Kashmir, the declaration merely stated that "Jammu and Kashmir were discussed and each side set forth its respective positions." The declaration solved none of the outstanding disputes between India and Pakistan, but it put an end to the state of undeclared war between the two countries with the withdrawal of troops to prewar positions.[14] Neither India nor Pakistan was wholly satisfied; in Pakistan the conference, widely and violently criticized, marked the beginning of the fall of Ayub Khan. The Soviets' satisfaction, however, was immense: the Tashkent Conference made the Soviet position unique in the subcontinent until 1970. During the conference the Soviet attitude was described by both sides as impartial and fair, and Ayub and the Pakistani delegation were impressed by Kosygin's handling of one of the most complicated international rivalries on the contemporary scene.

Only Foreign Minister Bhutto and Foreign Secretary Aziz Ahmad—the hawks who had prevented Pakistan from faring better at Tashkent—complained about the Soviet conduct. But many conference participants complained of Bhutto's conduct. When Bhutto continued to rail about Kashmir's plebiscite, Foreign Minister Gromyko had to remind him that since Pakistan had failed to achieve its goal by war, Bhutto should not expect the Soviet Union to be able to deliver Kashmir to Pakistan at the conference table. Similarly Gromyko pointed out to his volatile Pakistani counterpart that the withdrawal of troops was more important for Pakistan than for India; the former occupied desert lands of India near Sind, but India held the strategic areas near Lahore and Sialkot.

Despite his complaints, Bhutto was one of those who prepared the declaration, and he immediately defended it both inside and outside the National Assembly of Pakistan. It was only after his dismissal by Ayub in 1966 that he became a great opponent of the Tashkent agreement and began threatening to disclose the "secrets" of Tashkent. In the course of his political attacks on Ayub in the winter of 1968–1969, Bhutto stressed these "secret clauses" of the agreement and claimed that Ayub had "sold" Pakistan's interests under crude Soviet pressure. At the time, the Soviet government made the unusual gesture of officially denying the existence of secret clauses.[15] Later, after his retirement, Ayub told me that the only "secrets" about the Tashkent Conference were Bhutto's irrational attitude and statements; Ayub said that he had to seek the help of the Soviet Premier to overcome the obstacles to agreement imposed by his own Foreign Minister.

TRIPS TO MOSCOW AND ARMS TO PAKISTAN

The Tashkent Declaration disappointed many people because it brought final solution to the Indo–Pakistani problems no nearer. After Tashkent India's attitude hardened, as evidenced by its refusal even to discuss the Kashmir dispute at the subsequent Indo–Pakistani ministerial conferences in January–February 1966. Thus Tashkent, like such other Indo–Pakistani agreements as the Liaquat–Nehru pact of 1950, produced no more than a short pause in the course of perennial Indo–Pakistani disputes and tensions.

As the architect of Tashkent, the Soviet Union was not happy to see its souring, and it urged both sides to keep up "the Tashkent spirit." Pakistan tried again to persuade the Soviet leaders that the stumbling block to improvement in subcontinent relations was India's refusal to discuss the basic issues. In previous years the U.S.S.R. had invariably heaped blame on Pakistan, but now, thanks to the better understanding between the two countries, Pakistan was not blamed alone for the evaporation of "the Tashkent spirit."

Moreover, the Soviet Union, while not admitting it publicly, seemed to feel that Pakistan's fears over the massive arms buildup in India were both genuine and reasonable. The Pakistani leaders believed that the Soviet Union, having finally grasped the complexities of the situation, realized that if peace in the subcontinent was to be maintained, something must be done to alleviate their apprehensions arising from the new military imbalance. The Soviet Union did not wish to reduce or curtail its military shipments to India, but it could no longer be flatly indifferent to Pakistan's requests for military supplies.[16]

"The improvement of our relations with Pakistan is cause for satisfaction," Premier Kosygin reported to the Supreme Soviet in 1966. "The Soviet Union, for its part, intends to take further steps to expand Soviet–Pakistan ties."[17] Indicative of the new Soviet open-mindedness required for such an expansion of ties was an article by S. Mikoyan that appeared in *Mirovaya ekonomika i mezhdunarodnye otnosheniya* (*MEMO*) (No. 2, 1966). This discussion of the Tashkent Conference included references to the history of Kashmir that, like earlier Soviet writings, discussed the "invasion" of Kashmir by armed tribesmen from Pakistan in October 1947. But, in a marked departure from earlier Soviet writings, the article summarized Pakistan's case on Kashmir as well as India's. Both sides must display fortitude, flexibility, and good will, said the author. "If India categorically refused to speak about Kashmir at all," Mikoyan added, "one could hardly expect Pakistan's president to remain at the conference table."[18]

In this changed atmosphere both Mrs. Indira Gandhi and Ayub traveled to the U.S.S.R.

Mrs. Gandhi paid her first visit to Moscow as the Indian Prime Minister from July 12 to July 16, 1966. She received at least as warm a welcome as had her predecessors since 1955, and she held talks with the Soviets in what was reported by the Indian and Soviet press to be an "atmosphere of friendship and understanding." Indo–Soviet bilateral relations were discussed, and the two sides expressed identical views on many major international issues. On these, Mrs. Gandhi seemed to have gone farther than had Nehru and Shastri in endorsing the Soviet viewpoint. *Pravda* reported on July 17:

> The two sides expressed concern in connection with the deterioration of the international situation and the growth of the danger

of war that has taken place recently as a result of aggressive actions of imperialist and other reactionary forces. . . .

The *Pravda* article went on to detail Indo–Soviet agreement on "the dangerous situation in Southeast Asia" and on the "obstacle in the path to cooperation among states" imposed by foreign military bases. (The tensions caused in many parts of the world by *Soviet* policies, actions, and military bases were conveniently forgotten.)

Earlier, from April 23 to April 30, talks were conducted in Moscow among the chiefs—First Secretary Brezhnev among them—of the Communist parties of the Soviet Union and India. On May 1, 1966, *Pravda* noted that India "pursues a policy of non-alignment which is in its vital interest and promotes the preservation of peace and security"; and the Communist party of India, *Pravda* reported, "expressed satisfaction with the strengthening of friendship and economic cooperation between the Soviet Union and India and expressed the hope that this friendship would continue and develop. . . ." The CPI, under the direction of the CPSU, thus endorsed Mrs. Gandhi's policy.

Mrs. Gandhi made a twelve-day tour of Eastern Europe in October 1967, and the Soviet press paid her high tributes.[19]

Ayub journeyed to the U.S.S.R. for the third and last time in September 1967. He told Kosygin—who among Soviet leaders seemed particularly aware of Pakistan's difficulties—his version of Indo–Pakistani relations, and the Premier recalled his recent talks with the Foreign Minister and other Indian officials. "What they say," remarked Kosygin, "is 180 degrees different from what you have stated."[20] Both Indians and Pakistanis wanted the same goods from the U.S.S.R.; with the Soviet attitude toward his country considerably relaxed, the President was seeking Soviet arms. Moscow did not need to be told that the U.S. decision to cut off military supplies to the subcontinent[21] had hurt Pakistan more because its Chinese military assistance was no match for the huge Soviet military shipments to India.

The Soviet leaders listened to Ayub's pleas with greater understanding if not with more sympathy than in 1965, and they were not happy to see Pakistan becoming solely dependent upon China for military assistance. Kosygin's question for Ayub, however, was blunt: "Does Pakistan believe that it could stay in the pacts and yet ask for the assistance of the Soviet Union for the solution of its problems with India?" Pakistan had already begun the process of disengagement from the pacts, Ayub replied, but did not want to incur the wrath of the United States by wrecking the pacts through a formal walk out. To satisfy the Soviets, Ayub indicated that he would give notice of termination for the U.S. intelligence communications center at Badabar. This was a significant move, and Ayub secured Soviet assurance that his request for arms would be given due consideration. For his part, Ayub expressed readiness to promise that Pakistan "will not misuse the arms supplied by the Soviet Union"; Ayub was prepared to "give any guarantee—any that will satisfy you or any reasonable person that peace will not be disturbed in that part of the world." He concluded: "Our policy is very clear: we wish security; our main problem is economic development. We do not wish to retard that process."

Having promised to consider seriously the question, the Soviet leaders asked for more time to decide on Pakistan's request for arms. Ayub pointed out that Pakistan had been seeking an answer for two years, and Brezhnev interjected, "Pakistan has already waited for two years, now that period may be reduced by one-fourth, i.e. wait for another six months." The decision came seven months later.

The notice of closure for the Badabar base was given in early 1968, and promptly in April 1968 Kosygin made the first visit to Pakistan by a Soviet head of state or government. The Premier expressed great satisfaction with Pakistan's decision regarding the Badabar base, which had been maintained for activity against the U.S.S.R. Kosygin also noted his concern about Pakistan's growing ties with Peking. (Similarly, the Chinese warned Pakistan about friendship with Moscow. "Just as you know India in a better way," the Chinese leaders told Ayub, "so we know the Soviet Union better than you." Pakistan was beginning to experience great difficulty in maintaining good relations with both Moscow and Peking—as much difficulty as that of the early 1960s when it sought to have friendship with both Washington and Peking. For a nation of the subcontinent to maintain good relations with two major powers can be as tricky as for a major power to maintain good relations with the two leaders of the subcontinent.)

It was during this visit that Kosygin agreed to sell a modest quantity of arms to Pakistan. This marked a grand success for Ayub's diplomacy. It had been a long and complicated journey from Khrushchev's threats of rocket annihilation to arms supplies from

Moscow. Analyzing the objectives of the Soviet decision, the *Financial Times* (London) wrote on July 23, 1968:

> The Soviet decision . . . seems to have been motivated from three considerations: (1) A collusion of interests between the Soviet Union and the U.S. to maintain the *status quo* in the Indian subcontinent; in other words, helping India and Pakistan in turn with military equipment just enough to ensure that one does not become so strong as to present a threat to the other. . . . (2) The Soviet Union was becoming so worried about the increasing dependence of Pakistan on Chinese military aid that Moscow thought it best to wean Pakistan away from Peking by offering her arms; the Soviets knew that this would offend India but they thought it was a risk they would have to take. (3) One direct concession which the Soviet Union probably hopes to win from Pakistan is permission to establish observation posts in Pakistan, particularly East Pakistan. Moscow has been getting increasingly worried about the Chinese influence in Cambodia, Burma and the Himalayan region and observation posts in East Pakistan would be a very valuable asset to Moscow in its long-term plans to check Chinese moves in the area. . . .

With the decision to sell arms to Pakistan, which wrought new and powerful leverage, the Soviet Union emerged as the most important and influential of the three major powers in the affairs of the subcontinent. It was a remarkable diplomatic achievement; within fifteen years the Soviet Union had risen from a state of hardly any power in either India or Pakistan to become the dominant foreign agent, and perhaps the most menacing, both in the South Asian subcontinent and in the Indian Ocean.

That dominance was only possible, of course, through gingerly treatment of India in the wake of the announcement of the Pakistani arms deal, and gingerly treatment was applied. An episode in U.S.–Pakistani relations provides an interesting contrast here. President Kennedy assured Ayub that Pakistan would be consulted if and when the United States decided to give arms to India; but in 1962, when the United States initiated military aid to India, that pledge was not honored.[22] The Pakistani reaction was hysterical. Bitter debates raged in the National Assembly, a United States Information Service library at Rawalpindi burned, and much good will, laboriously built up over a number of years by both countries, went up in the flames that consumed the effigies of President Kennedy in city streets.

Both the Soviet Union and India showed much greater maturity and wisdom six years later, demonstrating that their friendship could stand time's test and that their diplomats could handle the most delicate issue in Indo–Soviet relations with the care it required. Kosygin expected adverse reaction from India over the decision to sell arms to its neighbor, and on his return from Pakistan he stopped at New Delhi to consult with Mrs. Gandhi. The Premier stressed that arms sales to Pakistan neither harmed India's vital national interest nor vitiated its ties with Moscow. Mrs. Gandhi officially protested the arms sales, but she accepted the Soviet assurances. In her first public statement on the question, the Prime Minister said in Calcutta on July 9, 1968, that although "naturally we are not happy with the Soviet decision," there would be no change in India's policy toward the Soviet Union."[23] In Lok Sabha, the Indian Parliament, members of the opposition Swatantra party sought to censure the government for what they called the "failure of its foreign policy as evidenced by the Soviet decision to give arms to Pakistan"; in response, Mrs. Gandhi stated that India was bound to state its "misgivings and apprehensions," but she noted that she did not question the Soviet Union's right to supply arms to Pakistan or doubt that the Soviets acted in good faith. The opposition's adjournment motion was rejected on July 22, 1968, by 206 to 61.[24]

INDIAN RELATIONS FROM 1968

The most significant Soviet excursion to India in the post-Nehru period was Kosygin's trip in January 1968. The invitation had been extended a year and a half before, during Prime Minister Gandhi's visit, and the timing of the Kosygin trip gave rise to two schools of thought: the Soviets and Indian opponents of the Prime Minister claimed that Mrs. Gandhi pressed Kosygin to come at this time in order to strengthen her position at home; others held that Kosygin took the initiative to investigate for himself disquieting reports that the right wing of the Congress party had become dominant and Mrs. Gandhi was losing her hold. Whichever the case, many believed that Kosygin's presence on Indian Republic Day, January 26, 1968, was intended—by one if not both sides—to boost Mrs. Gandhi's position. Meeting with the Indian communist leaders, Kosygin advised them not to create any problem for Mrs.

Gandhi, who, in the Soviet view, made a better Prime Minister than anyone who might succeed her.

The Soviet aim was to bolster India's economy and thereby bolster Mrs. Gandhi in relation to her rightist opponents, who were anxious to make India lean toward the West. To alleviate India's balance-of-payments difficulties, Kosygin promised to double Soviet trade with India by 1970–1971 and to take more manufactured goods than before—including enough railroad cars to absorb India's surplus capacity until 1995. He agreed to import as well such manufactured and semimanufactured articles as heavy electrical and jute products. Kosygin also secured Indian agreements on a coordination of development plans: Soviet planners would take into account India's productive capacity, and India would take into account Soviet requirements.[25]

India's economic difficulties no doubt stemmed in part from its heavy military spending, and by this time the Soviet Union was the largest supplier of the most costly sophisticated weapons. Kosygin gave Mrs. Gandhi the same advice he had been giving Pakistan since 1966: peacefully settle the Indo–Pakistani disputes in accordance with the Tashkent Declaration. Any breach of the peace, Kosygin told the Indians, would be viewed with the utmost concern and disfavor by the Kremlin—which, like Washington, felt that any increase in Indo–Pakistani tensions would be harmful to its global policies because of China's growing influence in Pakistan. Kosygin seemed to be trying to impose a pax Sovietica—there was no chance of a pax Britannica or pax Americana—in the subcontinent. If this was Kosygin's goal, he could not have been discouraged by President Ayub Khan's January 28 message, delivered to him by the Pakistani Ambassador in New Delhi, urging him to use his influence to settle the Indo–Pakistani disputes, including Kashmir.[26]

When the Soviet Union led the Warsaw Pact invasion of Czechoslovakia in August 1968, the Indian reaction was critical but cautious. Mrs. Gandhi's dependence on the Soviet military assistance muted her protest, and the Indian press termed the invasion a blunder rather than an outrage. In Pakistan, the reaction to Soviet actions in Czechoslovakia was also mild.

During the preceding one and a half decades, the Soviet Union had achieved considerable success in India through economic and military aid, diplomatic support on India's vital national issues, extensive cultural exchanges, trade relations, and various other means. Of late, military assistance has been the Soviets' most effective tool for increasing influence and power.[27] Since the United States banned military shipments to the subcontinent in the wake of the 1965 war, the Soviet Union has become the largest supplier of India's military. By 1966 Soviet military aid to India was valued at about $300 million annually. Since 1961 contracts valued at between $800 million and $1 billion have been signed, and deliveries, though sometimes delayed, have been substantial. The Indian Air Force is now predominantly supplied with Soviet aircraft, including MIG 21s made in India and SU-7 fighter bombers. The navy was expanded in the period 1966–1968 with Moscow's submarines, escort vessels, torpedo boats, and patrol boats, and the Soviets provide a sizable number of T-55 tanks. On Indian Republic Day, January 26, 1969, Soviet aircraft, tanks, and other military equipment were conspicuously displayed. India has always been unwilling to rely heavily upon a single country for military supplies, but since 1965 its dependence on the Soviet Union has grown considerably.[28] Soviet influence in India has grown along with it.

I discussed in Chapter 2 the substantial Soviet economic aid to India since the latter's third five-year plan. The U.S.S.R. has maintained a fairly extensive aid program to India since 1969, with the bulk of the assistance in loans rather than grants. *Pravda* noted on February 6, 1970:

> It is 15 years since the signing of the first Soviet–Indian agreement on economic cooperation. The agreement envisaged Soviet financial aid and technical cooperation for India in the construction of Bhilai Metallurgical Plant . . . by now 65 large plants, power stations and other projects of importance to the Indian economy have been built or are under construction on Indian soil with the aid of USSR.

(The Soviet economic aid to India, however, has never matched that of the United States. From 1954 to 1967, in fact, it equaled only about one-fourth of American aid.)

In addition, the two countries concluded in 1967–1968 agreements for scientific exploration, shipping, and joint space research, and in recent years they have expanded considerably their trade with each other. From the Soviet side, aid, joint ventures, and trade have been intended to increase leverage in South Asia through special links with the dominant power in the area.

THE IMPACT OF SINO–SOVIET TENSIONS

With subcontinent affairs moving generally to its satisfaction, the Soviet Union undertook several definitive steps to thwart China in South Asia, part of a worldwide effort to contain its communist enemy.

In 1969, a year that witnessed serious fighting on the Sino–Soviet border, the effect of the growing Soviet campaign began to be felt in Pakistan, which was greatly dependent upon China for military supplies and other support. The Soviet Defense Minister, Marshal Andrei A. Grechko, came to Pakistan in February and told Foreign Secretary S. M. Yousuf "you can not have simultaneous friendship with the Soviet Union and China." Yousuf noted that the Soviet Union had sought friendship with India and Pakistan, but Grechko ruled the point irrelevant. "What is permissible for a superpower," he said bluntly, "is not possible for a country like Pakistan."[29] At a May meeting of the Pakistani envoys to neighbors and to major powers, Ambassador to Moscow Salman Ali said that moves against China were the main factor of recent Soviet policy in South and Southeast Asia; countries such as Pakistan that sought good relations with Peking as well as Moscow, warned the Ambassador, would be put to "crude pressures." The experts on the Soviet Union at the Ministry of Foreign Affairs, including myself, also expressed concern over growing Soviet pressure "to unite against Mao."[30]

Interestingly, at roughly the same time that the U.S.S.R. began a serious effort to curtail Chinese ties with Pakistan, China expressed concern over Pakistan's desperate wooing of the Kremlin and its "being exposed to the Soviet influence." The Chinese leaders' warnings about the Soviet Union were proving accurate, as it now began to demand political payment for its arms supplies to Pakistan: it pushed for Pakistani membership in groupings that ostensibly would serve economic and security ends but in reality would be primarily designed to contain China. As evidenced by the visit of Nikolai V. Podgorny, Chairman of the Presidium of the Supreme Soviet, to North Korea and Mongolia in early 1969 and by Kosygin's visit to India, Pakistan, and Afghanistan, also in early 1969, the anti-China campaign had become a key to Soviet foreign policy. The subcontinent—India as well as Pakistan—could not help but be affected.

KOSYGIN'S REGIONAL ECONOMIC GROUPING

The idea of such a regional grouping was not new when, in early 1969, Kosygin suggested in Kabul that a cooperative organization be established by Pakistan, Afghanistan, India, Iran, and the Soviet Union. The Afghan Foreign Minister put forth a similar proposal in 1966, and the United States endorsed the idea for the subcontinent in 1967 when it resumed economic aid to Pakistan and India.[31] Pakistan itself was an exponent of regional cooperation, taking the initiative for collaboration and development among Iran, Turkey, and itself. But Kosygin's plan only appeared innocuous: it was intended to consolidate the Soviet position and to contain the Chinese in South Asia. Moreover, Pakistan had always maintained that meaningful economic cooperation was not possible when political relations among the potential partners were strained—as were its own with Afghanistan and India.

During his second Pakistani visit within thirteen months in May 1969, Kosygin met at length with Yahya Khan, who had assumed the presidency on March 25, and urged him to accept the regional grouping proposal.[32] Kosygin shrewdly stressed only the economic aspects. He said that in the past the Pakistani government, aided by the capitalist countries, had engaged in "vain efforts" to eliminate the nation's widespread poverty—in this context he apparently sought to please Yahya by referring to the failure of Ayub's economic policy. Pakistan welcomed Kosygin's offer of Soviet development aid and trade, but the President was warned by his foreign policy experts, including me, "to be cautious of involvement in the Soviet Union's more far-reaching economic proposals with political overtones." Kosygin pushed ahead, pressuring Yahya to accept his proposal for a conference of Pakistan, India, Afghanistan, and the Soviet Union at the Deputy Foreign Minister level "to discuss the question of transit trade." He added that "Iran and Turkey could also be brought into this arrangement [the conference of deputy ministers]." Yahya, a simple man and a novice in diplomatic dialogues with a major power, accepted Kosygin's conference proposal in the belief that this acceptance did not represent a commitment to join the proposed grouping; the Soviet Premier got the impression that Pakistan had endorsed his economic proposals.

In the meantime, the Pakistani Ministry of Foreign Affairs as well as the military intelligence pointed out to Yahya the grave implications of a Soviet-built political grouping on China's southwest flank. Such publications as *Dawn* and the *Pakistan Times* also lambasted the idea of Pakistan's joining the Soviet-sponsored economic community, and Yahya finally realized his mistake.

When the Soviet Ambassador in Pakistan began to remind him of his previous intention to send representatives to the deputy foreign ministers' conference, the President tried to avoid the issue. On July 10, 1969, a Foreign Ministry spokesman, calling the Soviet plan of "little economic advantage," said that Pakistan would not join an "alliance opposed to China."[33] Analyzing Pakistan's turn away from the Kosygin plan, the Indian newspaper *Hindustan Times* on May 23, 1969, mentioned Pakistan's concern that a system of cooperation which includes a "giant-like Soviet Union" might work to the disadvantage of the Asian countries. It was, however, the suspicion that Moscow was forming a political league against China that was the main factor in Pakistan's refusal. Kosygin himself had firmly planted this suspicion. "China is not interested in peace in this region," the Premier told Yahya during their talks on the proposed group, "while the Soviet Union wants peace and stability in the region." The Pakistanis found it as hard to agree with this assessment as they did to believe what Kosygin said to Yahya next. During their meeting in Peking in fall 1964, said Kosygin, Mao told him that "China should be given a free hand in Asian affairs while the Soviet Union should have a free hand in Europe." Kosygin claimed that the Soviet Union could not agree and that this refusal caused "friction between the Soviet Union and China." Kosygin also leveled charges concerning "China's involvement in East Pakistan." Yahya replied, "there is no such evidence." In fact, Pakistan was more worried about direct Indian and indirect Soviet involvement in East Pakistan.

New Delhi and Kabul received Kosygin's proposals more favorably. This was evident from the joint communiqué issued after Mrs. Gandhi's visit to Afghanistan in June 1969 and from an Indo–Soviet agreement signed in March 1970. Under this agreement India agreed to finance a road from Kandahar in Afghanistan (linked by road to the Soviet border) to the Iranian border, there to join an Iranian-built road to the Persian Gulf port of Bandar Abbas. The Soviet Union would thus obtain an outlet, much needed since the closing of the Suez Canal, for its trade to South and Southeast Asia—the route would pass through Afghanistan and Iran but bypass Pakistan. In July 1970 the Soviet Union also completed another sector of highway in Afghanistan, a highway that ultimately will lead from the Soviet Union to modern roads reaching down to Pakistan; the Soviets may hope to use this route, in preference to the sea route via Vladivostok, for the delivery of naval stores to their growing Indian Ocean fleet.

BREZHNEV'S ASIAN COLLECTIVE SECURITY SYSTEM

One of the ironies of the feud with China is that it led the Soviets to the very "Dullesism"—the propagation of military pacts—that it had damned for more than fifteen years. The proposed Soviet collective security system in Asia was introduced to the world by First Secretary Brezhnev in his speech to the international meeting of the Communist parties in Moscow on June 7, 1969.[34] A few days before, *Izvestia* gave some details of the proposed security plan, which was described as a defensive measure to safeguard the independence of Asian countries against "imperialist aggression and neo-colonialism."[35] That its real aim was to restrict Chinese influence becomes clear from an analysis of the Soviet envoys' and leaders' diplomatic dialogues with the Pakistanis, the Indians, and others. In fact, as I told Yahya after carefully reading the minutes of his July 1969 talks with the Soviet Ambassador, the plan called for nothing but "the Russian version of SEATO."[36]

Following a Moscow conference of Soviet envoys, the Ambassador to Pakistan called on Yahya as well as the Pakistan Foreign Secretary to try to sell the Brezhnev scheme. He described the proposed plan in lofty terms, stressing such features as "noninterference in internal affairs of signatory countries" and "economic, cultural and scientific cooperation." The Ambassador pointed out to the Foreign Secretary "the inadequacy of economic collaboration" under SEATO and CENTO in contrast to the more worthwhile collaboration under the Soviet plan.

But upon being questioned about security aspects of the plan, the Soviet Ambassador had to reveal its main purpose, which had to do, not with economic cooperation, but with China. The specifics of the proposed security agreement also made this plain. For example, the signatories would not enter into any alliance, formal or informal, with a third country that might be hostile to any member countries, nor should they "make any commitment inconsistent with the proposed Asian Security Plan"; in addition, the signatory countries "will consult each other in case of an aggression by a third party." The anti-China slant was also indicated by the fact that Brezhnev announced the plan only three months after the most serious armed conflict to date on Sino–Soviet borders; the chances of a full-scale Soviet attack on China could not be ruled out, and there was speculation, not entirely baseless, that the Soviets might strike at the Chinese nuclear installations. Moreover, if the proposed security plan could be used against a nation that Pakistan considered a friend, it apparently could *not* be used against Pakistan's true enemy. Yahya wanted to know what help, if any, the Brezhnev plan would offer "in case of an aggression com-mited by one member country against another"—such as would be the case in a repetition of the 1965 Indo–Pakistani war. The answer was as evasive as it was rhetorical: "The Asian Security Plan will put an end to such regional conflicts which the Imperialist countries like U.S.A. and expansionist ones like China encouraged."

Pakistanis were practically unanimous in opposing the Brezhnev plan. The army made it clear to the policy makers that it would not allow them to respond favorably (although they were not in-clined to do so anyway), and the press also scorned the plan.[37] Yahya sent one of the top members of his military junta, Air Marshal Nur Khan, to assure Peking that Pakistan would never be a party to any direct or indirect anti-China move, economic, political, or military. "Pakistan shall not succumb to Soviet pressure," Nur Khan told Premier Chou En-lai during extensive talks on July 13 and 14.

Reaction to the proposed Asian collective security system was not much more encouraging elsewhere. On a September 1969 Moscow visit to discuss the plan, Indian Foreign Minister Singh first commented rather favorably: "India welcomes the proposal . . . the essence of the Soviet Plan is the development of cooperation among the Asian countries for the purpose of strengthening peace".[38] But in view of India's traditional opposition to any form of military pact, Singh had to modify his position after he returned to New Delhi. Enthusiasm for the plan in other Asian countries was no greater than that for Dulles's Manila Pact (SEATO) in the mid-1950s.

The Soviets continued to extol the proposed security system's virtues and advantages to Asian countries—just as they denounced any form of alliance to which "the imperialists belong"—but without much apparent effect. The Soviet press launched a major campaign in December 1969, when the third ministerial meeting of the Association of South East Asian Nations (ASEAN) took place in Malaysia. On December 15 Moscow Radio proposed that a new regional grouping be formed with the assistance and participation of the Soviet Union as a "state with territory both in Europe and Asia." The Soviet claim that it was not merely a European power was first advanced, as we have seen, in 1964 by India in the attempt to include the U.S.S.R. in the Second Afro–Asian Conference, and since the Tashkent Conference the Soviet Union had been working particularly hard to establish its Asian credentials. During his visit to Pyongyang in the summer of 1970 Brezhnev claimed that Soviet ideas on European security were gaining approval and support from European publics and governments; "in the opinion of the Soviet Government," he said, similar ideas would also prove "quite acceptable" for the Asian continent.[39] But the Asian countries approached about the Soviet collective security system remained unimpressed.

President Yahya Khan scheduled a five-day visit to Moscow beginning June 22, 1969, and both the Soviet Ambassador to Pakistan and the Pakistani Ambassador in Moscow indicated that the Kremlin leaders would give top priority to the Asian security system in the dialogues. I was among those advisers in the ministries of Foreign Affairs, Defense, and Economic Affairs who prepared the President for the trip; having joined his Cabinet in October 1969, I was in active consultation with Yahya in his final planning sessions before heading for Moscow. Since joining the Ministry of Foreign Affairs in 1967, I had consistently warned both President Ayub Kahn and President Yahya Kahn of the Soviet designs in South Asia: I harbored no illusion about Soviet "friendship" for Pakistan.

During Yahya's lengthy talks with Kremlin leaders, Pakistan was assured of larger Soviet economic aid for the fourth five-year plan (1970–1975). Soviet assistance was promised for several industrial projects, including a million-ton steel-melting plant in Karachi.

But when Yahya raised the question of continued arms shipments to Pakistan, the Kremlin leaders demurred. Kosygin told Yahya, "You cannot expect Soviet arms while you are unwilling to endorse our Asian Security System." He added that the system would be "the best guarantee for her [Pakistan's] territorial integrity," pointing ominously to an "explosive situation in East Pakistan," "dangers of foreign involvement there," and "China's role." Yahya and his government disagreed. "China," said the President, "is sincerely interested in Pakistan's territorial integrity and sovereignty." Yahya, who by this time was acquainted with the technique of dealing with Soviet blackmail and blandishment, ended the dialogue with a polite but firm rejection of the Brezhnev and Kosygin proposals.

The Russians also sought to establish a radio relay communication center near the site of the former American Badabar base. While innocuous in theory, the proposal was revealed upon closer scrutiny as another clever Soviet device to make Pakistan sacrifice much more than it could hope to gain. As Communications Minister of the Yahya Cabinet, I examined the Soviet proposal and warned Yahya on the eve of his visit to the U.S.S.R. In a note to the President, I referred to the proposal as nothing but a "Russian version of the Badabar base" and worse; while it was easy to give notice to a Western country such as the United States to close a base, I said, "once you are in the Russian parlour, you are there forever."

Pakistan's rejection of the various proposals put forth by the U.S.S.R. as the "price" of military supplies doomed the era of better understanding and warmer relations between Moscow and Islamabad. In addition to their unwillingness to conform to Soviet plans and proposals, the Pakistanis annoyed the Soviet Union by providing links between Washington and Peking; their middleman's role was begun at the request of President Nixon during his twenty-two-hour visit to Pakistan in August 1969, and it culminated in the secret trip of Henry Kissinger to Peking via Rawalpindi in July 1971. The Soviet attitude toward Pakistan waxed harder and harder. On February 7, 1970, even before Yahya's June visit, *New Times* wrote a highly unfavorable article on Pakistan, thus reversing the attitude of the Soviet press, which had stopped its hostile comments on Pakistan after 1965.

Thus the Soviets were frowning at Pakistan when the Bangladesh crisis began in 1971. The relationship between this soured attitude and the prompt Soviet support for the Bangladesh movement was more than casual.

NOTES

1. *New Times,* January 19, 1965.
2. Based on my research and personal interviews in Pakistan, 1967–1971.
3. See Ayub's speech on Sept. 23 in *Dawn,* Sept. 24, 1965.
4. "Soviet Press Comment," *Central Asian Review,* no. 4, 1965, pp. 372–373.
5. *Ibid.*
6. *Pravda,* Sept. 18, 1965.
7. See Chapter 9.
8. See Chapter 5.
9. *The Times* (London), Sept. 7, 1965.
10. See Chapter 9.
11. See *New York Times, Christian Science Monitor, The Times* (London), and *The Guardian* (London), January 1966.
12. See Choudhury, *op. cit.,* pp. 216–222.
13. See the statement of F. Jinnah (the founder's sister and Ayub's opponent in the 1964 presidential election) in *Dawn,* Jan. 12, 1966.
14. See the text of the declaration in *Dawn* and *Pravda,* Jan. 11, 1966.
15. The Soviet news agency Tass made the denial, reported in *Dawn* and *Pravda,* Feb. 4, 1969.
16. Based on my research and personal interviews in Pakistan, 1967–1971.
17. *Pravda,* Aug. 4, 1966.
18. "Tashkent Conference," *Central Asian Review,* no. 3, 1966, pp. 274–278.
19. The Soviet reaction was reported in *The Statesman,* Oct. 20, 1967; *Pravda,* Oct. 25, 1967.
20. Except where otherwise indicated, the following account of Ayub's Moscow visit and Kosygin's return visit is based on my research and personal interviews in Pakistan, 1967–1971.
21. See Chapter 5.
22. Oehlert, *op. cit.*
23. *The Statesman,* July 10, 1968.
24. *Ibid.*

25. Based on my research and personal interviews in Pakistan, 1967–1971.

26. *Ibid.*

27. For an American interpretation of the Soviet penetration in India, see Palmer, *op. cit.*, pp. 31–32.

28. *Ibid.*

29. Based on my research and personal interviews in Pakistan, 1967–1971.

30. *Ibid.*

31. See Chapter 6.

32. Except where otherwise indicated, this section is based on my research and personal interviews in Pakistan, 1967–1971.

33. *Pakistan Times* (Rawalpindi), July 11, 1969.

34. *Pravda,* June 8, 1969.

35. See V. V. Matveyev, "A Filled Vacuum," *Izvestia,* May 29, 1969.

36. Except where otherwise indicated, the remainder of this section is based on my research and personal interviews in Pakistan, 1969–1971.

37. See *Pakistan Times* and other Pakistani newspapers, June–July, 1969.

38. *Pravda,* Sept. 21, 1969.

39. *Ibid.,* Aug. 16, 1970.

Part Two

The United States and the Subcontinent

Chapter Four

THE INITIAL PHASE, 1947–1960

FRIENDSHIP BUT MINIMAL INVOLVEMENT

WHEN INDIA AND PAKISTAN emerged as two independent dominions on August 15, 1947, the United States, unlike the Soviet Union, greeted the two countries warmly and also paid tribute to Great Britain for voluntarily and peacefully transferring power to the people of the subcontinent. President Truman told India's leaders, "We welcome India's new and enhanced status in the world community of sovereign independent states and assure the new dominion of our continued friendship and goodwill." Equally warm was the American President's message to the first Governor-General of Pakistan, Mohammed Ali Jinnah: "On this auspicious day which marks the emergence among the family of nations of the new dominion of Pakistan, I assure you that the new dominion embarks on its course with the firm friendship and goodwill of the United States of America."[1] The United States had watched the struggle for national independence with sympathy and interest and had sometimes encouraged the national aspirations of the Indian people, especially in the 1940s under President Franklin Roosevelt. Roosevelt was regarded by many Indians as a true champion of freedom and democracy, and stories persist about his concern and help for the freedom movements in India.[2]

Diplomatic relations with the two countries were established at the earliest opportunity. On October 24, 1946—about a year before the formal attainment of independence—it was announced that the Indian diplomatic mission in Washington and the American mission in New Delhi would be raised to the rank of embassies.[3] Soon the United States appointed a senior diplomat, Henry F. Grady, as its first Ambassador, and Nehru sent one of his Cabinet colleagues, Asaf Ali, to represent India in Washington. When it was decided that India would be divided and a separate state would be created, the United States was prompt in announcing that Pakistan would have the same diplomatic status as any other member of the British Commonwealth. On August 15, 1947, the United States extended full diplomatic recognition to Pakistan.[4]

But South Asia, a region of major American involvement by the mid-1950s, at first received little attention from the policy makers in Washington; in 1947 the United States, like the U.S.S.R., was preoccupied with more urgent problems in Europe and the Far East. The major problem of U.S. foreign policy now was relations with the Soviet Union. Since South Asia was comparatively free from immediate Cold War tension, Washington could afford to confine its role in this area to pious and friendly gestures of good will. Possibilities of assistance, particularly in the economic sphere, soon began to be explored, but in American eyes no major diplomatic, political, or military involvement was necessary. And none was contemplated.

U.S.–INDIAN POLITICAL RELATIONS, 1947–1952

Two main sets of factors dominated the relationship: (1) world and Asian affairs, and (2) Indo–American cooperation in various fields, especially economic. To grasp the impact of the first set of factors, it is necessary to refer to broad foreign policies of the United States and India during this period.

Postwar developments in Eastern Europe and the determined Russian attempts to consolidate and strengthen the communist bloc, attempts evidenced by the coup d'état in Czechoslovakia in 1948 and by the communist threats in France and Italy, convinced the policy makers in Washington that the Soviets would not honor agreements and pledges made at the wartime Tehran and Yalta conferences. The Americans were seriously concerned over Russian expansionism, and containment of international communism became the pivot of U.S. foreign policy. The result was the Truman Doctrine, the Marshall Plan, the Rio Pact, and the North Atlantic Treaty Organization (NATO). The Asian countries, on the other hand, saw not communism, but colonialism and racism as the menace; they saw the rising tide of nationalism as the dominant issue. Asian nationalist leaders were not much concerned by Soviet policies and actions in Europe. More important to them was the Soviet Union's unqualified support for anticolonialism both inside and outside the UN, support that seemed to contrast starkly with the American friendship for the very Western colonial powers that the nationalists were fighting. Invigorated by the voluntary liquidation of the British raj in India, Burma, and Ceylon, Nehru and other Asian nationalist leaders clashed with the adamant French and Dutch over Indochina and Indonesia.[5] The dominant, largest, and most stable country in the region, India could bid for leadership in the nationalist movements in Asia, and it did.[6]

The Indian Prime Minister was not unmindful of Russian moves and designs. Internally, he took firm measures against the Indian communists who sought to create violent problems for the government in southern India; he put thousands of Indian communists in jail. But on the international scene, Nehru was convinced of neither the righteousness of the Western cause nor the wrongs of the communist side. Aiming to keep clear of either bloc, he wished to be on good if not friendly terms with both Moscow and Washington.[7] Many Americans were disappointed that Nehru, with his strong liberal ideals, failed to support the forces of the "free world" and made no distinction between democracy and totalitarianism.[8] There was criticism of the Prime Minister's "double standard."[9] Nehru preached peace and understanding between East and West, Americans complained, but he did not hesitate to take firm steps where India's national interests were concerned—in Kashmir, Hyderabad, Nepal, Bhutan, Sikkim.[10] Although economic relations remained good, an area of misunderstanding was growing between Washington and New Delhi.

By the dawn of the 1950s Nehru differed more with Washington than with Moscow or Peking on Asian problems.[11] As noted in Part I, India took issue with the United States on the Korean War and on the Japanese Peace Treaty. (American annoyance was reflected in the long debates in 1951 on wheat loans to India, during which some Congressmen called Nehru a "hypocrite.")[12] Moreover, Indians did not like U.S. Kashmir policy, which they interpreted as "pro-Pakistan."[13] When the Kashmir issue was brought before the Security Council in January 1948, both the United States and the United Kingdom favored the idea of a UN-supervised plebiscite, an idea that India soon opposed after initial endorsement. But India wished the Security Council to declare Pakistan an aggressor for its alleged role in the "tribal invasion" of Kashmir in late 1947, and the Western powers demurred, assuming correctly that such a declaration would only lessen the chance of effecting a peaceful settlement. (India made a similar assumption during the Korean War, when the United States wished to brand China an aggressor. Unfortunately, there is always a wide gap between principle and practice when national interests are involved.) When India took what it termed "police action" in annexing another princely state, Hyderabad, the American and British press criticized India's resort to arms. Indians were irritated by the British and American attitude, much preferring the Soviet neutrality on both Kashmir and Hyderabad.

Indo–American differences, however, were not fundamental. Both countries believed in the principles of freedom, democracy, human rights, and international peace and security, though security for Nehru was to come through a "doctrine of defense by friendship," for Dulles through alliances. There was no clash of principles or vital national interests (at least until 1954), and prospects were good for understanding and amicability. What was needed was for both countries to avoid lecturing the rest of the world on the righteousness or superiority of their policies and actions. The United States, disillusioned with the U.S.S.R. had opted for a balance of military strength; Nehru had less experience with Kremlin leaders and, like Jan Masaryk and Eduard Benes of Czechoslovakia, was an idealist.

The United States made considerable efforts to promote better understanding with India. India's role in Asian affairs, particularly after the communist victory in China, received more and more attention in Washington. In December 1949 an Indo–American Conference, sponsored by the American Institute of Pacific Relations and the Indian Council of World Affairs, explored the possibilities of greater bilateral cooperation and understanding in political, diplomatic, economic, and cultural relations; Nehru was among those who addressed the conference.[14]

The Prime Minister's visit to the United States at the personal invitation of President Truman was an event of great importance.

On October 13, 1949, addressing both houses of Congress, Nehru declared that "however the voice of India and the United States appear to differ, there is much in common between them." He said that the objectives of India's foreign policy "are the preservation of world peace and enlargement of human freedom." He reaffirmed his policy of nonalignment, but he significantly concluded: "We are neither blind to reality nor do we propose to acquiesce in any challenge to man's freedom from whatever quarter it may come. Where freedom is menaced or justice threatened, or where aggression takes place, *we cannot and shall not be neutral*" [italics added].[15] This speech was well received in the United States, but the Soviet press took exception to the statement that India would not remain neutral in all circumstances. The Soviet interpretation was that Nehru had endorsed U.S. policy. However, an analysis of Nehru's speeches in the United States indicates that he repeatedly stressed nonalignment, Asian concern over colonialism and racism, and the urgent need of Asian countries for economic aid.[16] Nehru's visit helped to bring Indo–U.S. relations into proper perspective as characterized by community of ideals, cordiality, and a mutual desire to help.

U.S.–INDIAN ECONOMIC RELATIONS, 1947–1952

Despite divergent Indian and American views on political and diplomatic issues, economic development aid to India was given high priority. Apart from broad humanitarian considerations, its global policy of "enlightened self-interest" motivated the United States. The struggle in Asia between democracy and communism was considered to be heavily dependent upon Nehru's success in solving his country's huge economic problems through the process of free enterprise rather than by totalitarian methods; for this reason, there were hardly any differences among the American policy makers on the necessity of helping India economically.[17]

Following initial Indo–American agreement on December 28, 1950, U.S. technical assistance began to flow to India under the first bilateral economic pact, a fruit of the Point Four Program.[18] Chester Bowles was appointed U.S. Ambassador to India in September 1951. Seeking to relax the tension arising as a result of the

Korean War, India's refusal to sign the Japanese Peace Treaty, and the unfortunate debate on the wheat loan for India in the U.S. Congress, he made a significant contribution to Indo–American understanding. A new economic assistance agreement signed by Nehru and Bowles on January 5, 1952, provided for U.S. contributions of $50 million by June for Indian development projects; another agreement for U.S. aid of $38,350,000 was signed for the fiscal year 1952–1953.[19]

THE UNITED STATES AND PAKISTAN, 1947–1952

The first U.S. Ambassador to Pakistan, Paul H. Alling, arrived in Karachi in 1947, and Governor-General Jinnah referred to the great tradition of American democracy while accepting his credentials.[20] America's lack of interest in the new state, however, was indicated by the delay until 1950 of the replacement of the first Ambassador, whose stay in Karachi was limited to five months because of illness and subsequent death. The United States had no doubt attached greater importance to India because of its larger size and past history. Whereas such Indian leaders as Gandhi and Nehru were well known, those of Pakistan were hardly familiar to Americans. On the eve of Liaquat Ali Khan's visit to the United States in 1950, the American press frankly admitted that Americans knew little about Pakistan.[21] Indeed, Pakistan was so preoccupied by regional problems that it could scarcely play any role in international politics, and it had no illusions about its lack of capacity to do so—much less was heard in Karachi than in New Delhi about the new "spirit" of Asia. Nor did Pakistan appear much interested in the East–West tensions. Although Pakistan, like India, gave consistent support to anticolonialism, it had no pretensions about its role in Asian affairs and did not entertain ideas of building an Asian grouping—which it knew would come in almost any case under Indian leadership, an intolerable prospect.

Pakistan and its leaders continually sought to strengthen ties with Washington. The largest Muslim state, as Pakistanis proudly referred to themselves, was ideologically aligned with the West; "Pakistan can never go communist,"[22] declared Fazlur Rahman, a prominent Bengali member of the Cabinet. In the early years of nationhood, Finance Minister Ghulam Mohammad, subsequently the third Governor-General and a key actor in the alliances of the mid-1950s, was engaged in strenuous efforts to secure American capital and investment for solving the country's desperate economic problems.[23] The Defense Secretary, Iskander Mirza, who became the fourth Governor-General and the first President of Pakistan, led in July 1949 a military mission to the United States to explore the possibilities of securing arms supplies.[24] The Truman administration, however, refused; the United States worked for settlement of Indo–Pakistani disputes, but as long as they remained unresolved, the State Department wanted to preserve "complete neutrality" in matters such as arms supplies.[25] After Indians expressed "concern" over what they termed the "large scale of American ammunition" sent to Pakistan, in June 1950 Secretary of State Dean Acheson assured Ambassador Vijayalakshmi Pandit (who came to Washington in 1949 following her Moscow service) that "Pakistan was given no permission which also had not been given India."[26] Both nations, in this early period, bought ammunition from the United States as from other countries, but neither yet received American military aid.

Americans repeatedly expressed the hope that Indo–Pakistani relations would become normal, if not friendly. A group of American senators who visited the subcontinent in November 1949 expressed dismay that "the air of both dominions was charged with unusual tension, making one doubtful of the existence of peace in these two countries." This injected, the senators believed, a "disturbing factor" in the consideration of foreign aid. "Aid to one Dominion alone would create misunderstanding between the aiding country and the country not receiving it."[27] The assessment was correct, as subsequent developments proved.

There were, however, fewer differences on world affairs, and thus less chance of misunderstanding, between the United States and Pakistan than between the United States and India. Pakistan did not assail U.S. policy or actions in the Cold War. On the contrary, feeling threatened by Afghanistan and India, Pakistan appreciated problems inherent in the "search for security" and the "doctrine of defence by friendship."[28] Its attempts to form a union among the Middle Eastern Islamic countries seemed reasonable to the policy makers in Washington, since the United States was already thinking in terms of defense arrangements in the Middle East as well as Southeast Asia.[29] Pakistan's geographic location afforded it special strategic significance: West Pakistan borders on the region surrounding the Persian Gulf, while East Pakistan had a vital interest in problems affecting the countries of Southeast Asia.

Prime Minister Liaquat Ali Khan deemed his visit to the United States in 1950 "an impressive success,"[30] and his speeches sparked favorable comment in the American press.[31] President Truman's invitation to Liaquat seemed to be a natural sequel to Nehru's visit of the preceding year—a courteous intimation that the United States was equally the friend of Pakistan and India. Truman wanted assurance that the subcontinent would not give passive support to the extension of Soviet influence in the direction of Central Asia,[32] and, as far as Pakistan was concerned, he received it: "No threat or persuasion," Liaquat told the U.S. Congress, "no material peril or ideological allurement," could deflect Pakistan from its chosen path of free democracy. These words were interpreted to mean that Pakistan could be "counted among those who are devoted to freedom, regardless of the cost."[33] Liaquat's visit no doubt left U.S. policy makers with a better understanding of Pakistan and its policy and problems, but the immediate results were not spectacular. Liaquat was unable to obtain a promise of arms shipments, and he could not line up private capital and investment[34]—the only economic aid pledged was through the government's Point Four program, which also supported India.

Nevertheless, developments in the Middle East and Southeast Asia were bringing closer the United States and Pakistan.[35] While Liaquat, assassinated in 1951, did not live to see the fruits of his plans for U.S. military and economic assistance, the last two years of the Truman administration indicated a trend toward forging closer links with Pakistan that assumed formal shape in 1952 when Republican Dwight D. Eisenhower took office. Pakistan's role during the Korean War and its enthusiastic participation in the San Francisco Conference arranged to sign the Japanese Peace Treaty made a favorable impression on Washington in contrast to India's role on these issues. On the U.S. side, Henry A. Byroade (who became Assistant Secretary of State for Near East, South Asian, and African Affairs), Theodore Tannenwald (Deputy to Mutual Security Administrator Averell Harriman), and Major General George Olmstead (Director of the Office of Military Assistance) favored closer military ties with Pakistan.[36]

In November 1952, Admiral Arthur W. Radford, Chief of the U.S. Naval Staff, arrived in Pakistan for discussions with Governor-

General Ghulam Mohammad and Commander-in-Chief General Ayub Khan, the two architects of Pakistani military alliance membership. These discussions, as well as previous negotiations between Major General Shahid Hamid and American Army officials in Washington, laid the foundations for subsequent military pacts between the two countries.[37] A careful analysis of the unpublished papers relating to these talks uncovers proof that these pacts were not solely what George J. Lerski labelled a "brainwave of John Foster Dulles,"[38] although it was indeed Eisenhower's Secretary of State who provided the vision, clarity, and purpose to bring about the pacts. The defense scheme for the Middle East was yet to take definite shape, but it was clear by late 1952 that Pakistan would be included. Similarly, the idea of a Pacific pact, which had earlier been considered infeasible by the Americans,[39] was revived after the Korean War.

Pakistan's policy of noninvolvement in the East–West Cold War, a policy initiated by Jinnah and faithfully followed by Liaquat up to 1950, was coming to an end along with the American policy of noninvolvement in the subcontinent. The United States and Pakistan were moving in the same direction for different reasons: the United States was guided by its global policy of containing international communism, and Pakistan was motivated by problems of national security and defense. In U.S. relations with the subcontinent a new phase that had a profound impact on the South Asian Triangle had begun.

DEEPER INVOLVEMENT IN THE SUBCONTINENT

Although the Republicans had been the opposition party for twenty years, President Dwight D. Eisenhower and his Cabinet did not make any radical changes in U.S. foreign policy once they assumed power in January 1953. They no doubt made a fresh assessment of the international situation, but containment of international communism continued to be the keynote. The Truman Doctrine, the Marshall Plan, NATO, and the Point Four program had all been effected to achieve the main foreign policy objective— the prevention of Soviet expansion. By this time, the European scene had stabilized in two formal camps, and the division was complete between Western Europe and the Soviet satellites of Eastern Europe.

In Europe, the problem of Russian expansion was thought to have been solved by the military alliance of NATO. But the NATO-type defense could not be applied to either the Middle East or Southeast Asia for three reasons: (1) as already discussed, the Asians and Arabs were not as worried about communism as was Western Europe; (2) partly because of (1), the Asians and Arabs saw their regional concerns as problems apart from great power politics—if the British feared the Soviets, it was colonialism that inflamed Indonesia and Egypt—and (3) Asians and Arabs were more reluctant than West Europeans to enter into major commitments with the United States because their cultural bonds with the Americans were much weaker. Despite the inapplicability of a NATO arrangement, however, something had to be done to protect the countries of the Middle East and Southeast Asia—or, to put it bluntly, something had to be done to protect the interests of the Western powers in these regions.

A VISIT AND A VISION

On May 9, 1953, new Cabinet officer Dulles set out on a twenty-day fact-finding mission to Egypt, Israel, Jordan, Syria, Lebanon, Iraq, Saudi Arabia, India, Pakistan, Turkey, Greece, and Libya—the first visit of this kind ever undertaken by an American Secretary of State.[40]

In India, Dulles's first discussions with Nehru dealt with bilateral Indo–American relations, particularly the U.S. assistance to India's development projects. These talks went well, but basic differences came out when Dulles began the dialogue on broad international issues, concentrating on the American plan of military groupings in the Middle East or in Southeast Asia. It is safe to assume that Nehru made it plain that any military bloc violated the fundamentals of India's policy of nonalignment;[41] he did not need to add that an American-sponsored bloc, because it would probably include Pakistan, would violate as well the fundamentals of India's national interests. India would not be carried along by Dulles's enthusiasm for fighting the "menace" of international communism and abandon its cherished policy, a policy endorsed in Moscow, accepted in Peking, and embraced in the new countries of Asia.

In Pakistan, Dulles found a completely different climate. Eager to line up allies, the Pakistanis promptly responded to the plan for a collective security pact. Dulles's talks with Pakistan's new government[42] were cordial, and he was impressed not only by the people's apparent friendship for the United States but also by what he termed, in his report on his visit, their "strong spiritual faith and martial spirit" that made them a "dependable bulwark against communism."[43] Of new Prime Minister Mohammad Ali (Bogra), who was noted for his strong pro-American views, Dulles said that "he energetically leads the new government." The Secretary stressed Pakistan's strategic position:

> Communist China borders on northern territories held by Pakistan, and from Pakistan's northern border one can see the Soviet Union. Pakistan flanks Iran and the Middle East and guards the Khyber Pass, the historic invasion route "from the north into the subcontinent."[44]

Despite both the Pakistanis' enthusiasm for security pacts and Dulles's enthusiasm for the Pakistanis, the path toward closer association between the two countries proved to be circuitous, complicated not only by U.S. policy in the Middle East and Southeast Asia but also by Indo–American relations. Involving as they did India's immediate and unfriendly neighbor, the proposed military pacts severely strained U.S. relations with New Delhi.[45] Dulles and the Eisenhower administration, not for a moment underestimating India's importance and growing influence in Asian affairs and probably willing to go to any length to induce Nehru to join the collective security schemes, counted India out of their new global plans only because India itself did. But this did not mean that India was not a factor in U.S. calculations on South Asia. During the speech quoted above in which Dulles paid tribute to Pakistan, he also said:

> India has 7,000 miles of common boundary with China. There is occurring between these two countries a competition as to whether ways of freedom or police-state methods can survive. This competition affects directly 800 million people in these countries. In the long run the outcome will affect all of humanity including ourselves.[46]

Pakistan, only too eager to respond to Washington's new moves in the subcontinent, had to wait, sometimes in great suspense, for many months before it became America's "most allied ally in Asia" through bilateral and multilateral agreements and pacts. Not effected until 1955, full alignment was the result of a long and complicated process, a string of many hesitations and reservations on both sides.

ALIGNMENT

What made the U.S. policy makers turn to Pakistan? When Dulles toured the Middle East in 1953, his assessment of the prospects for a Middle East defense organization was far from encouraging. It was "a future rather than an immediate possibility," he said.

> There is a vague desire to have a collective security system. But no such system can be imposed from without. It should be designed and grow from within out of a sense of common destiny and common danger.[47]

Dulles proposed a defense organization for the "northern tier": Pakistan, Turkey, and Iran. This scheme had a much better chance of success than did a Middle Eastern grouping, as Dulles pointed out in the report on his tour: "there is more concern where the Soviet Union is near. In general the northern tier of nations shows awareness of the danger."[48] U.S. policy makers were anxious to foster such an awareness among these countries, linking them with each other and with the United States to form a barrier against Soviet encroachment.[49] If Turkey and Pakistan were molded into bastions of defense on either flank, the prospects of denying the key areas of the Middle East to Soviet attack would be greatly improved, provided the center of the front—either Iran or, if possible, Afghanistan—could be sufficiently strengthened. The region comprising northern tier countries was highly important as it abuts that part of Soviet-controlled territory, the Central Asian Republics of the U.S.S.R., that, after Eastern Europe, caused the Soviet government the most anxiety about security.[50] A glance at a map shows that bases or airstrip facilities on the northwest frontier of Pakistan would place the Americans in a favorable position on the periphery of the Soviet Union. Along with the government, the American press, too, was stressing Pakistan's strategic importance in any defense scheme against the Soviet Union.[51]

Possible repercussions in Afghanistan and, more important, in India were the chief factors that gave the policy makers in Washington second thoughts about military aid to Pakistan. On November 2, 1953, the *New York Times* published reports of arms negotiations between the United States and Pakistan, but it was not until February 25, 1954, that President Eisenhower announced that the United States would give arms to Pakistan.[52]

The arms deal between the United States and Pakistan in 1953–1954 is an interesting episode in the history of the South Asian Triangle. Crucial negotiations between Pentagon and State Department officials and Ayub Khan began in late September 1953, when the Pakistani Army Commander-in-Chief went to Washington as a guest of the U.S. government for talks that, as he later recorded, were "highly complicated" and "sometimes extremely slow and hesitating," but "in the end successful."[53] India attempted to persuade Canada to intercede with the United States, but the arms negotiations continued; in London on November 13, 1953, an official spokesman of the Commonwealth Relations Office confirmed that the talks were in progress.[54] Ayub, Governor-General Ghulam Mohammad, and Defense Secretary Iskander Mirza (subsequently Governor-General and finally President of Pakistan in 1955–1958) were the chief architects on the Pakistani side of the arms deal. The Pakistani Parliament and Cabinet received no information and played no role, although Prime Minister Mohammad Ali and Foreign Minister Zafrullah actively participated.

Toward the end of Ayub's visit, Ghulam Mohammad arrived in Washington, ostensibly for a medical checkup, and joined Ayub in discussion with Eisenhower and Dulles and other officials. Ayub made a favorable impression on the top officials at the Pentagon, and they gave him full support. In a discussion on October 15 with General Walter Bedell Smith, the U.S. Under Secretary of State, Ayub said that "military assistance to Pakistan is a matter of mutual benefit in the defense of the area in which Pakistan is situated." On October 22 Ayub had another fruitful discussion, this with Assistant Secretary of State Henry Byroade, who became an enthusiastic supporter of arms aid to Pakistan. Similar support was given by General Olmsted, Director of the Office of Military Assistance, with whom Ayub also had lengthy discussions.

On the other hand, Ambassador Bowles in New Delhi, Senator William Fulbright, and other friends of India expressed serious doubts about the wisdom of arming Pakistan, given the vehement opposition of India. It was also feared that arming Pakistan would drive Afghanistan into Moscow's arms.[55] At his press conference on November 19, 1953, Eisenhower hinted that the United States would be cautious about giving aid to Pakistan because of the adverse effect such a move would have on India.[56] Eisenhower's comments were interpreted by the Pakistanis to mean that the long negotiations had reached stalemate as a result of India's vigorous opposition. Pakistani Ambassador to Washington Amjed Ali, who had developed a good personal relationship with Vice-President Richard M. Nixon, geared up a counteroffensive against Indian moves, but in his reports in November he presented a dismaying and frustrating picture.

The situation brightened for Pakistan when Nixon went to Karachi in December 1953. An examination of the papers relating to his talks with Pakistani leaders including Ghulam Mohammad, Mohammad Ali, and Ayub Khan gives the impression that Nixon, more than anybody else in the American hierarchy, sympathized with Pakistan's urgent problems of security and defense. He assured the Pakistani leaders of his full support. Nixon kept his pledge when the matter was discussed in the U.S. National Security Council in February; he was reported by Ambassador Ali to have endorsed Pakistan's application for arms. Nixon's biographer, Ralph Toledano, explains that Nixon fully supported Pakistan's cause in 1953–1954 not only for defense against the U.S.S.R. but also to strengthen Pakistan "as a counter force to the confirmed neutralism of Jawaharlal Nehru's India."[57] Fifteen years later, when President Nixon visited Pakistan in August 1969, he reminded his friends of his special affinity for the country, which was greatly appreciated.[58] No other American leader is loved more in Pakistan than Nixon, and his personal feelings for Pakistan might, apart from the new China policy, help explain U.S. policy during the Bangladesh crisis of 1971.

In line with Dulles's notion of the northern tier and with Pakistan's need to retain and expand U.S. military assistance, Pakistan—under direct U.S. initiative and guidance—signed an agreement of mutual cooperation with Turkey on April 2, 1954, and a mutual defense assistance agreement with the United States.[59] Pakistan thus formally abandoned its policy of neutrality or noninvolvement in the Cold War.

Now the Pakistanis had what they considered vital—ships loaded with American arms began to stream into the port at Karachi, and the United States committed itself to Pakistan's defense through bilateral agreements. But the Americans wanted more, and here unresolvable disagreement arose. The military alliance between the United States and Pakistan was based on different expectations and aims from the two sides: the United States gave military aid to Pakistan in the context of its global policy of containing communism; Pakistan considered the whole deal from the angle of its problems of security and defense vis-à-vis India. Mainly concerned with its 3,000-mile frontier with India, Pakistan was compelled by forces of history and geography to cultivate closer links with a great power. It could not meet its defense requirements from its own meager resources, and at this point the only power from which it could expect military help was the United States. Pakistan's entry into the American-sponsored pacts, both bilateral and multilateral, was mainly due to its desperate urge to improve the balance of power in the subcontinent.

Although the *formal* U.S. commitments related to communist aggression or threats, *informal*—and confidential—diplomatic notes between the United States and Pakistan gave rise to expectations in Pakistan that U.S. military help would be available even in case of a noncommunist threat, such as from India. These expectations, as time told, were ill founded. Why did not the U.S. government make clear at the beginning that these agreements with Turkey and the United States were not for Pakistan's defense against India, as the Kennedy and Johnson administrations began to intimate in the 1960s? One may conclude that because of Pakistan's importance to their global strategy, U.S. policy makers made false promises in an attempt to placate Rawalpindi. The result was frustration and bitterness in Pakistan that had great impact on patterns of relationships in South Asia in the 1960s.

Pakistan's next moves in the direction of becoming America's most allied Asian ally were its entries into SEATO, in September 1954, and into the Baghdad Pact (CENTO), in July 1955. The history of Pakistan's adhesion to these pacts, particularly SEATO, was one of hesitancy, reservation, and doubt.

SEATO

Just as most Arab states remained unconvinced by American arguments in favor of a defense organization to counter Soviet "threats," so the more important countries in Asia, such as India and Indonesia, were totally opposed to any idea of regional military pacts in South Asia. Leaders of new Asia regarded the American scheme for collective security as moves toward a new form of "domination" or "exploitation." Just as the original plan of a defense organization for the whole of the Middle East had to be modified into a modest scheme of northern tier countries, so the eventual Southeast Asian organization turned out to be a truncated version of the original concept. There was determined opposition from the Asian neutral countries; only three Asian countries, the Philippines, Thailand, and Pakistan, could be induced to join SEATO.[60]

Pakistan's military authorities—particularly Ayub Khan, who had been so enthusiastic about the bilateral defense pact between the United States and Pakistan—were not in the least interested in an Asian security organization such as SEATO. The Pakistani Cabinet agreed to participate in the Manila Conference, but it stipulated certain conditions to membership in SEATO. Mulling over the notion of such a pact, Pakistanis worried most about whether they were in a position to make any military commitment in an area fairly remote from their frontier. Was it prudent, Pakistan's leaders wondered, to have military obligations not only to pact members but also to other nations, such as those of Indochina, that were "protected" by SEATO? American emphasis that SEATO would defend against *communist* aggression and other SEATO partners' insistence that they could not be expected to enter Pakistan's disputes with India hardly fostered Pakistani confidence in the organization. "If America wishes us to help countries outside Pakistan," said a skeptical Ayub, "an agreement has to be reached as to what we shall be required to do and what force will do it." On another occasion, he described SEATO as "a political stunt so far." Even after ratification, Foreign Secretary J. A. Rahim (once a Cabinet Minister in Prime Minister Bhutto's government) made a frontal attack on Pakistan's adhesion to SEATO. The treaty, he felt, militarily and politically committed Pakistan in an area fairly remote from its frontiers; other members of the pact did not commit themselves to defending Pakistan except in the event of a communist attack, which Pakistan considered unlikely. Rahim's and other Pakistani leaders' fears were not eliminated by the note, replying to a letter from Mohammed Ali, written by Dulles in December 1954:

Even if the attack were non-communist aggression, the United States would by no means be disinterested or inactive. As the U.S. understanding makes clear, we would in the event of any such attack, consult immediately with other parties in order to agree on the measures which would be taken for the common defense as contemplated by the provisions of Article IV, paragraph 2 [of the treaty].

Pakistan's adhesion to SEATO was due to only one person, Zafrullah Khan, who exceeded the mandate of the Cabinet and scorned the advice of the military. Once Zafrullah had signed the Manila Pact on September 8, 1954, Pakistan had no choice but to ratify it in order to avoid the displeasure of the U.S. government, whose economic and military help it urgently needed. Mohammad Ali questioned Zafrullah's signing of the treaty in a lengthy communication on September 9, 1954. Zafrullah sought to justify his actions in a reply two days later. He mainly argued that a refusal to sign the treaty would have been greatly misunderstood by the United States, particularly by Dulles, and that this would have jeopardized Pakistan's prospects for increased military aid and economic aid. Quite different from his own explanation, there is an uncharitable interpretation of Zafrullah's actions: with his position as Foreign Minister ended as a result of religious agitation against his community the Ahmadis, Zafrullah put self before country; Dulles secured for him a judge's post at the International Court of Justice soon after the Manila Conference. In fact, Zafrullah did not return to Karachi, but flew straight to the United States from Manila.

CENTO

Let us now turn to the Baghdad Pact—CENTO. Here again Pakistan was unenthusiastic, though less so than in the case of SEATO. CENTO developed out of the treaty of cooperation signed by Iraq and Turkey on April 2, 1954. The Baghdad Pact did not grow from the northern tier concept—it was created at Iraq's initiative with the full support of Britain—but it was close enough to Dulles's concept to warrant enthusiastic American support.[61] The British and the Americans began a vigorous campaign to induce Middle Eastern countries to join CENTO, but vehement opposition from the Soviets and from leaders such as Egypt's Nasser persuaded all the Arab countries to shun the pact. After Britain joined in March 1955, the Arab leaders and press opened a chorus of condemnation of the pact, which was looked upon as a device by the Western powers to retain their old hold in the region.

The United States did not adhere to the organization even though it had done so much to promote a regional pact in the Middle East. The U.S. Ambassador in Baghdad, Walderman J. Gallman, noted in his memoirs that he recommended joining the pact because the United States had originated the northern frontier concept and because U.S. membership would demonstrate Anglo–American cooperation in the Middle East.[62] The U.S. ambassadors in Ankara, Tehran, and Karachi also favored American membership. According to Gallman, the United States stayed out in order to avoid antagonizing Egypt, to sidestep objections from Israel, and to preclude a Senate fight over ratification during an election year.[63]

It was feared in both Pakistan and Iran that without the United States the Baghdad Pact would drift into obscurity as had its predecessor, the Sadabad Pact of 1937.[64] For several months there were lengthy debates in Pakistan on whether to join the pact. Here again Ayub raised all sorts of queries and reservations. Then Defense Minister, he argued before the Cabinet that Pakistan had already given proof of its solidarity with Iraq and Turkey by initiating the Turko–Pakistani pact. "In our opinion," said Ayub, speaking for the army, "this pact can only be saved if the Americans join in. We shall join as soon as the Americans do. Our joining in it earlier will be premature and do no good to us or them." But Iraq, Turkey, and Britain, in addition to the United States, pressed Pakistan to join the pact, and Pakistan finally entered on June 30, 1955. Iran soon followed suit, and the Baghdad Pact thus formally came into existence. The United States welcomed the creation of the organization, but its position was ambiguous: it was a member of most of the committees without having signed the pact.

Under SEATO and CENTO, Pakistan's military commitments extended from Turkey in the West to the Philippines in the East. The Pakistan Ministry of Defense considered it absurd to take on such extensive commitments; it seemed to subscribe to the Bismarckian axiom that it is unwise to be militarily committed on two fronts simultaneously.

Thus Pakistan—despite its reservations about SEATO and CENTO—truly became "America's most allied ally in Asia."

U.S.–INDIAN RELATIONS, 1953–1959

Since 1947 there had been periods of coldness as well as warmth in Indo–American relations and areas of misunderstanding on a number of international issues, particularly relating to Asia. But in 1953–1954 relations suffered their most serious strain up to that time. India concluded that the provision of U.S. arms to Pakistan was a direct threat to its security; Nehru expressed his country's concern over American arms for Pakistan on a number of occasions. He regarded the arms shipments as a serious blow to his concept of "an area of peace" in Asia.[65]

New Delhi Ambassador George Allen's testimony before the U.S. Senate Foreign Relations Committee gave a good account of the Indian reaction to the U.S. decision to arm Pakistan: "The most important question that really excites American–Indian relations at the present time is the question of granting military aid to Pakistan." While reviewing the divergent views of the United States and India on collective security through military alliances, Allen told the Senate:

> All those matters are questions on which the United States and India can differ and still maintain, I believe, friendly relations. The one which has most emotion in it is the question of military aid to Pakistan. . . . The chief objection of the great majority in India is to the strengthening of Pakistan.

Asked why India, a recipient of huge amounts of U.S. economic aid, reacted so violently against another form of aid to Pakistan, Allen remarked that the distinction between economic and military aid was not so much financial as political.[66] It was evident from Allen's Senate testimony that the United States and India might have, at least, "agreed to disagree" on U.S. policy in the Middle East or in Southeast Asia if that policy had not involved Pakistan. The Indian correspondent of *Round Table* bluntly wrote:

> As long as Pakistan is an enemy, any strengthening of the enemy is to be resisted violently. . . . This is, after all, a reasonable attitude as the West confirms in its policy and trade with communist bloc in strategic goods . . . it is of no avail to point out that India is much more powerful militarily than Pakistan; that she is spending twice as much on it [military expenditures] as her neighbour.[67]

Thus Eisenhower administration policy in the Middle East and Southeast Asia in 1953–1956 irritated New Delhi as it satisfied Karachi; U.S. policy rooted more deeply into the Cold War the unfortunate tensions between India and Pakistan. Just as India's relations with Washington began to deteriorate, so its relations with Moscow began to improve. Moscow's wrath against Pakistan was also manifested.

The Pakistanis received arms as part of the global U.S. policy in the 1950s of containing communism—certainly not for use against India, whose importance and friendship the United States always stressed. In fact, the Americans did everything in their power to ease Indian apprehension. Eisenhower announced the decision to give military aid to Pakistan, but he also made the unusual gesture of writing Nehru to assure him of U.S. friendship and to indicate that if India should ask for military assistance, the United States would give the "most sympathetic consideration."[68] Ambassador Allen spoke in similar terms.[69] One of the paramount concerns of U.S. policy was to prevent neutral countries such as India from slipping into the communist orbit. On the assumption that the United States could not afford to discontinue economic assistance to India, the flow of U.S. economic aid for India's second five-year plan continued. During the fiscal year 1954–1955, when Indo–American political relations were at their lowest point, U.S. aid to India amounted to about $84 million—more than its aid to the ally, Pakistan, although Pakistan's U.S. economic aid was more calculated on a per capita basis. The U.S. policy makers seemed to have realized that to cut off aid or attach strings to it would not soften India's policy, but only push India farther in the direction of Moscow.

Successfully resisting U.S. pressure to line up as another Asian ally, India pursued its policy of nonalignment and became eligible for friendship and aid from both the Western and the socialist blocs. The policy also lent prestige to India as "independent" compared with "subservient" Pakistan. The new countries of Asia and Africa, seeing the success of Nehru's policy, were encouraged to espouse the neutralism to which Dulles was opposed. The "soft" policy toward India, which was dictated by the "enlightened self-interest" of the United States, proved the failure of Dulles's policy of making neutrals into allies and forming regional pacts.

By 1956, the Indians seemed convinced that U.S. policy was not hostile, and Pakistan likewise realized that its expectation that the

United States would invariably support an ally against a neutral was incorrect. U.S. policy on Kashmir, for instance, did not change markedly in favor of Pakistan once it adhered to the pacts. Pakistani Foreign Minister Malik Feroz Khan Noon met Dulles in Washington on November 23, 1957, and discussed the question of U.S. help if Pakistan were subjected to noncommunist aggression (presumably Indian). Noon claimed afterward, "He [Dulles] left me in doubt that the United States would promptly and effectively come to the assistance of Pakistan if it were subjected to armed aggression[,] which, however, the United States did not anticipate."[70] Although this American ambiguity or uncertainty was formalized in a letter on April 15, 1959, from the U.S. Ambassador to the President of Pakistan, the U.S. government requested that the letter *not be made public*.[71] It was not, but Pakistan's frustration with U.S. policy continued to be expressed rather bitterly. In a foreign policy debate in Pakistan's National Assembly in March 1958, Noon, now Pakistan's Prime Minister, severely criticized the "Western allies" for their alleged "lack of sympathy and understanding" of Pakistan's difficulties. He told the National Assembly that if the people of Pakistan found their freedom in jeopardy, they would break all the pacts and "would go and shake hands with those whom they made their enemies for the sake of others."[72]

As Pakistan's frustration with the United States grew, Indo–American relations began to show signs of improvement. India's fear that the United States would actively support Pakistan in its dispute with India proved unfounded, but this fear still remained the greatest source of misunderstanding between Washington and New Delhi.

Then, in 1956, two major international crises—Suez and Hungary—made Nehru reassess his attitude toward East–West relations. On the Suez crisis, the United States was more in agreement with India than with Britain and France, two principal NATO and SEATO allies, and Israel. The pressures the United States applied to end the fighting and effect a withdrawal both surprised and gratified Indians, many of whom had counted the United States as a defender of old-line imperialism. On Hungary, Nehru's condemnation of Russia was not as strong and forthright as was his condemnation of Britain and France on Suez. Yet Nehru, a liberal and democrat, must have been appalled by the Soviet brutalities in Hungary. The Suez and Hungary events of 1956, the continued U.S. interest in the economic development of India, erosion of fears regarding a U.S. role in Indo–Pakistani disputes—all these factors led to a better U.S.–Indian understanding. There remained, of course, many points of disagreement. For example, Dulles's joint statement with the Portuguese Foreign Minister in December 1956 referring to Portuguese territories in India was bitterly resented in New Delhi and fully exploited by Moscow.[73]

In late 1956—December 16–21—Nehru went to the United States at the invitation of President Eisenhower. Nehru seemed to be favorably impressed by Eisenhower. Their talks led to a friendly relationship between the two; each came to understand the other better. The result was that Indo–American relations, which had been bogged down by suspicion and fears at least since the Republican victory in 1952, took a favorable turn, as indicated by diplomatic sources in Washington, New Delhi, and Karachi.[74] When India faced an acute financial crisis in 1957–1958, the United States stepped in to help. President Eisenhower and Indian Food and Agriculture Minister S. K. Patil signed an agreement in March 1958 providing large-scale U.S. food sales to India under Public Law 480. The United States promised to provide over a four-year period 16 million tons of wheat and 1 million tons of rice. It was further agreed that the rupees accruing to the United States in payment for the wheat and rice would be made available to the Indian government to finance economic development projects; one-half of the rupees would be in the form of a loan, and the rest would be a grant.[75]

The military coup in Iraq in July 1958 led to the defection of that country from the Baghdad Pact. When the next Council meeting was held, without Iraq, in London on July 28 and 29, 1958, the pact was renamed the Central Treaty Organization and its headquarters was shifted from Baghdad to Ankara.[76] Most significant at this London meeting was America's demonstration of continued interest in the pact, seemingly to compensate for Iraq's defection. With Dulles in attendance, it was at this meeting that the United States undertook cooperation in the defense and security of CENTO members. The United States virtually undertook the same obligations that the full members countries had already agreed to among themselves. Subsequently, bilateral defense agreements between the United States on the one hand and Turkey, Iran, and Pakistan on the other were signed in Ankara, on March 5, 1959. The United States made a definite commitment that in case of aggression against Pakistan, the government, in accordance with the American Constitution, "will take such appropriate action, including use of armed forces as may be mutually agreed upon . . . in order to assist the Government of Pakistan at its request."[77]

India expressed concern over this agreement, but the United States assured Nehru that the agreement was governed by the "Eisenhower Doctrine," which was concerned solely with aggression from communist countries. India was also informed by Ambassador Allen in New Delhi that no additional military aid would be given to Pakistan except under previous commitments.[78] Nehru was "satisfied" with the assurance, which he reported to Lok Sabha on March 13 along with the pledge of the U.S. authorities that there was no secret clause or secret supplementary agreement.[79] In contrast to his reaction after Eisenhower's similar assurances in 1954, Nehru's reaction demonstrated the success of recent U.S. policy in India.

Eisenhower's visit to India during his eleven-nation tour in December 1959 further brightened relations with India. The personal trust and friendship between Eisenhower and Nehru developed earlier were cemented. The significant feature of Eisenhower's visit was the intimate and frank exchange of views with Nehru on international issues. This paralleled Nehru's U.S. visit in 1956, when he was the first foreign statesman to discuss foreign policy with the President without Dulles being present. Eisenhower addressed a joint session of both houses of the Indian Parliament on December 10 and declared, "Above all, our basic goals are the same."[80] More important, deteriorating relations between China and India during the autumn of 1959, a result of clashes on the Himalayan borders, made India realize the need of U.S. friendship. Thus a new era of Indo–American friendship and understanding began. It was to come to fruition during the administration of President John F. Kennedy.

NOTES

1. U.S. Senate and Department of State, *A Decade of Foreign Policy* (Washington: Government Printing Office, 1950), pp. 782–783.
2. See S. K. Banerjee, "American Interest in Indian Independence," *India Quarterly*, October–December 1968, pp. 311–332; M. S. Venkataramani and B. K. Shrivistava, "The United States and the Cripps Mission," *India Quarterly*, July–September 1963, pp. 214–265.
3. *The Statesman*, Oct. 25, 1946.

4. *Dawn,* Aug. 16, 1947.

5. See Henry M. Christman, ed., *Neither East nor West: The Basic Documents of Non-Alignment* (New York: Sheed & Ward, Inc., 1973); L. W. Martin, *Neutralism and Non-Alignment* (New York: Frederick A. Praeger, Inc., 1962).

6. George Fischer, "Political Ideas and Ideologies," in S. Rose, ed., *Politics in Southern Asia* (London: Macmillan Co., Ltd., 1963), pp. 279–353.

7. *Nehru's Speeches—Vol. III: 1953–1957, op. cit.,* pp. 280–288, 292–301.

8. See Martin, *op. cit.*

9. *New York Times,* Mar. 28, 1950.

10. See C. H. Alexandrowicz, "India's Himalayan Dependencies," in *Year Book of World Affairs* (1956), *op. cit.,* pp. 128–243.

11. See "United States and India," *Far Eastern Survey,* Jan. 25, 1950, pp. 9–20.

12. *New York Herald Tribune,* Jan. 29, 1951, and *New York Times,* editorial, May 4, 1951.

13. Choudhury, *op. cit.,* pp. 90–140.

14. For a full account of the conference, see "United States and India," *op. cit.*

15. *Nehru's Speeches—Vol. II: 1949–1953, op. cit.,* pp. 590–591.

16. *Ibid.,* pp. 161–266.

17. See Secretary of State John Foster Dulles's speech of May 29, 1953, after his return from a fact-finding trip to the Middle East and the Asian subcontinent, cited in *Documents on International Affairs, 1953* (London: Royal Institute of International Affairs, 1956), pp. 258–259.

18. *The Statesman,* Jan. 29, 1950; see also President Harry S. Truman's Point Four speech in *Documents on American Foreign Policy, 1949* (Boston: World Peace Foundation, 1950), pp. 238–243.

19. *The Statesman,* Jan. 6, 1952.

20. *Dawn,* Oct. 9, 1947.

21. *Christian Science Monitor* and *New York Herald Tribune,* May 2, 1950.

22. *New York Times,* Oct. 13, 1947.

23. *Ibid.*

24. *Ibid.,* July 24, 1949.

25. Based on my research and personal interviews in Pakistan, 1967–1971.

26. *Hindu* (Madras), June 17, 1950.

27. *The Statesman,* Nov. 18, 1949.

28. See Choudhury, *op. cit.*, pp. 222–250.

29. Avra M. Warren, "Pakistan in the World Today," *Department of State Bulletin,* June 20, 1949, pp. 1011–1012.

30. Liaquat Ali Khan, *Pakistan, the Heart of Asia* (Cambridge, Mass.: Harvard University Press, 1951), p. xi.

31. *New York Times,* May 5, 1950; *Christian Science Monitor,* May 4, 5, and 10, 1950.

32. Based on my research and personal interviews in Pakistan, 1967–1971.

33. *New York Times,* editorial, May 5, 1950.

34. Based on my research and personal interviews in Pakistan, 1967–1971.

35. *Documents on International Affairs, 1953, op. cit.*, p. 263.

36. Based on my research and personal interviews in Pakistan, 1967–1971.

37. *Ibid.*

38. George J. Lerski, "The Pakistan–American Alliance: A Re-evaluation of the Past Decade," *Asian Survey,* May 1968, pp. 400–415.

39. See *Survey of International Affairs, 1951, op. cit.*, pp. 478–480.

40. See Dulles's speech of May 29, 1953, *Documents on International Affairs, 1953, op. cit.*, pp. 258–259.

41. Based on the report of the Pakistani High Commissioner in New Delhi, May 25, 1953, uncovered in my research and personal interviews in Pakistan, 1967–1971.

42. In April 1953, the month before Dulles's trip, Governor-General Ghulam Mohammad, backed by army chief Ayub Kahn, dismissed Prime Minister Khawaja Nazimuddin, and Mohammad Ali (Bogra), who had been Ambassador to the United States, was appointed Prime Minister on Apr. 17.

43. See Dulles's speech of May 29, 1953, *Documents on International Affairs, 1953, op. cit.*

44. *Ibid.*

45. *Nehru's Speeches—Vol. III: 1953–1957, op. cit.*, pp. 366–376.

46. Dulles's speech of May 29, 1953, *Documents on International Affairs, 1953, op. cit.*, p. 266.

47. *Ibid.*

48. *Ibid.*

49. *Ibid.*

50. *Defences in the Cold War* (London: Royal Institute of International Affairs, 1950), p. 39.

51. See Selig S. Harrison, "India, Pakistan and the United States: Case History of a Mistake," *New Republic*, Aug. 10, 1959; *New York Herald Tribune*, Apr. 17, 1953.

52. *New York Times* and *Dawn*, Feb. 26, 1954.

53. Except where otherwise indicated, the remainder of this section is based on my research and personal interviews in Pakistan, 1967–1971.

54. *Pakistan Times*, Nov. 14, 1953.

55. M. S. Venkataramani and Harish Chandra, "America's Military Assistance with Pakistan: The Evolution and Course of an Uneasy Partnership," *International Studies* (New Delhi), July 1966, pp. 73–125.

56. *New York Times*, Nov. 20, 1953.

57. Ralph Toledano, *Nixon* (New York: Henry Holt and Company, Inc., 1956), p. 164.

58. Based on my research in Pakistan, 1967–1971.

59. *Dawn*, Apr. 3, 1954.

60. Except where otherwise indicated, this section is based on my research and personal interviews in Pakistan, 1967–1971.

61. John C. Campbell, *Defense of the Middle East* (New York: Harper & Brothers, Council on Foreign Relations, 1958).

62. W. J. Gallman, *Iraq under General Nuri: My Recollections of Nuri al-Said, 1954–1958* (Baltimore: Johns Hopkins University Press, 1964), p. 58.

63. See *Ibid.;* John C. Campbell, "Doctrine to Policy in the Middle East," *Foreign Affairs*, April 1957.

64. The remainder of this section is based on my research and personal interviews in Pakistan, 1967–1971.

65. See *Nehru's Speeches—Vol. III: 1953–1957, op. cit.*, pp. 94, 205.

66. Hearings before the U.S. Senate, Committee on Foreign Relations, Mar. 12, 1954 (Washington: Government Printing Office, 1954).

67. "Foreign Policy of Nehru," *Round Table*, June 1954, p. 267.

68. *Documents on International Affairs, 1954, op. cit.*, pp. 178–179.

69. See George V. Allen, "American–Indian Relations," *India Quarterly*, January–March 1954.

70. Based on my research and personal interviews in Pakistan, 1967–1971.

71. *Ibid.*

72. G. W. Choudhury, "Pakistan's Relations with the West," *Eastern World*, July 1958.

73. *Nehru's Speeches—Vol. III: 1953–1957, op. cit.*, pp. 372–377.

74. Based on the report of the Pakistani High Commissioner in New Delhi, Dec. 24, 1956; *The Statesman,* Dec. 23, 1956.

75. Norman Palmer, *South Asia and United States Policy* (Boston: Houghton Mifflin Company, 1966), p. 21.

76. *The Times* (London), July 30, 1958.

77. See the text of "Bilateral Agreements between the United States and Pakistan," in *Documents on American Foreign Relations, 1959* (New York: Council on Foreign Relations, Inc., 1960).

78. Based on my research and personal interviews in Pakistan, 1967–1971.

79. *The Statesman,* Mar. 14, 1959.

80. *Ibid.,* Dec. 11, 1959.

Chapter Five

TILTING TOWARD INDIA, 1960–1965

FAVORING THE NEUTRAL

KHRUSHCHEV once was reported to have predicted that military pacts like CENTO and SEATO would "burst like a bubble."[1] Instead, CENTO and SEATO have unraveled, as it were. Significantly, this has been due not so much to the success of Soviet diplomacy or policy as to the changed attitude of the United States; much water has flowed since Dulles described neutralism as "immoral."[2] With the coming of the Kennedy administration, the keynote of the American subcontinent policy became favorable treatment of neutrals, such as India, to the disadvantage of allies, such as Pakistan. As noted earlier, Indo–American relations had already taken a good turn in the last two years of the Eisenhower administration.

President Kennedy himself was largely responsible for the new cast of Indo–American relations. As a Senator, Kennedy had expressed his interest in the welfare of India and his reservations about forming military pacts that earned for the United States the friendship of weaker, unstable, and military-run Pakistan at the expense of warm relations with India. In his speeches in the Senate on March 25, 1958, and November 1, 1959, he strongly advised giving greater attention to India. "We want India," he explained, "to be a free and thriving leader of a free and thriving Asia."[3] These speeches epitomize the Kennedy administration's early policy toward the subcontinent.

The Pakistani Ambassador in Washington sent reports in early 1961 expressing "grave concern" over the new U.S. policy. The

"Harvard intellectuals" who were close to the Kennedy administration were reported to be favorably disposed toward "free and democratic" India as against "theocratic and military" Pakistan. India's American friends—such as Chester Bowles (Under Secretary of State in the Kennedy government), Professor J. K. Galbraith (one of Kennedy's principal economic advisers, in 1961 appointed Ambassador to India), Adlai Stevenson (Ambassador to the United Nations), Averell Harriman (Ambassador at Large and later Assistant Secretary of State for Far Eastern Affairs), and W. W. Rostow (Deputy Special Assistant to the President for National Security Affairs), and others—were all urging better understanding between Washington and New Delhi. India, it was feared by Pakistani officials in Washington in 1961–1962, "figured prominently in the U.S. policy and thinking."[4]

Apart from the admiration of Kennedy and those around him for "free India," there were other factors that led to the new U.S. South Asian policy, such as the prospects for an East–West détente, the Sino–Soviet ideological split, and of course the Sino–Indian border conflicts. Advances in nuclear technology also affected America's policy toward allies as against neutrals: the development of the ICBM and of the Polaris submarine much reduced the value of military bases at the periphery of the Soviet Union. Perhaps most important to the U.S. policy change was the common objective of the United States and the U.S.S.R. to contain China and the role that India was expected to play in that containment. This chain of events and trends shook the subcontinent policies and roles of the major powers and consequently shook alignment and nonalignment policies of India and Pakistan.

For the developing countries, President Kennedy enunciated "new alliances for progress" in lieu of military alliances. He wanted to help these countries cast off the "chain of poverty," and he made a pledge of larger economic aid.[5]

Obviously, Nehru was pleased with Kennedy's policy and program, and in India there were new hopes for better understanding and closer cooperation with the United States. Pakistan, on the other hand, expressed concern over the new U.S. policy, as much concern as New Delhi had voiced over the policy of the Eisenhower–Dulles era. Prospects of increased U.S. economic aid to India, which President Kennedy was determined to make a "showpiece" of what the Western world should do for an Asian country,[6] were also resented in Pakistan, which saw little difference between economic and military aid. According to this interpretation, economic aid from the United States and other countries enables India to divert huge resources for the purchase of arms. Both forms of aid, economic and military, effect savings in foreign exchange that then become available for purchase abroad either of machinery and capital goods or of military equipment. Thus, according to Pakistan, there was little difference between India's "purchasing" military equipment and Pakistan's receiving it in the form of aid. Ayub made a number of speeches in 1961–1962 expressing his country's sense of frustration at being let down by "the Western allies," meaning the United States.[7]

The news of proposed amendments to the United States Mutual Security Act, amendments that would facilitate the flow of arms to neutrals such as India, caused additional anxiety in Pakistan. There was fear in Pakistan that once the terms of the Mutual Security Act were reframed (as they were during President Kennedy's tenure), India might secure arms from the United States on terms as advantageous as those enjoyed by "loyal ally" Pakistan.[8]

In early 1961 President Kennedy invited both President Ayub and Prime Minister Nehru to visit the United States. Ayub was so perturbed over the change he perceived in American policy that at his request his visit to the United States was brought forward by about six months to July 1961.[9] Meanwhile, in May, Vice-President Johnson visited India and Pakistan on his tour of Asia. His talks with Nehru were largely concerned with economic assistance for Nehru's third five-year plan. As was expected, Johnson assured Nehru of a substantial American contribution. The U.S. economic assistance to India in 1961–1962 was about $400 million (excluding surplus food). The U.S. Government tried to ensure that other members of the "Aid to India Consortium" and the International Bank for Reconstruction and Development would give an additional $600 million for 1961–1962, so that the $1 billion annual requirement in foreign aid for India's plan would be available; the ambitious third plan envisaged huge expenditures, including a total of $5 billion in foreign aid.[10] Nehru was reported to have found the United States deeply interested in the economic development of India, and Johnson's assurance of substantial aid was greatly appreciated by the Indian government and the press.[11]

In Karachi, where Johnson was given a big reception by Ayub, there were "free and frank discussions" between the two. Ayub wanted to find from Johnson if there were any actual changes in

U.S. policy toward Pakistan; Johnson assured Pakistan of "continued friendship" but was cautious in discussing any "new commitments." An analysis of the Johnson–Ayub dialogue reveals that Johnson's "assurances" to Ayub were of a general nature, and Ayub could get no clues about the policy changes over which he was so worried. A communiqué was issued at the end of the visit on May 20, but it, like the conference itself, evidenced no significant statements; "Kashmir" was not even mentioned, which must have been a source of dismay to Pakistan.[12]

The atmosphere in Pakistan was so bogged down in suspicion and prejudice that a statement erroneously attributed to Johnson— to the effect that "at President Kennedy's request, he urged Nehru to extend his leadership to other areas in Southeast Asia"—caused an uproar in the Pakistan press.[13] What was regrettable was that neither the government nor the press in Pakistan took the trouble to check the authenticity of Johnson's statement. The Pakistani Ambassador in Washington, Aziz Ahmad, sent cables to try to stop the agitation against Johnson, who was at that stage one of the few members of the Kennedy administration disposed toward Pakistan, but later clarifications did not repair the damage that had been done to Pakistani–American relations.

AYUB AND NEHRU VISIT WASHINGTON, 1961

Ayub arrived in Washington in July 1961 with a good deal of apprehension, aware that Kennedy's close advisers had more respect for Nehru than for him. Ayub was given a "pompous and ostentatious reception"—but not so much out of regard for him as from the belief that the "Field Marshal President" would be "more effectively tackled" by an outward show than by the sort of serious and quiet discussions reserved for Nehru's visit.[14] But Kennedy's advisers had misjudged Ayub. He was indeed a soldier and could hardly compare with Nehru in intellectual attainment or in knowledge of world issues, but he understood his country's problems and needs. He made a favorable impression on the U.S. Congress in his forthright speech of July 12, declaring bluntly that Pakistan was the only country in Asia on which the United States could count in a crisis.[15]

The two presidents had free and wide-ranging discussions. Of all his visits abroad, Ayub later told me, this was one of the most important and decisive. Ayub in his autobiography has reported that during his visit he emphasized that without a just settlement of the Kashmir dispute there could be no peace in the subcontinent. Kennedy was reported to have agreed that there was an urgent need to solve the Kashmir problem, but the American President made it clear that he was not in a position to play an active or direct role. Ayub pleaded for U.S. pressure on India to settle the problem, hinting that the United States had considerable leverage because of its massive economic aid to India. Kennedy apparently did not like the idea of putting any pressure on India, first because it would be ineffective and second because the U.S. Government was not prepared to miss the opportunity—which arose as a result of developments after 1959, particularly in the context of growing Sino–Indian tensions—of developing good relations with India. Ayub endeavored to discover from Kennedy what shift had occurred in American policy toward neutrals as compared with allies, particularly regarding the proposed amendments to the U.S. Mutual Security Act. Kennedy "assured" his guest that he attached "importance" to such collective security arrangements as SEATO and CENTO, that he had been "misunderstood" on the question of aid to neutrals, and that he was not thinking in terms of "abandoning friends" and "embracing neutrals."[16]

President Ayub made a number of speeches while in the United States, and all highlighted Pakistan's anxiety over the possibility of U.S. military aid to India; he pointed out that any arms aid to India would put a "real strain on Pakistan–U.S. relations as Pakistan would have genuine grounds of concern for . . . [its] security."[17] In a television broadcast on July 9 Ayub hinted that Pakistan might have to reexamine its membership in SEATO and CENTO and adopt neutralism "as the only guarantee of her security," though he still hoped that a choice between security and Western alignment would not have to be made.[18]

At the end of Ayub's visit, a joint communiqué on July 13, 1961, declared:

> The two presidents reaffirmed the solemn purpose of the bilateral agreements signed by the two governments on 5 March 1959 which declare among other things that "The government of the United States regards as vital to its national interest and to world

peace the preservation of the independence and integrity of Pakistan. . . ."

They also reaffirmed the value of "existing collective security arrangements" as an instrument for defense against aggression. As explained earlier, the formal U.S. commitments under the bilateral agreement of March 1959 and under arrangements such as SEATO and CENTO were confined to communist aggression, and there was nothing in these commitments to mollify Pakistan's fears over alleged threats imposed through Indian arms buildup. Ayub could not wrest any new public assurances from Kennedy. The communiqué added, however, that President Kennedy desired "to see a satisfactory solution of the Kashmir problem and expressed his hope that progress towards a settlement would be possible at an early date."[19] Although rather vague, the reference to Kashmir made, for the Pakistanis, this communiqué an improvement over the Ayub–Eisenhower communiqué issued on December 10, 1959, and the Ayub–Johnson joint message of May 20, 1961.

Kennedy seemed to have calmed Ayub's apprehensions, at least for the time being.[20] Ayub was pro-Western, but he had been subjected to mounting criticism not only by his political opponents but also by some of his close associates, such as Bhutto, who had concluded that the Kennedy administration favored India at the expense of Pakistan. Kennedy promised Ayub "continued" military aid: some of the commitments made by the previous administration to supply F104 aircraft (only twelve) and other sophisticated items were assured of early fulfillment. When Ayub raised the critical issue of whether the United States intended to give military aid to India, Kennedy, according to Ayub, said that India would not receive military aid unless the security of the subcontinent was threatened; what is more, if the United States extended such aid, Ayub would be consulted *in advance*.[21] I, who not only read the minutes of the Kennedy–Ayub talks but also had lengthy discussions with Ayub, am in no doubt that Ayub received such assurances. The point is stressed because this pledge was broken when the United States rushed military help to India after the Sino–Indian border war in the autumn of 1962, thus considerably damaging American relations with Pakistan.

The people of Pakistan no doubt welcomed the apparent halt in the deterioration of the relationship between Pakistan and the United States, a halt effected through, and symbolized by, Ayub's

Washington visit, but their mood was one of watchfulness rather than rejoicing. Soon Ayub and the Pakistanis realized that this dialogue between the two presidents was merely an interval before the next worsening stage in the two countries' relationship.

The news of agreement on military supplies to Pakistan, as well as the actual delivery of F104 aircraft following Ayub's visit to Washington, caused some misgivings in New Delhi before Nehru went to the United States in November 1961. The U.S. Ambassador in New Delhi, however, had been authorized to divulge the exact nature and quantity of military supplies to Pakistan. There was no new commitment, merely the delivery of the twelve aircraft promised by the previous administration. Ambassador Galbraith convinced Nehru and his government that the delivery did not represent any change in policy and was not in any way comparable to the massive economic aid from the Western countries (mainly the United States) for India's Third Plan.[22] Nehru was thus able to say in Lok Sabha on August 13, 1961, "The United States could not be considered to be 'unfriendly' towards India—unfriendly in the sense in which it was used in international usage—because of her giving arms aid to Pakistan." He added that the U.S. Government had exhibited on many occasions an attitude of friendliness and cooperation.[23]

Nehru arrived in the United States on November 5 for his ten-day visit. Although he was given a less ostentatious reception than Ayub, Kennedy paid much more attention to him. Four lengthy talks the President held with Nehru were described as "pleasant and rewarding." Each tried to explain the rationale of his country's foreign policy. The leaders discussed the Berlin crisis, the situation in Southeast Asia, India's third five-year plan, nuclear tests, disarmament, the United Nations, the Congo crisis, and finally Indo–American relations.[24]

It was expected that Kennedy, with his intellectual cast, would be more impressed by India's philosopher Prime Minister than by Pakistan's soldier President, but the meeting with Nehru did not match the high expectations prevailing at the White House. One of Kennedy's close associates, Arthur M. Schlesinger, Jr., reported Kennedy as describing Nehru's visit as a "disaster . . . the worst head-of-state visit I have had," and said that "Kennedy's vision of India had been much larger before the visit than it would ever be again." Though Kennedy was determined to pursue his policy of helping India in a massive way in its development projects, "He gave up hope, after seeing Nehru, that India would be in the next years a great affirmative force in the world or even in South Asia."[25] The Pakistani Ambassador's reports on Nehru's visit—a visit that had roused great fears in Rawalpindi—gleefully concurred that its results were disappointing. His assessments were derived from diplomatic sources as well as his contacts with pro-Pakistan lobbies in Washington.[26]

Within five weeks of Nehru's visit to the United States India took what was described as "police action" to liberate the Portuguese colony of Goa in December 1961. Both the British and U.S. governments had urged India not to use force and recommended a political settlement. Washington had made a specific proposal pledging diplomatic pressure on Portugal in exchange for a six-month standstill by India. India, however, decided to resort to arms to settle the issue and faced little resistance in completing the military operations; the Portuguese garrison surrendered at Panjim, the capital of Goa. Both the British and American governments deplored the use of force by the Indians. At the UN, U.S. delegate Adlai Stevenson, who was normally a great supporter of India, bitterly criticized India, and the U.S. press was also highly critical.[27] The reaction in India was an outburst of anti-American feeling and a bitter attack against the "colonial powers" of the West. Nehru himself resented the Western outcry, calling colonialism "in itself permanent aggression."[28] There was a temporary setback in the improving U.S.–India relations.

In January 1962 Dr. Henry Kissinger came to India as President Kennedy's "special representative on international affairs." His mission was to heal the damage in relations caused by the U.S. reaction to Indian armed intervention in Goa; he made some unkind remarks about Pakistan's foreign policy while in India—one of the easiest ways to please India or Pakistan is to attack the other. When asked what the U.S. attitude would be if the Kashmir dispute was referred again to the Security Council, Kissinger's reply was, "We are not going to spite India because of Goa." Talking about Pakistan's growing relations with China, he said, "If Pakistan were stupid enough to enter into an alliance with China, how long could she survive without a strong independent India?" It was during this trip to India that Kissinger described the defense pacts of the previous American administration as a disease called "pactitis."[29]

The United States made another major contribution to India's third five-year plan, though in 1962 the debate on foreign aid in the U.S. Congress was unusually prolonged and bitter. There were also some harsh criticisms of India, which were well publicized in the Indian press.[30] In the end both India and Pakistan got substantial economic aid for the next fiscal year, but the U.S. government began to put pressure on Pakistan to give more attention to the economic development of East Pakistan. The growing dissatisfaction over regional economic disparity between East and West Pakistan was pointed out by the American experts and advisers attached to the Pakistani Planning Commission. Instead of appreciating the friendly counsel and advice, the Pakistanis accused the Americans of encouraging secessionist movements in East Pakistan;[31] this unfounded allegation contributed to the worsening relations between the United States and Pakistan.

Jacqueline Kennedy's trip to the subcontinent in the spring of 1962 did good public relations work in the two countries. Mrs. Kennedy was not initially interested in going to Pakistan, but her husband's administration turned to the First Lady to demonstrate its "policy of non-discrimination" toward India and Pakistan.[32]

In 1961 and 1962 President Kennedy was, on the whole, successful in maintaining simultaneously good relations with India and Pakistan—a task perhaps ranking in complexity with pleasing both the Arabs and the Israelis. Kennedy seemed to have modified his attitude toward Pakistan after entering the White House. Ayub's visit in the summer of 1961 contributed to this change, as did America's global strategic considerations; on the other hand, a number of factors sullied Kennedy's earlier image of India. Idealism and reality do not often go hand in hand.

SINO–INDIAN WAR AND ITS REPERCUSSIONS

The whole situation dramatically changed when full-scale armed conflict between China and India broke out. As soon as the hostilities started in October 1962, Nehru sent urgent requests for military aid to the British and United States governments. Both governments, to the pleasant surprise of many Indians, responded most promptly: the first consignments of British aid arrived in India on October 29, and the first American aid reached India from depots in Western Europe on November 1. As the Chinese advances continued in the direction of the plains of Assam along the North-East Frontier Agency (NEFA), the Indian government panicked and Nehru made desperate appeals to the United States and Britain to give him fifteen bomber squadrons to attack the advancing Chinese troops. Before any action could be taken on his request, the Chinese declared their unilateral withdrawal. Nehru's request might have meant direct Western involvement in the Sino–Indian border conflict with the potential consequence of a third world war.[33]

With the cessation of fighting, Great Britain, the U.S., and other Western countries began to strengthen India's armed forces so as to prevent a repetition of the disasters of October 1962. Subsequently, the U.S.S.R. and other socialist countries also joined in the military buildup. On December 29, 1962, President Kennedy and Prime Minister Harold Macmillan agreed at Nassau to continue to supply India on an emergency basis with military aid of up to $120 million.[34] On July 27, 1963, Nehru disclosed that in accordance with the Nassau agreement a British–Canadian air mission went to India to study its requirements; so also did a separate American military mission.[35] On June 30 at Birch Grove, the United States and Britain decided on further aid, worth $60 million.[36] Then came the five-year agreement of military aid between the United States and India, whereby the latter was to receive $100 million in assistance per year.[37] This agreement reached an early end when the United States banned military shipments to the subcontinent with the outbreak of the 1965 war.

The exact quantity of the U.S. arms aid to India, either on an emergency basis or through the sustained programs begun in 1963, is debated. The Pakistani press and members of the Pakistani National Assembly later termed the aid "massive."[38] Bhutto, in his *Myth of Independence*, gave the most exaggerated estimates of the volume of aid, aid that he said "threatened the territorial integrity of Pakistan"[39]—a view echoed by many responsible Pakistani leaders. During 1962–1964, President Ayub repeatedly bewailed the imbalance of power in the subcontinent.[40] Just as President Eisenhower was confronted with a dilemma in 1954 when he ordered the arming of Pakistan, President Kennedy faced serious problems in the early 1960s as weapons flowed to India. At a press conference on September 12, 1963, he said: "Everything we give India adversely affects the balance of power with Pakistan, which

is a much smaller country. We are dealing with a very, very complicated problem, because the hostility between them is so deep."[41]
Defense Secretary Robert S. McNamara also acknowledged that
the U.S. military assistance provided to India for its conflict with
China "deeply troubled" Pakistan, but he justified arms aid to
India in the context of the U.S. global policy of containment of
communism in Asia.[42]

According to Bhutto, the United States at first made the grant
of military assistance to India conditional on the settlement of the
Kashmir dispute but subsequently withdrew the condition because
of Nehru's objection. Bhutto claimed that Ambassador Galbraith
informed the Indian government that "aid to fight China was not
contingent upon a Kashmir settlement."[43]

As the fighting raged on India's China front, President Kennedy
wrote a long letter to Ayub Khan on October 28, 1962, explaining
the rationale of the U.S. policy of arms assistance to India but
affirming continued U.S. interest in the security and territorial integrity of Pakistan. Kennedy also asked Ayub to make a gesture
to India by saying that Pakistan would not take any action on the
Kashmir frontier; in this way it was hoped that India could be
persuaded to withdraw troops on the borders with Pakistan and
concentrate its military strength against China. Similar requests
were made in letters to Ayub from Macmillan and Australia's Prime
Minister R. G. Menzies. Ayub published the text of his reply to
Kennedy in his autobiography, *Friends Not Masters*.[44] In accordance
with official Pakistan policy, Ayub could not agree to Kennedy's
suggested gesture toward India. Yet through diplomatic channels
Ayub indicated that Pakistan would not aggravate India's problems,[45] a move for which he was later criticized by extremists such
as Bhutto, who thought that Pakistan missed a "grand opportunity"
to "liberate" Kashmir in 1962.[46] Ayub showed statesmanship in re-
fraining from such militant steps, which would have broken Pakistan's ties with the West.

Ayub confined himself to criticizing the policy of arming India,
referring with great anguish to the pledge given by Kennedy that he
would be consulted *before* arms were given to India.[47] As pointed
out earlier, the lack of consultation led to bad feelings on both
sides. U.S. policy makers could claim, justifiably, that Pakistan had
no right to object to U.S. military help to a country that was, at
that time, engaged in armed conflict with a communist country;
Pakistan had already committed itself to a number of treaties and

pacts that were instruments of the U.S. policy of "containment" of the communist countries. On the other hand, the Pakistanis could claim, truthfully, that the United States had broken its word. Former U.S. Ambassador to Pakistan Oehlert put the whole episode as follows:

> It was because of the implacable hatred between India and Pakistan and Pakistan's fears both of India's superiority of arms, men and economic capability and of India's often-expressed determination to merge Pakistan into India, that Pakistan extracted a promise from the United States that it would not furnish arms to India without prior consultation with Pakistan. . . . At the time of its 1962 border clash with China, India panicked and so did the United States. Fearing a full-fledged Chinese sweep into India, the United States rushed substantial arms aid to India without prior consultation it had promised Pakistan. This action, by their ally, in violation of its pledged word, deeply concerned the Pakistanis and caused them to reassess their position of alignment with the United States against their neighbors, Russia and China.[48]

Although the Western arms aid to India was not conditional on the settlement of the Kashmir issue, a serious new attempt was made to solve this complicated dispute that has acted as the poisoned well infecting every point of contact between the two countries. Mainly at the initiative of U.S. Assistant Secretary of State Harriman and British Commonwealth Secretary Duncan Sandys, on November 29, 1962, a joint communiqué issued simultaneously from New Delhi and Rawalpindi stated that a renewed effort was to be made to resolve the Kashmir dispute.[49] This Western-sponsored attempt at conciliation, like many similar attempts, demonstrated the sincerity and earnestness of the British and American governments in trying to maintain good relations with both India and Pakistan. But unfortunately it was not a success. Six rounds of ministerial talks were held during 1962 and 1965 between Bhutto and Swaran Singh. All conventional solutions to a territorial dispute, such as plebiscite, partition, internationalization, and other forms of political settlement, were explored and examined, and all were rejected. During the course of talks Pakistan signed the boundary agreement with China, which provoked India, while the Pakistanis interpreted Nehru's readiness to talk on Kashmir as only a shallow gesture to get reassurance of continued Western aid. After the talks' conclusion Nehru declared, "Kashmir was, is and will continue to be an integral part of India."[50]

THE WANING OF ALLIANCE AND THE FACADE OF NEUTRALISM

So the paradox of the United States' arming India (to defend against China) while counting Pakistan as its most "allied ally in Asia" continued. Sincere in wanting friendship with Pakistan, President Kennedy sent in late 1963 a number of emissaries to mollify Pakistan as well as to work toward an Indo–Pakistani rapprochement. Harriman, Presidential adviser Rostow, Presidential military representative General Maxwell Taylor, Secretary of State Dean Rusk, Under Secretary of State George Ball, and Assistant Secretary of State for Near Eastern and South Asian Affairs Philips Talbot all visited Pakistan and held discussions with Ayub and his government.[51] Having read the minutes of these discussions, particularly those including Foreign Minister Bhutto, I have no doubt that the Americans went out of their way to reassure Pakistan. It is tragic that the usually wise and moderate Ayub did not accept genuine assurances, mainly because of the influence of Bhutto, and thereby helped to destroy the friendship and confidence of a superpower—a friendship which had been built up over the past decade and of which Ayub was one of the chief architects.

George Ball gave "further assurance against aggression from any area," adding "our assurance of assistance to Pakistan against Indian aggression is [already] there." Ayub's reply was, "Guarantees are easy to give but difficult to implement." The discussion with Ball was continued by Foreign Minister Bhutto in Washington on October 4, 1963. Ball, reaffirming U.S. pledges, told Bhutto, "The U.S. has already assured Pakistan that if there was aggression from India or any other quarter the U.S. would lend assistance to Pakistan to meet such aggression." He added that Pakistan should "conceive of American arms as for the integrity of Pakistan's borders." When Bhutto raised the question of determining or defining aggression, Ball's reply was, "There is some confusion and ambiguity about the question of identifying aggression." But the Under Secretary of State tried to convince Bhutto of American good faith by stating that a violation of Pakistan's international border by India would clearly constitute aggression, and "there would be *immediate U.S. response.*"[52]

General Taylor, in his discussion with Ayub on December 20,

1963, said, "Pakistan has U.S. assurances against Indian aggression."
From Washington, Pakistani Ambassador Ahmad reported that on
March 16, 1964, Harriman said his

> Government failed to understand why Pakistan did not take
> at their face value the assurances already given by the United
> States about the nature of aid to India: he could not see why
> Pakistan should persist in disregarding U.S. assurance that the
> U.S. would come to Pakistan's aid should India use U.S. weapons
> against Pakistan.[53]

Here Harriman perhaps referred to a 1963 *aide-mémoire* passed
along by the American Ambassador in Pakistan that, according to
Oehlert, gave this categorical assurance:

> Under instructions from the White House and Department of
> State acknowledging positively and without equivocation that our
> formal agreement to assist Pakistan in the event of aggression,
> even with our own armies, was not limited to Communist coun-
> tries but indeed specifically included India.[54]

In fact, President Kennedy had written a letter to President Ayub
on January 26, 1962, before the Indo–Chinese border conflict, in
which he reaffirmed the U.S. commitments. "On the subject of
aggression against Pakistan," he wrote, "my Government certainly
stands by these assurances." But Kennedy added, "I trust that you
will agree, however, that a public statement to this effect would not
be fruitful at this juncture."[55]

The American emissaries failed in their efforts. Not only did
Pakistan's fears persist, but Indo–Pakistan tensions remained; and
they even increased as a result of Pakistan's growing friendship
with China, which began to play an active role in the affairs of the
subcontinent, and as a result of India's huge military buildup following the 1962 war.

The press in Pakistan, particularly in West Pakistan, continued
to cast aspersions upon U.S. policy. Prominent among the anti-
American lobby were Bhutto, Foreign Secretary Dehlavi, and Ayub's
(Principal) Secretary, Q. Shahab. Pakistan's policy makers, all West
Pakistani civilian and military officials, failed to appreciate the U.S.
position.[56] It was unrealistic to expect that the United States would
or could remain neutral in the Sino–Indian quarrel, judging from
the nature of both Sino–American relations and global U.S. policy
at that time. Pakistan's apprehensions about increased Indian
military strength were understandable in view of the unfortunate

tensions between India and itself, but the United States, as a reading of the records of the assurances by the U.S. emissaries shows, seemed to show full understanding and to do everything possible to retain the good relationship with Pakistan.

Pakistan's growing dissatisfaction with the West led it to shift from a policy of alliance to a policy of bilateralism, which, according to its author, Ayub, aimed for simultaneous good relations with the United States, the U.S.S.R., and China.[57] Friendship with China, which I shall treat in the next part, was an act of constructive diplomacy on Pakistan's part. In contrast to its sympathetic understanding of Pakistan's problems with India, the United States responded most unfavorably to Pakistan's attempts to improve relations with China. Ayub was extremely cautious in his moves toward Peking and Moscow until 1965, and the U.S. reaction to what was termed "Ayub's flirtation with Mao" was unduly harsh— just as Pakistan's reaction to the new U.S. policy toward India was unwise. After all, the military balance of power had changed to Pakistan's detriment, and it was the Soviet Union and not the Western powers that provided the bulk of the military supplies to India. In the changed South Asian Triangle, it was quite natural for Pakistan to look for friends elsewhere, and it got a quick response from Peking. Sino–Pakistani relations became the most serious complicating factor in the U.S. attitude toward Pakistan if not toward the whole subcontinent. Moves by Pakistan toward Peking, such as the border agreement, the aviation agreement, cultural exchanges, and the trade agreement, were a source of particular annoyance in Washington during the presidency of the intolerant Lyndon Johnson.

Annoying to India was much of the world's reaction to its 1962 China war. The reaction of India's best friend, the Soviet Union, was at least initially not free from ambiguity and uncertainty, as we have seen. Another big frustration for India during the war was the passive or even negative role of leading Afro–Asian countries, such as the U.A.R. (Egypt), Indonesia, and Nigeria, whose causes it had always tried to uphold. Nehru's foreign policy was openly criticized, and its rationale and basis were challenged both inside and outside the Indian Parliament. For Nehru it was a rude shock—his *panch sheel* (based on the five principles) seemed dead; his vision of Asian nationalism and the spirit of the Third World appeared shattered. His faith in the "doctrine of defence through friendship" appeared to be nothing more than a pious wish or an idealistic vision having no meaning in geopolitics.[58]

In contrast to the socialist nations and the Third World, Washington promptly responded to Nehru's call for help in the autumn of 1962, and the period following the war was perhaps the peak in U.S.–Indian relations. At one stage it was believed in some quarters that India might be persuaded to join in some form of alliance with the West[59]—in particular, Moscow worried over growing U.S. military involvement in the subcontinent.[60] But the Indian policy of nonalignment proved to be fully acceptable in Washington. When, after initial hesitancy, the U.S.S.R. openly supported "neutral" India against "fraternal" China, the policy makers in Washington seemed to come to appreciate the impact of India in the Sino–Soviet conflicts. Far from deploring Indian ties with Moscow, the United States seemed to give tacit recognition to them in the expectation that they would serve both to contain China and to intensify Sino–Soviet differences. According to Ayub, India was "given to understand that it is in the Western interest that she should continue to remain 'non-aligned' and receive aid from the Soviet Union as well."[61] As one observer put it, "Just as India has a psychological vested interest in a stalemate with Pakistan, so there is utility in the China impasse as a factor keeping alive Soviet and American interest in New Delhi."[62] Soon there seemed to be an identity of interest between the two superpowers in grooming India to help them achieve their common objective of the containment of China in South Asia. In addition to these considerations, New Delhi Ambassador Galbraith was opposed to pressuring Nehru to change his policy of nonalignment because Nehru's position was already shaken; the Prime Minister had had to drop Defense Minister Krishna Menon, the most noted leftist member of his Cabinet, and any further pressure on Nehru would be detrimental to the Western powers as well as to India.[63]

Thus India retained the facade of nonalignment, but in fact it became increasingly dependent on both Moscow and Washington for defense and security. India could no longer play the role of the leader of any third bloc—"instead of striking an elusive, equidistant pose midway between the extremes of commitment, the object [of Indian foreign policy] is now to remain as near as possible to both patrons while displeasing neither."[64]

When Lyndon Johnson became President in November 1963,

the American policy of helping India to contain China continued. India reportedly asked in 1963–1964 for a huge military assistance grant from the United States in return for its acceptance of the Western air defense umbrella and the presence of the Seventh Fleet in the Indian Ocean.[65] In March 1964, Defense Secretary McNamara reaffirmed the American policy of military assistance to India. In February 1965, McNamara said, "China was trying to drive a wedge between Pakistan and the United States," and for this reason he saw "a very real need for India to improve the quantity of its defense against the Chinese Communist threat"; he also said, of the Indians, "it is in our interest to assist them."[66] India's old friend Chester Bowles, who had become U.S. Ambassador for a second time, assured India after China's first atomic bomb explosion in late 1964 that a closer military tie with the United States could bring the entire nuclear power of the Seventh Fleet into any frontier struggle on the side of India; India would have not only the atomic bombs but also hydrogen bombs at its disposal.[67]

India's attitude toward the presence of the American Seventh Fleet in the Indian Ocean was in marked contrast to its stand on such issues in the heyday of Nehru's policy of nonalignment, *panch sheel*, and the "Bandung spirit." When questioned on this presence, Nehru seemed to have quietly acquiesced: "It does not apply to us in any way," he said. In contrast to Nehru's views, Pakistan told General Taylor that it did not believe the security and stability of the region would be strengthened as a result of the presence of the Seventh Fleet. Ayub said:

> The USA claims that a move [the introduction of the fleet in the Indian Ocean] is aimed at providing protection to the area. Pakistan is closely assessing the situation to gauge whether the move will add to the troubles of the area or lessen them.[68]

Foreign Minister Bhutto was more blunt in his opposition to the American move.[69]

These divergent attitudes reflected the changing pattern of nonalignment and alignment in the foreign policies of India and Pakistan. India seemed to avoid working at cross-purposes with the United States, and partially as a consequence the U.S. policy toward India softened; the U.S. was glad to see the end of the irritating era of India's left-leaning neutralism. Reverse trends marked U.S.–Pakistani relations. George Ball candidly expressed to Ambassador

Ahmad Washington's displeasure over the "developing relationship" with China. A similar concern—or warning—was voiced by Dean Rusk, who had adopted a "rigidly doctrinaire approach to Peking."[70] Thus Pakistani–American relations began to deteriorate rapidly. References to the so-called Karachi–Jakarta–Peking axis were heard in Washington, particularly when the question of foreign aid to Pakistan came up.[71]

In 1965 the U.S. aid to India and Pakistan reflected the changed atmosphere. Economic assistance was sanctioned by the international "Aid to India Consortium" *prior* to congressional authorization, but the "Aid to Pakistan Consortium" meeting, scheduled to be held in July, was abruptly postponed for two months, at American request, on the grounds that U.S. congressional authorization had not yet been given. This postponement was interpreted by the Pakistani press and government as evidence of the growing American disapproval of their country.[72]

While communicating news of the postponement of the Consortium meeting from July to September, the U.S. Ambassador in Rawalpindi, Walter P. McConnaughy, conveyed to Ayub a message from Johnson suggesting that during the two months interregnum "other problems" in U.S.–Pakistani relations could be discussed. Bhutto later wrote that the American Ambassador told him that these problems "covered the whole range of Pakistan's relations with the People's Republic of China, with President Soekarno's regime and Vietnam."[73] Pakistan bristled; it regarded the postponement of aid as "crude pressure" on a nation following an independent foreign policy. The Soviet press gave a similar interpretation and talked about a "chain of dollar imperialism."[74] It was during this period that Ayub proclaimed, "We want friends, not masters," a phrase that later served as the title of his autobiography and a sentiment that presently echoed through Pakistan's press and Parliament.[75]

Demands were made by the press and some sections of the public that Pakistan quit SEATO and CENTO. Pakistan did not formally break away from these pacts but did begin a process of disengagement, particularly in military commitments. From Pakistan's point of view, there were three important military issues facing CENTO: (1) command structure, (2) basic assumptions about global war, (3) basic assumptions about local war. By the mid-1960s Pakistan differed with its Western partners on all these issues: it was not interested in CENTO's centralized command structure; in view of its improving relations with China and the U.S.S.R., it could not agree with the West on most likely potential foes in a global war; and in regard to local war it had to differ because the United Kingdom was unwilling to consider in CENTO the "Indian threat" as demanded by Pakistan.[76]

LYNDON JOHNSON'S FURY

In pursuit of his new foreign policy, Ayub Khan planned to visit China, the U.S.S.R., and the United States. By this time Pakistan, particularly Foreign Minister Bhutto, was very vocal in identifying with the Afro–Asian countries and was taking a leading part in organizing the abortive Second Afro–Asian Conference scheduled to be held in 1965.[77] Ayub was called an "Asian de Gaulle."[78] In 1965, Ayub visited China in March and the U.S.S.R. in April and was scheduled to visit the United States April 25 and 26. But Johnson abruptly, if not discourteously, postponed the trip just a few days before its scheduled date. In order to maintain the "policy of non-discrimination," as well as to express disapproval, Johnson also postponed Prime Minister Shastri's visit, scheduled to take place June 2 and 3.[79]

India regarded this as an "affront," and Shastri declared that he would never visit the United States. From New Delhi, Ambassador Chester Bowles cabled that fifteen years of patient efforts to build a working relationship between the United States and India had been undone.[80] Addressing the Indo–Soviet Cultural Association on April 20, four days after Johnson's cancellation of the visits, Shastri evidenced Indian resentment by lambasting U.S. Vietnam policy. "If the United States continues bombing of North Vietnam," he said, "there is hardly any point in President Johnson's favourable response to the 17 non-aligned nations' appeal [at the Cairo Conference, October 5–10, 1964] for unconditional negotiations." Shastri declared that the "bombing must stop before talks are possible."[81] The White House announced the next day that the invitation to Shastri still stood and that President Johnson hoped he would visit Washington in the late summer.[82] (The Prime Minister of India and Ayub both went to the United States in due course, but that Prime Minister was not Shastri: Shastri died suddenly in January 1966 at Tashkent.)[83]

Unlike Shastri, Ayub preferred to express his displeasure at Johnson's postponement in a subtle way; when I questioned him on the American postponement, he told me, "If a friend does not like to see my face, why should I impose myself?" But in fact the resentment in Rawalpindi was no less than that in New Delhi.[84]

The postponements of the Shastri and Ayub visits—and the resentment that resulted in New Delhi and Rawalpindi—were a function of President Johnson's apparent unwillingness to listen to his critics, particularly those who criticized his policy on Vietnam, particularly those who expected him to give U.S. foreign aid. "The President simply lost his temper," explained one man who was close to Johnson at the time he delayed the visits.[85] Johnson wanted to make India and Pakistan examples for all nations receiving or expecting U.S. aid; the idea was to punish two children that had been naughty (and that together had received $10 billion in U.S. aid) so that the other American wards would stay in line. India's and Pakistan's mischief, in Johnson's view, had been considerable. "Attacked" by China, India had asked for U.S. help in the fighting, received it, and then disagreed with America on China's role in Vietnam. Similarly, Pakistan had sought U.S. support, committed itself to join with the United States for the containment of China in Asia, and then tried to develop the friendliest relations with China—with Ayub attacking U.S. policy in Vietnam, though cautiously and in a muted voice, while touring China. This was too much for Johnson. If India and Pakistan expected U.S. aid, they should "appreciate," if not support, U.S. policy. But by the mid-1960s the Johnsonian technique of bullying India and Pakistan had no prospect of success.

THE INDO–PAKISTANI WAR OF 1965 AND U.S. POLICY

It is tragic that India and Pakistan have looked upon one another as enemies since their independence and that their relations are charged with an envenomed load of bigotry, prejudice, and hostility, both religious and nationalistic. This has been a bitter disappointment not only to the people of the two countries but also to their friends and allies. Instead of the peace and progress that the people of both countries needed urgently, the years since independence have brought warfare, vituperation, frustration, and fear.[86] Instead of devoting all their resources to economic development, both countries have spent millions of rupees on defense against each other. The United States gave military assistance to Pakistan and India to fight external enemies, but the two countries' military machines have been directed against each other instead. The United States has spent billions of dollars for the economic development of these two important South Asian countries, but their corrosive quarrels have much inhibited that development.

So when India and Pakistan began to move in the direction of armed conflict in 1965, there was genuine concern, dismay, and anger in Washington, as in many other capitals. During the early limited war in the Rann of Kutch, U.S. Ambassador McConnaughy, saying that "the party providing military assistance has certainly some responsibility," informed Foreign Minister Bhutto on April 30 that the United States was unwilling to permit the use of its military equipment by either side in the conflict.[87] (The Indian Government had already complained to the United States about the use of U.S. arms by Pakistan in the Rann of Kutch; as the fighting spread, the Pakistanis as well as the Indians would complain about American arms being used against them.) The Pakistani Foreign Minister referred to the U.S. assurance of aid against foreign aggressors and inquired about U.S. action "in the event of India implementing its threat of aggression." The Ambassador's reply was, "The Government stands behind its commitment and agreement," but he added, "The U.S. view is that the situation is somewhat confused and belligerence is not justified on either side." Both the inquiry and the response were to be repeated in the days ahead.[88]

Thanks to the mediation of the British Prime Minister, Harold Wilson, the Rann of Kutch conflict was settled by arbitration. But then began the larger, full-scale war of August and September over the Kashmir issue. Both countries produced extensive legal and moral arguments to support their action in the conflict of September 1965. India claimed the war started on August 5 when 4,000 to 5,000 Pakistani-trained and -equipped guerrillas crossed into Kashmir in an attempt to inspire and lead a general uprising. Pakistan held that the war started on September 6 when, without provocation, Indian troops crossed Pakistan's international border in the area of Lahore.[89] The United States was approached by its ally to come to its rescue as a "victim of the Indian aggression." Pakistan insisted that India's crossing of the international frontier on September 6 constituted a case of "real aggression" requiring, under America's commitments to Pakistan, aid from the United States.

An analysis of the numerous confidential U.S. pledges and assurances, those aside from the formal commitments under SEATO and CENTO, leaves no doubt that the United States had promised to help even if the aggression was noncommunist and Indian. An *aide-mémoire* handed to the U.S. Ambassador in Pakistan when he met President Ayub on September 6 invoked those assurances, calling for U.S. assistance "to meet aggression from India."[90] The U.S. Ambassador replied on September 10 that the United States

> regards India's strike across the Punjab frontier as a most serious development [but] India's attack across the Pakistan border must be viewed in an overall context—that immediate crisis began with a substantial infiltration of armed men from the Pakistan side to the Indian part of Kashmir. In accordance with our assurance to Pakistan, the U.S. is acting to meet this common danger by fully supporting immediate UN action to end hostility—the appeal of the United Nations' Security Council must be honored.[91]

In Washington, Ambassador Ghulam Ahmad, Aziz's brother, met Secretary of State Rusk on September 30 and reminded him that the United States and Pakistan were allies and that Pakistan wanted to know what the Americans would do to support it against Indian aggression. "What was relevant," Rusk replied, "was not alliances"; the U.S. had reservations about the SEATO treaty. More relevant to Rusk and his government was the bilateral arrangement (of 1954, renewed secretly in 1964), and this had been carefully "looked at." But the difficulty posed by the rapid development of events in the subcontinental conflict, according to Rusk, was that "the U.S. was being invited in on the crash landing without being in on the take off."[92]

In the American view, that "take off"—the action that triggered the September fighting—was Pakistan's alleged infiltration of guerrillas into Kashmir; India had then overreacted. The U.S. view, though not expressed fully to Pakistan, was that there was no clear Indian aggression against Pakistan (the U.S. did not share Harold Wilson's early opinion, which he later repudiated), and therefore the question of fulfilling U.S. assurances to Pakistan did not arise.[93]

Whatever the verdict of future historians as to who was the aggressor in the Indo–Pakistani war of 1965, the Pakistanis felt bitterly let down by their principal ally in their darkest hour. Not only did the United States fail to come to Pakistan's rescue, but on

September 8—within two days of the alleged Indian invasion—Dean Rusk announced that, after consultation with Congress, the administration had stopped all U.S. military aid to India and Pakistan, and would grant no further economic aid.[94]

The stoppage of arms supplies to both India and Pakistan was described as "even-handed" by the U.S. government as it applied to both, but in practice it hit Pakistan much harder. The U.S. military shipments to Pakistan since 1954, according to some reliable sources, had cost $1.5 billion and had provided all of Pakistan's fighters, bombers, and modern transport aircraft, nearly all of its combat tanks and much of its artillery; U.S. arms supplies to India since 1962, on the other hand, had totaled only about $75 million in value and for the most part had been lightweight, easily movable equipment and arms for high-altitude combat. Pakistan's armed forces were nearly 100 percent American-equipped, while India's equipment was not more than 10 percent American. India's best source of military supplies, the U.S.S.R., continued to provide it with military equipment.[95]

The cutoff of U.S. arms aid was decisive to both the war and the shape of the South Asian Triangle. Without U.S. replacements, spare parts, and ammunition, Pakistan would have been left defenseless in a few weeks, and Ayub had no choice but to accept the cease-fire.[96] Relations between the U.S. and Pakistan therefore reached their lowest point in history. India, on the other hand, was pleased to see proved hollow Pakistani expectations of U.S. assistance against it. India's worst apprehensions since Pakistan entered into military pacts and alliances in 1954 evaporated.

NOTES

1. Levi, *op. cit.*, p. 217.
2. See Rajan, *India in World Affairs, op. cit.*
3. John F. Kennedy, *The Strategy of Peace* (New York: Harper & Brothers, 1960).
4. Based on the reports of the Pakistani High Commissioner in Washington in early 1961, uncovered in my research and personal interviews in Pakistan, 1967–1971.
5. See John F. Kennedy's State of the Union message to the Congress, 1961, in *American Foreign Relations, 1961, op. cit.*, pp. 16–25.

6. Kennedy, *Strategy, op. cit.*

7. See Mohammed Ayub Khan, *Speeches and Statements, Vols. V and VI* (Karachi: Government of Pakistan Press, n.d.); Mohammed Ayub Khan, *Pakistan Perspective: A Collection of Important Articles and Excerpts from Major Addresses* (Karachi: Government of Pakistan Press, n.d.), pp. 63–77.

8. Based on my research and personal interviews in Pakistan, 1967–1971.

9. *Ibid.*

10. See the joint communiqué issued at the end of the Johnson–Nehru meeting, in *The Statesman*, May 20, 1961.

11. Based on the points of the Pakistani High Commissioner in New Delhi, May 27 and June 2, 1961, uncovered in my research and personal interviews in Pakistan, 1967–1971.

12. Based on my research and personal interviews in Pakistan, 1967–1971.

13. "Pakistan: President Ayub and President Kennedy," *Round Table*, September 1961, p. 418.

14. I was told this interpretation of Ayub's reception in the United States by a member of the President's entourage.

15. *Dawn*, July 13, 1961.

16. Based on my research and personal interviews in Pakistan, 1967–1971; also, see Ayub, *Not Masters, op. cit.*

17. *Dawn*, July 7, 1961.

18. See Ayub's speech before the National Press Club in Washington on July 13, 1961, in *Dawn*, July 14, 1961.

19. *Documents on American Foreign Relations, 1961, op. cit.*, pp. 287–288.

20. Based on my research and personal interviews in Pakistan, 1967–1971.

21. *Ibid.*

22. *Ibid.*

23. *The Statesman*, Aug. 14, 1961.

24. See *The Statesman* and *Times of India*, Nov. 6 to 16, 1961.

25. Arthur M. Schlesinger, Jr., *A Thousand Days: John F. Kennedy in the White House* (Boston: Houghton Mifflin Co., 1965).

26. Based on my research and personal interviews in Pakistan, 1967–1971.

27. See Adlai Stevenson's speech before the UN Security Council, Dec. 18, 1961, in Palmer, *United States Policy, op. cit.*, p. 23.

28. See Macadam, *Register of World Events 1961, op. cit.*, p. 86.

29. "Pakistan: Foreign Policy under Review," *Round Table*, March 1962, pp. 196–197.

30. *U.S. Foreign Aid in the Near East and South Asia* (Washington: Agency for International Development, n.d.), p. 12, cited in Palmer, *United States Policy, op. cit.*, p. 138.

31. Based on my research and personal interviews in Pakistan, 1967–1971.

32. *Ibid.*

33. Michael Edwards, "Illusion and Reality in India's Foreign Policy," *International Affairs* (London), Vol. 41, no. 1, 1965, p. 52, and Neville Maxwell, *India's China War* (New York: Pantheon Books, 1970), p. 410.

34. *The Statesman*, Dec. 30, 1962.

35. *Ibid.*, July 28, 1963.

36. *Ibid.*, July 1, 1963.

37. Choudhury, *Relations with India*, p. 266.

38. See the speech of Pakistani Foreign Minister Mohammad Ali (Bogra) in the National Assembly, Nov. 22, 1963, in *Dawn*, Nov. 23, 1963; see also editorials in *Dawn* and *Pakistan Times*, Nov. 23–24, 1963.

39. Z. A. Bhutto, *The Myth of Independence* (London: Oxford University Press, 1969), pp. 62, 68.

40. See *Sunday Times* (London), Oct. 20, 1963; see also Ayub, "Stresses," *op. cit.*

41. *Dawn*, Sept. 19, 1963.

42. Quoted in Bhutto, *op. cit.*, p. 69.

43. *Ibid.*, p. 63.

44. Ayub, *Not Masters, op. cit.*, pp. 140–141.

45. Based on my research and personal interviews in Pakistan, 1967–1971.

46. See Bhutto's speeches during the period of anti-Ayub agitation in winter 1969, *Pakistan Times*.

47. See Chapter 3.

48. Oehlert, *op. cit.*

49. *Hindu*, November 30, 1962.

50. *Ibid.*, June 16, 1963.

51. Based on my research and personal interviews in Pakistan, 1967–1971.

52. *Ibid.*

53. *Ibid.*

54. Oehlert, *op. cit.*

55. Based on my research and personal interviews in Pakistan, 1967–1971.

56. G. W. Choudhury, "U.S. Policy toward the Indian Subcontinent," *Pacific Community*, October 1973.

57. See Ayub, *Not Masters, op. cit.* The President compared pursuing his policy of bilateralism to walking a tight, triangular rope.

58. See Harrison, "Troubled India," *op. cit.;* "India after Chinese Aggression," *Round Table*, March 1963, pp. 177–181; and debates in Lok Sabha on May 6 and 7, 1963 (in *The Statesman*, May 7 and 8, 1963) and Aug. 16, 1973 (*The Statesman*, Aug. 17, 1963).

59. "After Chinese Aggression," *op. cit.*

60. See Chapter 3.

61. Ayub, "Stresses," *op. cit.*

62. Harrison, "Troubled India," *op. cit.*

63. "After Chinese Aggression," *op. cit.*

64. Harrison, "Troubled India," *op. cit.*

65. *Time*, Dec. 27, 1969, cited in Bhutto, *op. cit.*, pp. 68–69.

66. Bhutto, *op. cit.*, pp. 69–71.

67. *Ibid.*, p. 71.

68. "America in the Indian Ocean," *Round Table*, March 1964, pp. 175–179.

69. Bhutto, *op. cit.*

70. Based on my research and personal interviews in Pakistan, 1967–1971.

71. Based on reports from the Pakistani Ambassador in Washington, 1963–1964, uncovered in my research and personal interviews in Pakistan, 1967–1971.

72. *Ibid.*

73. Bhutto, *op. cit.*, p. 72.

74. *Pravda* and *Izvestia*, Aug. 14, 1965.

75. Ayub, *Not Masters, op. cit.*

76. Based on my research and personal interviews in Pakistan, 1967–1971.

77. Bhutto, *op. cit.*

78. *The Economist*, Aug. 15, 1959.

79. Cancellation of the visits of Ayub and Shastri was announced by the White House on Apr. 16, 1965. See *Dawn* and *The Statesman*, Apr. 17, 1965.

80. Philip L. Geyelin, *Lyndon B. Johnson and the World* (New York: Frederick A. Praeger, Inc., 1966), p. 266.

81. *The Statesman,* Apr. 21, 1965; see also *New York Times,* Apr. 21, 1965.

82. *The Statesman,* Apr. 22, 1965.

83. *Ibid.,* Jan. 11, 1966.

84. Based on my research and personal interviews in Pakistan, 1967–1971.

85. Geyelin, *op. cit.,* pp. 266–268.

86. For details, see Choudhury, *Relations with India, op. cit.*

87. Based on my research and personal interviews in Pakistan, 1967–1971.

88. *Ibid.*

89. See U.S. House of Representatives, Committee on Foreign Affairs, *The Report of the Special Study Mission to the Far East Asia, India and Pakistan (November 7–December 12, 1965)* (Washington: Government Printing Office, 1966), p. 36.

90. Based on my research and personal interviews in Pakistan, 1967–1971.

91. *Ibid.*

92. *Ibid.*

93. *Ibid.*

94. *Dawn* and *The Statesman,* Sept. 9, 1965.

95. Based on my research and personal interviews in Pakistan, 1967–1971.

96. *Ibid.*

Chapter Six

"TO ENCOURAGE SELF-RELIANCE, NOT DEPENDENCE," 1965–1970

THE LOWERED PROFILE

THOROUGHLY DISQUIETED by trends in the subcontinent since 1960, the United States began a new period in its relations with India and Pakistan, a period in which it lowered its profile. India's image after its wars of 1962 and 1965 was damaged seriously, and Americans no longer hoped to build up India against China. Similarly, the good will and friendship for Pakistan was lessened. Johnson seemed to have wanted to make it clear to both countries that the United States gave substantial economic and, until recently, military aid for purposes other than fighting each other, and the United States seemed to begin a process of disengagement from military commitment in the subcontinent. The threat of another Sino–Indian armed conflict had gradually receded; Pakistan's growing ties with Peking and its process of disengagement from SEATO and CENTO meant that it was no longer Dulles's bulwark against communism—if it ever had been. The subcontinent became of less importance to U.S. planners also because the war in Vietnam made Southeast Asia a top-priority area in American policy and because the rapid expansion of Soviet influence among the Arab countries after the Arab–Israeli war of 1967 heightened Middle East tension and, like the Vietnam War, diverted American attention.

On the other hand, the Soviet Union and China began to play increasingly active roles in South Asia, and the character of the South Asian Triangle changed considerably after 1965. The Soviet

Union had improved its position by the mid-1960s through special relations with the larger, dominant power and, since the Tashkent Conference, through developing relations with the other power. China came still closer to Pakistan after the war of 1965, as the latter became almost solely dependent upon China for military supplies after the 1965 U.S. cutoff of military supplies.

Despite its disillusionment with both India and Pakistan and its preoccupation elsewhere, however, the United States neither wanted nor could afford to cease to play its role in South Asia. South Asia may not have been a major crisis area until the conflict in Bangladesh erupted in March 1971, yet through the middle and late 1960s and beyond it retained great political significance in the global politics of the major powers, particularly in relation to the Third World; the U.S. could not be entirely unmindful of the fate of nearly 700 million people living in South Asia. Thus, although a new phase of U.S. policy began after the Indo–Pakistani war of 1965, both Ayub and Mrs. Gandhi had meetings with Johnson within six months of the war.

THE AYUB–JOHNSON MEETING, DECEMBER 1965

Johnson applied the technique of what the Pakistani Ministry of Foreign Affairs referred to as "bluff and bluster as well as of placating and persuading" in his dialogue with Ayub.[1] In Pakistan there was apprehension that because of its links with Peking, Johnson wanted to "cut Pakistan down to size," and one of Ayub's close advisers suggested, "It would pay to use the same technique [of bluff and bluster] in reverse in dealing with him." Ayub, however, performed cautiously and well; according to his entourage, he presented "a good exposition of Pakistan's geopolitical compulsions" to seek friendly relations with China. As a result, the Americans seemed to gain a better appreciation of Pakistan's relations with China, which had been the major complicating factor in U.S.–Pakistan relations. Ayub shrewdly asked the pragmatic Johnson, "If you were in my predicament, what policy alternatives would you follow?" A tacit understanding apparently evolved by which Pakistan, in its dealings with China, would not tread upon U.S. interest and sensitivities, while the United States would recognize that Paki-

stan had to maintain amicable relations with Peking. This understanding represented a success for Ayub's highly reputed personal
diplomacy, a success evidenced on March 23, 1966, when the display
of Chinese arms in Pakistan's National Day parade drew little protest from Washington. Ayub did not want to antagonize the United
States; he knew that U.S. economic aid, even unaccompanied by
military aid, ameliorated his country's problems. At the same time,
Pakistan had to forge increasingly close links with China: as long
as it had genuine apprehensions about India's arms buildup, Pakistan had to look to Peking because neither the U.S.S.R. nor the
United States shared Pakistan's assessment of India's threats to its
security.

During the Ayub–Johnson talks, the former complained about
the lack of U.S. support when India crossed the international
boundary on September 6, 1965, and he explained that the people
of Pakistan were greatly agitated over U.S. policy. When Johnson,
in turn, complained of hostile Pakistani remarks about U.S. policies,
particularly press comments on Vietnam, Ayub replied that such
criticism was a natural reaction of the people to the unsatisfactory
U.S. attitude toward Pakistan.

On Indo–Pakistani relations, Ayub tried to assess India's policies
and actions toward Pakistan and maintained that India had no
desire to resolve the Kashmir issue. It was evident, however, that
the United States, like the U.S.S.R., was interested in maintaining
the status quo in Kashmir rather than taking an initiative to bring
new pressures on India. The bitterest complaint from Ayub related
to the total ban of U.S. military supplies to Pakistan. Johnson was
not moved, as public opinion in the United States would not have
favored a lifting of the ban when Indo–Pakistani tensions were still
so high.

At the end of the talks on December 14, 1965, a joint communiqué was issued in which "President Johnson reaffirmed that the
United States regards as vital to world peace preservation of the
independence and integrity of Pakistan."[2] During their dialogue
Johnson had told Ayub: "If Pakistan was threatened by another
power, the U.S. would be there to protect its [Pakistan's] integrity—
just as it was on the scene in Vietnam. The U.S. would not allow
Pakistan to be gobbled up."

Ayub made a reference to Johnson's oral assurance in his press
conference in Karachi on December 19 after his return from Washington.[3] But after their frustrating experiences with such assurances

during the war of September 1965, neither Ayub nor any other Pakistanis with a memory attached much importance to Johnson's oral assurance or to the "reaffirmation" of the joint communiqué. Pakistani Ambassador in Washington Ghulam Ahmad, in his report on January 3, 1966, was incorrect in contending that the conference provided "the only assurance so far given by the United States unconditioned by the stipulation that the threat to the integrity of Pakistan must arise from international communism if it is to attract U.S. intervention." As pointed out earlier, the United States had given such assurances to Pakistan on at least six occasions between 1962 and 1964.

MRS. GANDHI TO WASHINGTON, MARCH 1966

In November 1965, before Ayub and Mrs. Gandhi visited Washington, the White House indicated that resumption of U.S. economic aid to India and Pakistan, aid that had been cut off along with military assistance in September, would depend upon the following factors: (1) maintenance of peace between the two countries, (2) pursuit of self-help policies and of a pragmatic approach to economic and industrial development (this applied to India rather than to Pakistan), and (3) avoidance of a military buildup that might lead to another conflict.[4]

During Ayub's visit in December Johnson had authorized the Agency for International Development to go ahead with certain projects in Pakistan, and Vice-President Hubert H. Humphrey, visiting Pakistan in February 1966, announced a commodity loan of $50 million.[5] Later it was indicated that the U.S. commodity aid to Pakistan in 1966–1967 would be about $140 million.

The main pressure to resume economic aid, however, came not from Pakistan but from India, which, in the grip of famine, issued urgent appeals in early 1966 for assistance to ward off impending economic disaster and widespread starvation; when Mrs. Gandhi arrived in the United States on March 27, 1966, she stressed India's emergency food grain requirements.[6] Within two hours of Mrs. Gandhi's departure from Washington, President Johnson sent a special message to Congress seeking approval for the emergency shipment to India of 3.5 million tons of American grain—a supplement to the 6.5 million tons that the United States was already providing. At the same time President Johnson announced the decision to establish a new and imaginative venture—the Indo–American Foundation, created to promote progress in all fields of learning. The foundation's main aims were to develop new techniques in farm and factory, to advance science, and to increase agricultural research.[7]

On Indo–Pakistani relations, Johnson impressed Mrs. Gandhi as well as Ayub with the need to lessen tensions and to reduce defense expenditures. India, like Pakistan before it, was urged to agree to specified levels of defense preparedness so as to establish between the two subcontinent nations a ratio in their military expenditures. How this ratio could be brought about was a question that would continue to receive American attention, as would proposals for placing agreed limits on the acquisition of weapons by the two nations, despite the fact that the United States could hardly achieve such a ratio or such limits. Johnson made it abundantly clear to both Ayub and Mrs. Gandhi that, with its deep involvement in Vietnam, Washington could not tolerate another conflict in South Asia; its reaction to the recurrence of conflict would be firm and would as a first step involve the prompt stoppage of economic aid.[8]

IN DEFENSE OF THE STATUS QUO, IN PURSUIT OF SIMULTANEOUS GOOD RELATIONS, IN OPPOSITION TO CHINA

In 1966 a new U.S. Ambassador to Pakistan endeavored to smooth out difficulties in the U.S.–Pakistani relationship, meeting Ayub on September 2, 1966, to convey a message from Johnson in reply to a recent letter. Johnson wrote Ayub, "Your letter of August 20 arrived at a time when my closest colleagues and I have been reviewing the manner in which our policies and attention in South Asia can best contribute to our common goal of peace and security." Johnson urged Ayub to establish "trusted communication between you and Mrs. Gandhi."[9] Johnson also suggested that India and Pakistan should hold arms limitation discussions that would be started independently of those on Kashmir. Ayub expressed the view that talks on arms limitations would be fruitless unless the basic political problems were simultaneously discussed.

It is clear from an analysis of the various American notes and

memoranda received in Islamabad in 1966–1967 that the United
States was deeply interested in the maintenance of the status quo
in the subcontinent. Despite Pakistan's repeated pleas, the United
States was not in a hurry to lift the ban on military supplies to the
two countries, though India continued to receive military supplies
from the Soviet Union, and Pakistan—frantically trying to procure
supplies from other sources, mainly China—could not match India's
military buildup. Like military supplies, economic aid under the
new U.S. policy was tied up with the American aim of promoting
better relations between India and Pakistan. In order to link directly
the economic future of the two countries to peace between them,
the United States was giving thought to the development of the
subcontinent *as a whole* through projects beneficial to both countries. The United States was also considering the joint use, through
the good offices of the World Bank, of the water of the Ganges.

If in some ways, such as through the suspension of military aid,
the U.S. status quo policy benefited India to the detriment of Pakistan, in other ways it did not. After the war of 1965, American
policy makers seemed to be loath to abandon Pakistan to Peking
just as they were unwilling to abandon India to Moscow. The United
States no doubt wanted India to be strong in the context of its
policy of containment of China, but it did not follow, as feared in
Pakistan, that America sought to make India, as Rostow put it, "the
most dominant [*sic*] power in Asia." Rostow, an important White
House aide, told the Pakistani Ambassador on September 7, 1966,
"The U.S. has no intention of depending upon India alone: it must
carry Pakistan with it [too]."

Throughout 1966 the United States conducted a review of its
policies—political, economic, and military—toward the subcontinent, and a number of State Department officials and members of
the policy-planning staff ·at the White House visited India and
Pakistan. These officials and staff members constantly stressed "Indo–
Pakistan amity and understanding." Pakistan told the emissaries that
the changing balance of power in the subcontinent and the lack of
progress toward settlement of the Kashmir dispute were the greatest hindrances to the U.S. goal of "Indo–Pakistan amity." Indians
believed that their nation was "committed to peace" and that its
defense preparations were not only against Pakistan but also against
China. A secret Pentagon report on Soviet military aid to India,
however, confirmed that

> all military equipment acquired by India since September, 1965, was intended for use against Pakistan. Tanks, artillery and naval aircraft acquired on procurement from the Soviet sources are of the kind that can not be used against China in the northern and northeastern mountainous areas.

Not only the nature but also the deployment of the bulk of the Indian Army and of India's most sophisticated aircraft lent further support to the contention that India directed its attention at Pakistan.

Yet the U.S. policy makers seemed to be determined not to "offend" India. Pakistan's growing friendship with China on the one hand and Indochina tensions on the other were two important factors limiting policy alternatives for the United States in South Asia. As long as the containment of China remained an objective of U.S. policy, Washington would not hurt India or let it succumb to political, economic, or military pressures. It is true that after Ayub's 1965 Washington visit American policy makers better appreciated Pakistani motives, but nevertheless the "threat of Chinese expansion" in Southeast and South Asia stayed uppermost in their minds.

The United States wanted to create a new regional grouping, ostensibly for economic reasons but in reality for political and diplomatic purposes against China. Pakistan, friendly with Peking, was opposed to such an organization. India also would not formally endorse any grouping for political and diplomatic reasons, but neither was it opposed to the U.S. policy of containment; its reaction to the new U.S. moves was far more mild than it had been when the United States had first formulated such groupings in the mid-1950s.

On February 9, 1967, President Johnson sent to Congress a message on foreign aid. While the message spoke highly of Pakistan's outstanding success in economic development and expressed the hope of future progress, it made no specific recommendation on economic assistance to Pakistan. On the other hand, the message urged all advanced nations to come to India's aid in resolving its difficulties. The U.S. aid program emphasized, among other things, self-help, multilaterism, regionalism, agriculture, balance of payments, and efficient administration; most of these had been incorporated into the amended Public Law 480. The foreign aid message's new element, an element laden with political implications, was "regionalism": "The future of many countries," read the document, "depends upon sound development of resources shared with their neighbors." The U.S. aid to India and Pakistan, explained U.S. officials in Washington, would be guided by this principle.[10] Pakistanis, rejecting American-sponsored "regionalism" just as they would scorn Kosygin's regional economic grouping in 1969, feared that U.S. economic aid would be directed to promote American political objectives in the area.

Another source of misgivings between the United States and Pakistan in the post-1965 years was alleged Central Intelligence Agency encouragement of East Pakistani secessionist sentiment. Some statements of high U.S. officials were partly responsible for this apprehension. Howard Wriggins, then a member of the State Department's policy-planning staff under the Johnson administration, stated, "To choose an identification of U.S. power with forces of public order in a recipient country may complicate our relationship with those who are now out of power but will be likely to form the next government." Dankwart A. Rustow, of the Brookings Institution senior staff, recommended American intervention in the domestic politics of the developing countries. According to Rustow, "Our aim should be to encourage not political stability but political evolution in a desirable direction."[11] Pakistani Ambassador Ghulam Ahmad was "assured" by CIA Director Richard Helms on August 26, 1966, that the "CIA is not engaged in any subversion activities in East Pakistan . . . or against President Ayub and his regime," but there persisted among Pakistanis a widespread feeling that Americans were not passive witnesses to their internal politics, particularly in East Pakistan. The U.S.–Pakistani relationship bogged down in suspicion, doubts, and prejudices from 1965 into 1969.

THE NEW ARMS POLICY

In April 1967, after much evaluation, the Johnson administration inaugurated its new arms policy for India and Pakistan. The professed purposes of the sustained limitations on shipments were to limit arms acquisition by both countries, to restrain military expenditure, to reduce the possibility of military confrontation, and to encourage higher priority in resource allocation to economic development. These objectives were good but almost impossible to attain. The effect of the new arms policy was to continue, if not to worsen, the military imbalance. India had been acquiring arms since 1962 from the Soviet Union and Eastern European countries as well as from Britain and France. Pakistani armed forces, on the other hand, equipped till September 1965 only with American supplies, faced tremendous problems as a result of the U.S. embargo.

The State Department announced:

> We have concluded an extensive review of our policy with regard to the provision of military equipment to India and Pakistan and have decided that we shall not issue grant of military assistance which has been suspended since September 1965.[12]

State Department spokesmen also announced the termination of the Military Assistance Adviser Group in Pakistan and the closing of the Military Supply Mission in India. They indicated as well that military policy would undergo careful, continuing review to ensure that it not contribute to an arms race between India and Pakistan. The new arms policy called for shipments of military equipment only in exchange for cash, not as a grant; for the supply of lethal spare parts and replacements only on a case-by-case basis; and for only indirect sale of lethal items of U.S. origin. Possibly allowable was "limited" sale on a case-by-case basis of secondhand American-made equipment owned by third countries but under U.S. control. As one official put it:

> We finally came out of the long intensive review to . . . remove ourselves from a position of being one of the suppliers—important suppliers—of military assistance to both countries to one in which we maintain a neutral relationship with both countries in this field.[13]

Both India and Pakistan expressed dissatisfaction with the new U.S. policy, but resentment was greater in New Delhi; in Islamabad it was regarded as a limited opening to urgently needed military supplies.[14] In fact, the Pakistanis should have been more annoyed. The policy meant little for India because it had relatively small quantities of equipment that required U.S. spare parts. On the other hand, while Pakistan got some U.S. spare parts from 1967, it garnered practically no secondhand tanks or other equipment.

Looking around among NATO countries and other nations to buy some used tanks to replace those that had worn out, Pakistan was turned down by one country after another, sometimes after initial agreement, usually because of political pressure from India.[15] Iran was ready throughout this period to help Pakistan, but the United States did not approve of its selling tanks to Pakistan; if

Iran were to sell its tanks to Pakistan, Johnson administration officials reasoned, it should purchase new tanks from the United States, and such expenditures would be inadvisable for Iran.[16]

During a seventy-minute refueling stop at Karachi on December 23, 1967, President Johnson, on his way home from Australia, assured Ayub at an airport meeting that arrangements would be made for Pakistan to purchase immediately 200 secondhand tanks. The American Ambassador received a telegram on March 1, 1968, from Dean Rusk instructing him to inform President Ayub that he could have 100 of these tanks now and 100 later. But no tanks arrived. How did this happen? According to Ambassador Oehlert, it happened "primarily because of deliberate foot dragging by the Department of State—that monolithic, power-unto-itself monstrosity which has been the despair of President after President." "Powerful" State Department personnel worked toward one objective—"don't help Pakistan"—as they felt that India would not be "pleased by a change in policy."[17]

DISENGAGEMENT FROM SEATO AND CENTO

As a result of the new arms policy announced in April 1967, the special relationship between the United States and Pakistan came to an end; the commitments made under bilateral military agreements of 1954 and 1959 virtually ended, though not legally or formally, and the process of disengagement from SEATO and CENTO, which Pakistan had begun after the 1965 war, was all but completed.

As a protest against the new arms policy, the Pakistanis abstained from the SEATO advisory meeting held in Washington the month the new policy was announced, advising their representative, Group Captain Kamal Ahmud, who had already arrived in Washington, not to attend.[18] At the SEATO discussions, two flags were missing, those of France and Pakistan. "The green and white flag bearing stars and crescent was whisked away from desk space allotted to Pakistanis . . . before reporters were allowed into the conference room."[19]

In making a new assessment of its membership in SEATO and

CENTO, Pakistan found that these pacts fell far short of its original expectations. The other members, particularly the United States and the United Kingdom, ignored Pakistan's primary need for firm and active assurance against armed aggression from any source, including India. Moreover, the economic benefits that were supposed to accrue were unrealized because of the low priority attributed by the United States to this aspect of SEATO—the preoccupation was with the containment of communism. Pakistan had proposed a number of projects to the SEATO Economic Council, including the improvement of Pakistani radio broadcasting facilities and the establishment of a marine diesel training center in East Pakistan, a technical center at Jhelum, a central mine rescue and safety station in Quetta, an education service for the National Museum, and a regional agricultural research center in East Pakistan. None of these projects passed beyond the stage of consideration by the member governments.

Turning to political problems, we find that Pakistan began to take an independent stand on the situation in Southeast Asia. In backing for Vietnam a peaceful and political settlement through negotiations, it disassociated itself from the position of the United States and its allies. This was evidenced in a special note to the communiqué issued at the end of the tenth Ministerial Council meeting of SEATO, held in London May 3 to 5, 1965, in which Pakistan, while expressing its concern over the consequences of armed conflict in Vietnam, advocated determined efforts to restore peace through negotiations on the basis of the Geneva agreements.[20] In 1966, the Pakistani delegation to SEATO took exception to certain paragraphs that condemned Peking and Hanoi for alleged subversion in Vietnam and Laos and for violating the Geneva agreements of 1954 and 1962. The gradual hardening of Pakistan's attitude on Vietnam was a clear manifestation of its reservations about membership in the pacts. The socialist countries took note of Pakistan's independence; China, indeed, expressed appreciation of Pakistan's role within these pacts.[21]

As Pakistan's "allies" made it clear—through their actions, such as America's role in the 1965 war, rather than through their words—that they would not participate in its defense against noncommunist aggression, Pakistan began to show indifference to Western military commitments. It gradually disengaged from those activities of the pacts that conflicted with its recent trends in foreign policy. In view of its friendly relations with China and the Soviet Union, it became inconceivable that Pakistan could join with other pact members in strictures against China and Russia and in support of U.S. policy over matters like Vietnam. Such a course would be inconsistent with its policy of bilateralism. Thus Pakistan came to act as an observer to rather than a participant in political or military cooperation—as demonstrated by the role it assumed at meetings of military advisers' groups, intelligence committees on counter-subversion and military intelligence committees. Pakistan ceased to take part in SEATO military exercises or in Intelligence Assessment Committee studies, and it banned the distribution in Pakistan of SEATO information materials because some of them were considered critical of China.

For similar reasons, Pakistan also reduced its participation in SEATO cultural programs. From 1960, it declined to host SEATO Council meetings and voiced reservations in SEATO and CENTO meetings and conferences' final communiqués on most of the political issues considered. In this it followed a policy of detachment like that of France, and its delegates neither participated in discussions nor took part in the drafting of communiqués.

In keeping with its policy of playing down the pacts, Pakistan was no longer interested, as we have seen, in participating in matters related to the command structure of CENTO or in defining the pact's assumptions for global or local wars. CENTO and SEATO had lost their value to Pakistan as a defensive shield. It felt they had been used by the Western powers, particularly the United States, to further global policies, with scant regard to the legitimate fears of regional members regarding their own problems. The Pakistanis saw evidence of this in CENTO's failure to support Turkey on Cyprus, to reassure Iran over the future of the Persian Gulf, and, of course, to back Pakistan against India. (Partly because of this indifference to regional members' problems, not only Pakistan but also other members, such as Iran and Turkey, came to enjoy better relations with Moscow or Peking.)[22]

On top of all these considerations, strong public sentiment against both pacts, particularly after the September 1965 war, rendered impossible full or active participation. In a policy statement in the National Assembly on June 28, 1968, new Foreign Minister Mian Arshad Husain summed up Pakistan's attitude to the pacts:

> With a change in the world situation these pacts have lost a good deal of their importance. Our own disenchantment with

them was completed by the failure of some of our allies to assist at the time of Indian aggression in September 1965. . . .

Our interest is . . . confined to their cultural and economic activities with which there are some beneficial and useful projects. If we are continuing our membership of the pact, it is out of deference to the wishes of other members, especially Iran and Turkey.[23]

Why did not Pakistan now formally withdraw from SEATO and CENTO as demanded by some critics, including Bhutto? As Husain said, one reason was deference to Iran and Turkey, which had always supported its cause and with which Pakistan has special bonds of friendship. Another important consideration was Pakistan's desire not to incur the blame for destroying the pacts. Third, its membership was no longer a handicap in relationships with China and the U.S.S.R. Chou En-lai and Foreign Minister Chen Yi stated that Pakistan's role in these defensive pacts was no longer a hindrance to friendly relations between China and Pakistan. It took the Soviets longer than it had the Chinese to appreciate Pakistan's new role, but Pakistan made it clear that it would leave these pacts should it find membership incompatible with friendship with either communist power.

It was at this stage in U.S.–Pakistani relations that Pakistan, mainly in response to Soviet pressure, decided to close the communications center at Badabar near Peshawar. Dean Rusk had told Foreign Minister S. Peerzada in October 1967 that special political relations with Pakistan had come to an end; now relations were "just normal," according to Rusk. If this were so, Pakistan concluded, then the communications center should be terminated as well. The center was a great source of embarrassment in Pakistan's new relations with the Soviet Union, as we have seen, and with China, and the Pakistani ministries of Foreign Affairs and Defense recommended its termination. When Ayub took this advice in early 1968, both the United States and Pakistan accepted the decision gracefully; the United States seemed to have been mentally prepared for such termination, and Pakistan made no fuss about it. There was no uproar in the press of either country as the base closing was carefully played down.[24]

Meanwhile, the sincere U.S. desire to slow the arms race in the subcontinent—so that both India and Pakistan could devote more of their resources to development projects—proved unsuccessful. The Soviet Union continued as the largest supplier to India and in

1968–1970 also dispatched a limited quantity of arms to Pakistan, which—despite Mao's cultural revolution—relied most upon China but acquired some arms from other sources such as France. On the whole, after 1965 the military balance of power changed fast to the advantage of India. "India's arms grow in quantity, in modernity and the degree of sophistication," noted Ambassador Oehlert. "Meanwhile Pakistan's arms grow older, fewer and more obsolete."[25] So it was on the eve of the Bangladesh crisis in 1971.

THE SUBCONTINENT AND NIXON'S NEW ASIAN POLICY

Richard Nixon's election to the presidency in 1968 was viewed with favor in Rawalpindi but with little pleasure in New Delhi. Pakistanis always feel that they get a better deal from the Republicans, just as the Indians feel that the Democrats are more friendly toward them.[26] Apart from this, Nixon was the most popular American leader in Pakistan on account of his past friendship toward the country, which he had visited five times.[27]

Thirteen months before his election Nixon, in an article in *Foreign Affairs*, gave his views on the future role of the United States in Asia. The United States was a Pacific power, Nixon claimed: "both our interest and our ideals propel us Westward across the Pacific not as conquerors but as partners." Nixon wrote that any discussion of Asia's future must ultimately focus on the role of four giants: India, the world's most populous noncommunist nation; Japan, Asia's principal industrial and economic power; China, the world's most populous nation; and the United States, the greatest Pacific power.[28]

As President, Nixon repeated the call for a new Asian grouping. Encouraged by American policy makers during the Johnson administration, regionalism had been repeatedly stressed by responsible officers of the State Department. There had been a phenomenal growth in the number of regional organizations, among them the Association of South East Asia (ASEA), which expanded and regrouped into the Association of South East Asian Nations (ASEAN), and the Asian and Pacific Council. These regional organizations, formed with U.S. encouragement, deliberately played down the military aspect so as to attract neutrals such as Burma, Ceylon, and perhaps even India. India's Deputy Prime Minister Moraji Desai was reported to be in favor of joining such a regional grouping.

During his trip around the world in August 1969, when he visited five Asian countries including India and Pakistan, Nixon enunciated his new policy, defining the future role of the United States in Asia. While the United States would of course honor its treaty commitments, the President explained it must avoid the kind of policy that would make Asian countries so dependent upon the United States that it would be dragged into conflicts such as the one in Vietnam. Nixon admitted that the policy would be difficult to conduct, but he believed that with proper planning it could succeed. Nixon recalled some advice that he had received in 1964 from former Pakistani President Ayub Khan: the role of the United States in countries such as Vietnam, the Philippines, and Thailand—or for that matter in any Asian country experiencing internal subversion—should be "to help them fight the war but not fight the war for them."[29] Nixon hoped to apply this general principle to America's policy throughout the world.

While Nixon held the view that the United States is a *Pacific* power, he wanted America to play an important role in the affairs of mainland Asia, hopefully in economic, political, and cultural rather than military spheres. The new U.S. policy favored the emergence of a viable organization in South and Southeast Asia that would be Western-oriented and would maintain a sociopolitical pattern favorable to the United States. While America was not willing to undertake Vietnam-type military operations to enforce such a pattern, the policy did not mean that the United States under Nixon would revert to isolationism of the traditional kind.[30]

Nixon's New Delhi meetings with Prime Minister Gandhi from July 30 to August 1 proved rather formal, but the atmosphere was cordial enough. The two leaders discussed a number of subjects of international importance, including Vietnam, East–West relations, China, the Kashmir problem, and collective security in Asia.

Coming to Pakistan on August 1 for a twenty-two-hour visit, Nixon's party engaged in a dialogue with its counterparts (I was a member of the Pakistani delegation), but the most important discussions were carried on between the two presidents unaided by their advisers. It was during this Nixon–Yahya meeting that Pakistan's relationship with China, which since 1962–1963 had been the most disruptive factor in U.S.–Pakistani relations, was endorsed by President Nixon. He asked Yahya to explore the possibility of providing links between Washington and Peking, an assignment that Yahya, who took little serious interest in his own administration, fulfilled most faithfully and with strict secrecy. Even the Ministry of Foreign Affairs and Yahya's closest military officers were excluded from his confidence. As usual diplomatic channels were forgotten, the messages from Peking were conveyed directly by the Chinese Ambassador in Pakistan, and Yahya forwarded them through his Ambassador to National Security Adviser Henry Kissinger and to Nixon.[31]

President Nixon seemed to be fully satisfied with his talk with Yahya, who impressed him by his simplicity and frankness. Good feeling developed not only between the two presidents on a personal level but also between the two countries. The relaxation in U.S.–Pakistani relations culminated in Nixon's October 1970 decision to lift the ban on the sale of military supplies to Pakistan, but conflict arose again at the outset of the Bangladesh crisis.

In his statement *U.S. Foreign Policy for the 1970's: A New Strategy for Peace* Nixon, elaborating on his new Asian policy, quoted from a speech he delivered in Pakistan during this trip:

> I wish to communicate my government's conviction that Asian hands must shape the Asian future. This is true, for example, with respect to economic aid, for it must be related to the total pattern of a nation's life. It must support the unique inspirations of each people. Its purpose is to encourage self-reliance, not dependence.

Elsewhere in *A New Strategy for Peace*, Nixon noted:

> The United States has a long-run interest in cooperation for progress in South Asia. The one-fifth of mankind who live in India and Pakistan can make the difference for the future of Asia.[32]

Both Indira Gandhi and Yahya Khan visited the United States on the twenty-fifth anniversary of the United Nations, but only Yahya traveled to Washington to see President Nixon and attend his banquet in honor of visiting heads of state and government. "Nobody has occupied the White House who is friendlier to Pakistan than me," said President Nixon to his Pakistani guest during their fruitful talks.[33] A month later, Yahya visited Peking (I was a member of his entourage), and his discussions with Chou En-lai concerned not only the bilateral relations between Pakistan and China but also ways of improving relations between Peking and Washington. Finally, Henry Kissinger made his secret trip to Peking via Rawalpindi in July 1971.

That the American role in the subcontinent from Nixon's inauguration up to the outbreak of the crisis in Bangladesh was characterized by warm relations with Pakistan and less than warm relations with India has been demonstrated above. That these relations had a crucial impact was most clearly evidenced in the American response to the turmoil of December 1971.

NOTES

1. Except where otherwise indicated, the remainder of this section is based on my research and personal interviews in Pakistan, 1967–1971.

2. *American Foreign Relations, 1965, op. cit.*, pp. 118–119.

3. *New York Times*, Dec. 20, 1965.

4. Based on my research and personal interviews in Pakistan, 1967–1971.

5. *Dawn*, Feb. 16, 1966.

6. For Mrs. Gandhi's speeches in the United States urging U.S. economic aid, see *The Statesman*, Mar. 28–31, 1966.

7. See President Johnson's appeal to Congress for emergency aid to India in *New York Times*, Mar. 30, 1966.

8. Based on my research and personal interviews in Pakistan, 1967–1971.

9. Except where otherwise indicated, this section is based on my research and personal interviews in Pakistan, 1967–1971.

10. *American Foreign Relations, 1967, op. cit.*, pp. 429–430.

11. See *Asian Survey*, March 1964.

12. See the text of the announced policy in *Department of State Bulletin*, May 1, 1967, p. 688.

13. *New York Times*, Apr. 13, 1967.

14. See editorials in *Dawn* and *Pakistan Times*, Apr. 14 and 15, 1967; *The Statesman* and *Times of India*, Apr. 14 and 15, 1967.

15. Based on my research and personal interviews in Pakistan, 1967–1971.

16. Oehlert, *op. cit.*

17. *Ibid.*

18. Except where otherwise indicated, this section is based on my research and personal interviews in Pakistan, 1967–1971.

19. *Washington Post*, Apr. 15, 1967.

20. *Dawn,* May 6, 1965.

21. See Chapter 9.

22. See Alvin J. Cottrell, "Iran, the Arabs and the Persian Gulf," *Orbis,* Fall 1973, pp. 978–988.

23. *Pakistan Times,* June 29, 1968.

24. The center was not a direct result of the bilateral agreement of 1959 between the U.S. and Pakistan, but it could not be detached from this agreement and the other pacts with the West. The formal agreement relating to the center had been signed in 1959, but the base functioned from 1955. Providing facilities for intelligence on the borders of the Soviet Union and China, it warned of strategic activities of the Soviet military, monitored important wireless transmissions and radar emissions from other countries in the region as well as from the U.S.S.R. and China, and tracked signals from the U.S.S.R.'s earth satellites, deep space probes, and missiles fired from ranges in the eastern and southeastern U.S.S.R. (Based on research and personal interviews in Pakistan, 1967–1971.)

25. Oehlert, *op. cit.*

26. Choudhury, "U.S. Policy," *op. cit.*

27. See *New York Times,* Aug. 11, 1974, in which Bhutto is quoted as saying that Pakistan would never forget Nixon's friendliness toward it during the 1971 crisis; see also *Dawn,* editorial, Aug. 10, and *Dawn,* Aug. 11, 1974.

28. Richard M. Nixon, "Asia After Vietnam," *Foreign Affairs,* October 1967, pp. 111–125.

29. *New York Times,* July 26, 1969.

30. Based on my research and personal interviews in Pakistan, 1967–1971. For the Nixon Doctrine, see *American Foreign Relations, 1969, op. cit.*

31. Based on my research and personal interviews in Pakistan, 1967–1971. On one occasion, Yahya showed me the mass of messages between China and the United States that he handled in absolute secrecy.

32. *U.S. Foreign Policy for the 1970's: A New Strategy for Peace,* A Report to the Congress by Richard Nixon, President of the United States, Feb. 18, 1970.

33. I was told of Nixon's remarks by President Yahya during his trip to China in November 1970.

Part Three

China
and the Subcontinent

Chapter Seven

CHINA'S RISE, 1949–1959

WITHIN TWO YEARS of Indian independence, China emerged as a united nation after prolonged wars with foreigners and among Chinese. A communist China under Chairman Mao Tse-tung, which pledged close alliance with the U.S.S.R., was a source of further anxiety to the United States, arising as it did at a time when tensions were at their height in Europe. But in Asia, notably in India, the rise of Communist China was greeted enthusiastically. Many Asians looked upon the emergence of a new and powerful China as a great feat of the spirit of Asian nationalism, not as the triumph of "international communism" controlled and directed by the Kremlin. Nehru, for one, believed that the Chinese communists could be weaned from the Soviet Union and that China and India together could form a third force, a bridge between Moscow and Washington.[1] India's sympathy for the Chinese national liberation movement, as well as the conviction that the Pakistanis were all the hostile neighbors she could handle, ushered in an era of initial Indian good will and friendship.

Indo–Chinese solidarity "against foreign imperialism" had been expressed as early as 1938 at a conference of "oppressed peoples" at Brussels: the delegates from the two countries denounced the use of Indian troops "to further British imperialist aspirations in China," and the leaders of the Indian independence movement promised to do "all in their power to coordinate their struggle with that of the Chinese people." During the Sino–Japanese war, the poet Sir Rabindranath Tagore, Nehru, and other prominent Indian leaders condemned Japanese aggression, and Nehru visited China in 1939. Indian intellectuals and nationalists took an idealized view of China

just as Indian Muslims, prior to independence, romantically adhered to the notion of pan-Islamism.[2]

During the civil war in China, the Indian press and leaders remained neutral, expressing the hope that China's bleeding would
soon end. Once it was over, however, they welcomed the victory of Mao, whom they regarded as a great agrarian reformer.[3]
Said Nehru:

> These hundreds of millions of people of China, after forty-five
> years of internal trouble, have got peace in China—at any rate
> there are no marauding armies about, there are no bandits about.
> . . . They feel that their great country which had been kicked and
> tossed about for generations has become unified and strong and
> can stand up on its own feet and look any other country in the
> face.[4]

How did the Chinese look upon India? Before the great political
changes of the late 1940s, they sympathized with, and supported,
the nationalist movement. In 1942, for example, Generalissimo
Chiang Kai-shek, trying to help bring about a political settlement,
flew to India to participate in the negotiations held during the
Cripps mission. But later on, in the first two years of the People's
Republic of China, the Chinese recognized the Soviet Union as the
only source of help against "American imperialism." In his article
"People's Democratic Dictatorship," Mao indicated that the Chinese
people must incline toward either imperialism or socialism. "To sit
on the fence," wrote Mao, "is impossible; a third road does not
exist, . . . not only in China but also in the world. . . . Neutrality is
mere camouflage. . . ."[5] Thus Nehru's avoidance of blocs had no
more appeal in Peking than it did in Moscow and Washington, and
China stood in opposition to India's government.

At the November 1949 Asian and Australian Trade Union Conference held in Peking, Liu Shao-chi, second only to Mao in the
hierarchy, pledged China's support for "wars of national liberation."
He predicted that in India, as well as Vietnam, Indonesia, Malaya,
the Philippines, Japan, and Korea, victory could be won through
armed struggle, following the path of the Chinese people.[6] China
thus seemed to assume the role of coordinator of communist movements in Asia. In 1950, Liu was quoted in the Cominform journal
For a Lasting Peace, for a People's Democracy to the effect that
Indian communists must use the Chinese precedent as an example
for their national liberation movement.[7] Earlier, on October 19,

1949, Mao himself cabled in reply to a greeting from the Communist party of India:

> I firmly believe that relying on the brave CPI and the unity and struggle of all Indian patriotes [*sic*], India certainly will not remain long under the yoke of imperialism and its collaborators. Like free China, a free India will one day emerge in the Socialist and People's Democratic family.[8]

Like the Soviet Union, then, the Chinese regime at first pilloried the government of India as "reactionary" and a "stooge" of the so-called imperialist powers of the West. But this attitude, distorted and unreasonable, was adopted in deference to the Kremlin, and it was soon to change.

DIPLOMATIC RELATIONS WITH NEW DELHI

Having agreed to let Burma be the first, India was the second noncommunist country to recognize the People's Republic. Announcing India's recognition on December 30, 1949, Nehru said:

> Very great revolutionary changes have taken place in that country [China]. Some people may approve of them and others may not. It is not a question of approving or disapproving; it is a question of recognizing a major event in history, of appreciating it and dealing with it.

He added that the new Chinese government was "in possession of practically the entire mainland of China" and that "there is no force which is likely to supplant it." Isolation of, or indifference to, new China would lead to "grave consequences," Nehru believed,[9] and he urged the Commonwealth foreign ministers at the Colombo Conference of January 1950 to recognize the People's Republic. Next to the Soviet Union, India under Nehru became China's chief spokesman in the UN and at international conferences. My study of the proceedings of the Commonwealth prime ministers' conferences reveals that Nehru provided almost unqualified support for China on a wide range of international issues between 1950 and 1956.

The exchange of ambassadors took place in 1950. K. M. Panikkar, who had been Ambassador to the Nationalist regime of Chiang Kai-shek, represented India in Mao's China, also serving as one of Nehru's few close advisers on foreign policy. As he relates in detail in his *In Two Chinas,* Panikkar enjoyed cordial contacts with the Chinese leaders, including Mao, as China evidenced a new desire to be on good terms with India.[10] Even though not all anti-India rhetoric had been curtailed, by 1950 the Chinese attitude toward India, and in particular toward Nehru, showed some signs of softening. On July 9, 1950, for instance, *People's Daily* (Peking), discussed India without unfavorable comment. The Chinese began to appeal to the Indians especially as fellow Asians—a theme, as already pointed out, that had great appeal in India.

China's change of heart toward India was a result of several factors. China recognized the realities and dynamics of politics in the new countries of Asia much sooner than the U.S.S.R. did. It realized that Indian support in various international gatherings was valuable in helping it establish credentials as a great Asian power. Peking had also apparently come to understand that because of the popular support for the Indian National Congress and its leaders, especially Nehru, there was very little prospect of armed peasant uprising. The CPI could hardly challenge Nehru effectively, as he demonstrated when he dealt firmly with communist-inspired trouble in the Telengana district of the former princely state of Hyderabad. At the Asian and Australian Trade Union Conference, the Indian communist delegation sharply criticized the government's imprisonment of 25,000 "democratic leaders," but the conference hosts were more impressed by actions than words. It was held in some quarters that Mao influenced the CPI's decision in 1951 to call off the Telengana uprising.[11]

Panikkar presented his credentials to Chairman Mao on May 20, 1950, and four days earlier he had a long and friendly meeting with Chou En-lai[12]—experiences that contrasted happily with the Soviet treatment of Mrs. Pandit in 1950–1951. When the Indian Embassy in Peking celebrated the first anniversary of the January 26, 1950, establishment of the republican parliamentary regime in New Delhi, Mao himself, to the pleasant surprise of the Indians and other diplomats in Peking, appeared at the reception. Declared the Chinese leader:

> The Indian Union is a great nation, and the Indian people is an excellent people. For thousands of years, excellent friendship had existed between these two nations, China and India, and between the peoples of these two countries. . . . India, China and the Soviet Union and all other peace-loving countries and people

unite together to strive for peace in the Far East and the whole world.[13]

With diplomatic ties established, Indo–Chinese relations became "an extensive friendly intercourse."[14] When India was threatened with famine in 1951, China offered to send rice—an expression, according to *People's Daily*, of growing friendship between the two great Asian peoples.[15] On January 1, 1951, a barter agreement involving Chinese rice and Indian jute was signed; another deal was concluded on May 27, 1952.[16] In the same year, as numerous goodwill and cultural delegations passed between the two countries, Mrs. Pandit led an Indian cultural mission and had talks with the top Chinese leaders. A number of Indo–Chinese friendship associations were set up in Indian cities, and the influx of Chinese communist literature was considerable.[17]

By and large, the initial period of diplomatic relations between China and India was noted for friendly gestures from both sides, though differences persisted in foreign policy and sociopolitical systems. Before we consider the first strain in Sino–Indian relations, let us turn to Sino–Pakistani contacts in the initial years.

EARLY RELATIONS WITH PAKISTAN

Although the People's Republic responded swiftly to Indian recognition, its reaction to Pakistan's recognition of January 4, 1950, was slow. The reasons were obvious. Unlike India, Pakistan had shown no special enthusiasm about new China. Unlike such Hindu leaders as Nehru and Tagore, no prominent Muslims had visited China before independence. Unlike the Hindus of India, the Muslims of India had had little contact with China; their attention before independence had been diverted to the Islamic Arab countries. But Pakistan, like most of Asia, was happy to see the end of war in China and the emergence of a united and powerful nation. On the Chinese side, if there was indifference there was no hostility. There was no talk of "a thousand years of bonds of friendship," as between China and India, but neither was there conflict. China and Pakistan were neither enemies nor friends, but strangers.

Following the May 10, 1951, announcement of the initiation of diplomatic ties Pakistan's first Ambassador, Major General N. A. M. Raza, arrived in Peking in November. Two months later, the first

Chinese Ambassador took up residence in Karachi.[18] When Raza presented his credentials to Mao, the contrast to Panikkar's warm treatment was marked. "I have great pleasure," said Mao in a sarcastic reference to Pakistan's dominion status, "in receiving the letters of credentials of the King of Great Britain, Ireland and the British dominions beyond the seas, presented by you."[19] (Ironically, Raza during his second term as Ambassador played a large role in creating the China–Pakistan friendship of the 1960s.)

Keeping in mind that Liaquat had visited Washington rather than Moscow and that Pakistan was hungering for U.S. economic and military help, China took it for granted that Pakistan was "in the imperialist camp"; but it was still farsighted in dealing with Pakistan. Geographic proximity (before the dismemberment of December 1971 China was the only country besides India geographically close to both East and West Pakistan), traditional trade and cultural ties and, most of all, current politics induced China as well as Pakistan to seek adequate if not friendly relations.

At the time diplomatic relations were established, Pakistan, as we have seen, followed a policy of noninvolvement in the Cold War. At the UN, it opposed a Nationalist Chinese resolution to withhold all aid from the People's Republic, supporting instead the "hands off" resolution calling for no outside interference in internal Chinese problems.[20] When the question of P.R.C. membership was first brought before the General Assembly in September 1950, Pakistani Foreign Minister Zafrullah Khan argued that debate on the question was missing the point. Too much stress, he said, was being placed on whether the new government in China "is peace loving or not; whether it is willing or able to discharge the obligations contained in the Charter." He contended that China was not applying for admission: "it is [already] a member state, a permanent member of the Security Council and one of the big five." The sole question was "who is entitled to represent China."[21] This was clear and forthright support of the People's Republic; here the Indian and Pakistani delegates spoke and voted in a similar way. But India was consistent in its stand, even after the Sino–Indian border war of 1962. Pakistan repeatedly shifted its position according to foreign policy commitments.

The Chinese seemed to realize that if there ever occurred a clash of interest between China and India—and my readings of the reports of the Pakistani Ambassador in Peking suggest that *even in the early 1950s* the Chinese believed such a clash might result—

they would be able to count on the help of India-hating Pakistan. China, therefore, was ambiguous toward Pakistan: it could not watch with equanimity Pakistan's annoying, deepening Westernism, but it wisely saw potential profit in keeping open its diplomatic options. Similarly, Pakistan took care to preserve at least some links with Peking. It too sensed that the romance between Peking and New Delhi was fragile for such reasons as competition for regional leadership and conflict of national interests in the Himalayas. When Indo–Pakistani trade came to a complete stop in 1949, Pakistan in its search for new markets sold jute and cotton to China in return for coal under barter agreements.[22]

The Pakistani press, like the Indian, considered the rise of new China not so much a triumph of "international communism" as another example of Asian resurgence, and the Pakistani policy makers, mostly West Pakistanis, agreed—but pan-Islamism meant more to them than did pan-Asianism. Pakistan tried to combine correct Chinese diplomatic relations with pan-Islamism and with economic and military assistance from the West (particularly the United States). Peking went along because it was unwilling to leave the diplomatic field in Pakistan to the Soviet Union, which had extended recognition in 1947. Another consideration for Communist China was its desire to cultivate relations with the Muslim countries of the Middle East through Pakistan.

TIBET, KOREA, AND RELATIONS WITH INDIA

The first major complicating factor in relations between the People's Republic and India arose over Tibet, whose international status was uncertain. The Chinese government claimed sovereignty over all regions formerly part of the Manchu Empire, and in January 1950 it announced that Tibet would be "liberated."[23] As decades of war and misrule sapped the power of Chinese central authority, Tibetan officials in Lhasa had declared independence. A clash seemed inevitable between Lhasa's aspirations and new China's firm determination to incorporate Tibet. India, which upon independence had assumed all rights and obligations of the British government with regard to Tibet (including the British mission in Lhasa), could not help but become involved.[24]

In recounting diplomatic exchanges with Peking on the matter, Nehru sounded conciliatory:

> We expressed our earnest hope that the matter would be set-
> tled peacefully by China and Tibet. We also made it clear that we
> have no territorial or political ambitions in regard to Tibet and
> that our relations were cultural and commercial. . . . We do not
> challenge or deny the *suzerainty* of China over Tibet.[25]

But the Indian Prime Minister added that India was anxious that Tibet remain autonomous for at least forty years. Reporting that the Chinese had said they would "very much like to settle the question peacefully but that they were in any event going to liberate Tibet," Nehru commented that he failed to understand from whom the Chinese were going to "liberate" the region.[26] (One might have pointed out to Nehru that there was not much difference between the Chinese desire to "liberate" Tibet and the Indian to "liberate" Hyderabad, Junagadh, Goa, and, in 1971, Bangladesh. The same considerations of national security or interest were perceived in all cases.)

The first conflict erupted on October 19, 1950, when China dispatched forces to Tibet. After some minor clashes these advanced to Lhasa without much difficulty. Nehru deplored the use of force. "Violence might perhaps be justified in the modern world," he said in a protest note to Peking, "but one should not resort to it unless there is no other way. There was another way in Tibet as we pointed out. That is why the action of China came to us as a surprise."[27] Peking replied that Tibet was an "integral part" of Chinese territory, and thus the present crisis was entirely a "domestic problem." Peking also alleged that the Indian reaction to its action in Tibet was "inspired by foreign influence"[28]—an allegation that triggered an indignant denial in a second Indian protest note on October 31.[29]

Despite its protests, however, India acquiesced to the Chinese military moves in Tibet. This was because it recognized both Chinese determination and its own limitations. As Ambassador Panikkar later wrote:

> knowing the importance that every Chinese government, includ-
> ing the Kuomintang, had attached to exclusive Chinese authority
> over that area [Tibet] I had, even before I started for Peking,
> come to the conclusion that the British policy (which we were
> supposed to have inherited) of looking upon Tibet as an area in

which we had special political interests could not be maintained.
The Prime Minister had also in general agreed with this view.[30]

At that time, India lacked the military strength to challenge China single-handedly—the bulk of its troops were poised in Kashmir against Pakistan. Nehru could perhaps have stood up to China had he been prepared to accept military support from the Western powers, but he would not sacrifice his policy of nonalignment for Tibet. The Chinese also soft-pedaled the whole affair, limiting press coverage to the publishing of diplomatic notes.

While Nehru would not or could not challenge China on Tibet, he was not unmindful of the repercussions for India's problems of defense in the north: Chinese troops were all over Tibet, and they took up positions along the 2,000-mile India–Tibet border. Nehru quickly consolidated India's position as a "South Himalayan power," relying on something more substantial than the "doctrine of defense through friendship" that he had urged the Western powers to adopt in their relations with the communist bloc.[31]

Having already signed a friendship treaty with Bhutan on August 8, 1949, India entered into a similar agreement with Sikkim on December 5, 1950.[32] The India–Nepal treaty of 1950 was different in content and tone. While the other treaties made firm India's hold on the two small Himalayan states, here the Indian government agreed to acknowledge and respect the "complete sovereignty, territorial integrity and independence" of Nepal. The treaty provided for consultation between the two governments if either faced an external threat.[33] Although there since have been some stresses in Indo–Nepalese relations from time to time, India has been successful in maintaining special rights in Nepal and has provided Nepal with military and economic assistance. Nehru saw the Nepalese border as India's strategic frontier. "Our interest in the internal conditions of Nepal," he told the Indian Parliament on December 6, 1950, "has become still more acute and personal because of the developments across our borders, to be frank especially those of China in Tibet. Besides our sympathetic interest in Nepal, we were also interested in the security of our own country."[34]

But even if New Delhi was moved to consolidate its position in the Himalayas, Indo–Chinese friendship survived the Indian shock over Tibet. In fact, the Korean War and the Chinese intervention in it overshadowed Tibet completely. In the troubled early 1950s, Ambassador Panikkar seemed to be the sole link between China and Western countries. India vigorously championed the cause of China during the Korean War,[35] and India's delegate at the UN acted almost as if he were China's spokesman.[36] Nehru stressed China's importance with regard to Korea in the following statement issued on December 8, 1950: "Whatever happens in Korea is of the utmost significance to the Chinese people. . . . We have always been of the opinion that the problems of Korea can only be solved with China's cooperation."[37] Nehru made a similar statement at the 1951 Commonwealth prime ministers' conference in London.[38]

HINDI–CHINI BHAI BHAI

Such Indian support led to a major shift in Chinese policy toward neutrals. Reverting from its doctrinal expectation that countries would lean toward either the "imperialist" or the socialist side, Peking now began to cultivate actively the friendship of countries such as India through "people's diplomacy." At an October 1952 Asian and Pacific Peace Conference held in Peking, the Chinese government proclaimed its new line of "peaceful coexistence." As one commentator noted, "Instead of talking primarily of violence and revolution and the necessity of backing the Soviet Union in the struggle between the two camps, the 1952 conference talked of peace and coexistence." The conference appealed to the UN to end the fighting in Vietnam, Malaya, and other countries, and, more significantly, it declared that "countries with differing social systems and ways of life can coexist peacefully."[39] This was a full year prior to the change in Soviet attitudes toward Asian neutrals as expressed in Malenkov's speech at the Supreme Soviet in 1953.

After the peace conference, the new policy promoting friendship with Asians and solidarity among them was first manifested in China's recognition of "Indian independence as a positive force" and Nehru and his government as "progressive."[40] Yet even before the peace conference, India's opposition to the Japanese Peace Treaty—among the reasons for opposition Nehru cited the failure of the treaty to give over Formosa to the P.R.C.—was hailed in the Chinese press; commenting on India's and Burma's refusal to attend the San Francisco Conference, *People's Daily* on August 27 said that it "reflected the will of all Asian peoples." The paper also stressed

"Indo–Soviet–Chinese solidarity," but this, at least as far as India was concerned, was misleading. Here, as on other issues, it was motivated more by a wish to demonstrate its independent role and to create a "third force" than by one to join any Indo–Soviet–Chinese front. This was the heyday of Nehru's espousal of nonalignment and "an area of peace" in Asia. That his policy in the mid-1950s helped the communist nations and crippled Western intentions in Asia (particularly through India's stern stance against the U.S. drive for military pacts) was a side effect, not an objective.

From 1952 through 1958 China showed flexibility in its dealings with the countries of South and Southeast Asia. There were some difficulties in the Indo–Chinese relationship, and it was not as warm as the Indo–Soviet relations that blossomed from 1955. Yet an era of good relations did begin, culminating in the Tibet agreement on the basis of *panch sheel*—five principles of peaceful coexistence. The agreement, signed in Peking on April 24, 1954, dissolved the special privileges in Tibet formerly enjoyed by the Indian government. New Delhi agreed to withdraw military escorts and, as a gesture of good will, also handed over rest houses and communications services. In return for trade agencies at Yatung, Gyantse, and Gartok, India allowed Chinese trade agencies in New Delhi, Calcutta, and Kalimpong. Most significant in the agreement were its five principles of peaceful coexistence: (1) respect for each other's territorial integrity and sovereignty, (2) mutual nonaggression, (3) noninterference in each other's internal affairs, (4) equality and mutual benefit, (5) peaceful coexistence.[41] The most popular slogan in India during this period was *Hindi–Chini Bhai Bhai*—the Indians and Chinese are brothers.

At the Geneva Conference, Chou En-lai proved flexible and an able negotiator. He secured a settlement that appeared, at the time, favorable to China: the dangerous situation in Vietnam was stabilized, and the risk of renewed fighting with the United States receded for the moment with the northern half of Vietnam formally coming under communist control. Even more important, the Geneva Conference

> marked the full emergence of China on to the world diplomatic stage as a great power. . . . The European great powers had tacitly conceded at Geneva that China could not be left out of settlements in East Asia and his [Chou's] Russian allies had let it be demonstrated that China was not to be regarded as a satellite.[42]

During the recess in the Geneva Conference, Chou paid friendly visits to India and Burma. (India was not an actual participant of the Geneva Conference, but through his emissary, Krishna Menon, Nehru played an important role behind the scenes; after the agreements were signed, tributes were paid India for its unofficial role and it was invited to be the Chairman of the International Supervisory Commission for Vietnam, Cambodia, and Laos. Canada and Poland also were appointed to the Commission.)[43] During his four-day stay in New Delhi, Chou had lengthy, harmonious discussions with Nehru. They discussed the prospects for peace in Southeast Asia and reaffirmed their faith in the five principles.[44]

Nehru paid his return visit to China October 19–24, 1954. (Before going to Peking, he visited Rangoon and met Prime Minister U Nu and had talks with Ho Chi Minh in Hanoi.) In Peking, Nehru and his entourage, which included his daughter Mrs. Indira Gandhi, were given a most enthusiastic welcome. Nehru had a series of discussions with Mao Tse-tung and Chou En-lai, and he signed trade and civil aviation agreements.[45] Having given his impression of new China, Nehru told his people when he returned home: "I shall have little respect for India if it follows blindly the American pattern or the Russian or the Chinese or the British. Then it would not be India but a pale imitation of somebody else." But he added that he was "well acquainted with China's history of the past few thousand years. . . . I think we can learn a good deal from Russia and China and more particularly now from China."[46]

Following the Geneva Conference, the Chinese government began a vigorous campaign to extend its contacts in Asia and other parts of the Third World. Having "discovered the potentialities of an active, positive diplomacy," Chou launched a freewheeling drive directed particularly at the nonaligned countries of South and Southeast Asia.[47] In this context, two conferences in 1955 gave unique opportunities. At an April New Delhi Conference of Asian Countries, the nongovernmental representatives, mainly communists and other leftists, proclaimed Asian solidarity "as the central theme of peoples' movements" in Asia. The conference marked the start of a new "peoples' diplomacy" campaign.[48]

But it was the Afro–Asian Conference at Bandung, convened by the Colombo powers, that gave Chou En-lai his best chance to demonstrate diplomatic skill and statesmanship in dealing with a large number of Asian and African countries. Attended by representatives of twenty-nine countries with a total population of about 1.4 billion, the Bandung Conference was astonishing in range of ethnicity and opinion.[49] Nehru was the conference's principal architect and was also much better known than his Chinese counterpart among the delegates, yet "it was Mr. Chou En-lai's week."[50] Pakistan's Prime Minister Mohammad Ali and Ceylonese Prime Minister Sir John Kotelawala challenged Nehru, and, according to some reports, the Indian leader lost his temper and created a poor impression. The Pakistanis gleefully watched the leadership of the conference pass from Nehru to Chou, who showed a surprisingly pleasant attitude to Pakistan; China's first serious contact with Pakistan was made in Bandung.[51] Not only the Pakistani account but also impartial sources confirmed that "for Mr. Nehru, the Bandung Conference was, perhaps, to a considerable extent a failure, but for Mr. Chou En-lai it developed into a diplomatic triumph of the first magnitude."[52]

From November 18, 1956, to the first day of the new year, Chou toured India, Pakistan, Burma, North Vietnam, and Cambodia. In New Delhi, he was welcomed by not only Nehru but also the Dalai Lama and the Panchen Lama of Tibet. There was no dearth of crowds shouting *Hindi–Chini Bhai Bhai;* there were many friendly remarks and speeches; there were reaffirmations of the five principles; there were references to "traditional Indo–Chinese friendship" and to the modern Indo–Chinese détente in the context of the "Asian spirit."[53] All this, however, had become almost ritual, and signs of cracks in the relationship were visible. Chinese maps showing some Indian-claimed territories irritated one side, while Nehru's advice to deal moderately with Tibet irritated the other.[54] In contrast to his visit to Pakistan, Chou's days in India yielded no joint communiqué.

CHINA–PAKISTAN RELATIONS, 1954–1959

Well into the 1950s, China was correct but cool toward Pakistan, though not as cool as the Soviet Union. From 1955 on, Sino–Pakistani relations sometimes showed warmth.

This warmth developed despite Pakistan's entry into SEATO. China expressed regret that Pakistan, alone among the Colombo powers, chose to become a member of this "aggressive military alliance," this "bulwark of capitalist inroads in the guise of collective self-defense," but Peking's disapproval was not so violent or threatening as was that of Moscow.[55] Upon joining SEATO, Pakistan conveyed through its Ambassador in Peking assurances that it would not be a party to any aggressive designs against China. Peking listened, but it was not altogether mollified—Chou summoned Pakistan's Ambassador in February and again in September 1954 to express Chinese resentment.

"One cannot strengthen one's country by getting foreign aid," the Premier cautioned. "The real strength should arise from within, and for the internal strength of a country it is essential to get rid of foreign elements." Chou said the Pakistanis should, with American assistance if necessary, develop their own military manufacturing capabilities rather than acquire tanks and planes. Weapons, he said, "become obsolete in no time and the recipient country remains always dependent on the donor country." He warned that the donor could threaten Pakistan with stoppage of aid to make Pakistan do its bidding, a danger the Pakistanis fully comprehended only eleven years later when the United States did exactly that. (China itself, once it began to give Pakistan military supplies in the mid-1960s, operated differently, as evidenced by the ordnance factory it set up in Dacca in 1970.)

Even as a SEATO member, however, Pakistan was not the special target of any public attack by the Chinese leaders, who showed considerable restraint in dealing with Pakistan at the height of its association with the West. An analysis of the Pakistani Ambassador's notes reveals that China was not willing to sacrifice relations with Pakistan for the sake of Indian friendship. Even in the days of *Hindi–Chini Bhai Bhai* China did not endorse India's claim to Kashmir—China was the only communist country that refused to follow Moscow's lead. Similarly, when the boundary talks with India began in 1960, China refused to discuss the frontier between it and Pakistani-held Kashmir, thus implying recognition of Kashmir as a disputed area.

At the Bandung Conference Chou En-lai had his first diplomatic dialogue with Prime Minister Mohammad Ali, and it was constructive. At Bandung Nehru denounced the military pacts with the object of vilifying Pakistan, but Chou did not condemn Pakistan directly or indirectly. On the contrary, he told the political committee of the conference that although Pakistan was a party to a military pact, it was not against China and would not commit any aggression against it. He concluded that his talks with Mohammad Ali resulted in better mutual understanding. Although an ardent supporter of close links with the United States, Mohammad Ali returned to Karachi to enter with other officials into a assessment of policy toward China. Pakistani deference to Dulles's policy of pacts and alliances precluded any real change of policy, but Pakistan took care to avoid offending Peking.

Traveling to China in 1956, new Pakistani Prime Minister H. S. Suhrawardy had an interesting dialogue with Mao Tse-tung. "We are not afraid of Pakistan, which is a friendly country," Mao said, but he voiced regret that Pakistan had joined with the United States in SEATO and CENTO. "Could you not evolve some other plans to solve your difficulties without joining these pacts?" Suhrawardy tried to stress that Pakistan's SEATO membership was not directed against China, which Pakistan considered a friendly neighbor. Perhaps Mao was not convinced. But he gained a good understanding of the difficulties that led Pakistan to join the pacts.

When Chou En-lai paid a return visit to Pakistan in December 1956, he was given a most enthusiastic welcome, particularly at Dacca. The joint communiqué issued at the end of his visit stated:

> The difference between the political systems of Pakistan and China and the divergence of views on many problems should not prevent a strengthening of friendship between [the two countries]. They [Chou and Suhrawardy] reaffirm their earlier conviction that with a view to promoting further the cordial and friendly relations existing between Pakistan and China, due importance should be given to commercial and cultural relations. They are happy to place on record that there is no real conflict of interests between the two countries.[56]

Some misunderstanding persisted, however—largely because of Pakistan's changed vote on Chinese UN membership. Having supported the P.R.C.'s claim when the matter first was raised at the General Assembly in 1949, Pakistan during 1955–1960 bowed to U.S. pressure and supported America's resolution to postpone action on the question of China's entry. This switch caused considerable strain in relations. On November 17, 1956, the Ambassador in Peking cabled the Pakistani Ministry of Foreign Affairs that it was difficult to rationalize Pakistan's UN vote—this was soon after Suhrawardy's China visit and on the eve of Chou's trip to Pakistan. Suhrawardy explained Pakistan's position to Chou in a lengthy message dated November 27. The Prime Minister also wrote President Eisenhower to describe the increasing problems involved in voting with the United States on the China issue. "There can be no doubt," he claimed, "that having recognized the People's Government of China, we cannot but concede that it is entitled to represent China in the UN." Eisenhower in his reply of December 19 bluntly told the Pakistani Prime Minister, "We do not alter our opposition to Chinese Communist entry to the United Nations. . . ."

The status of Taiwan (Formosa), which the Communist Chinese have always considered to be an integral part of their nation, was another irritant in the Pakistan–China relationship. On September 22, 1958, at a time when a clash between China and the United States over Taiwan seemed probable, the Chinese Foreign Office relayed the following query to Rawalpindi through the Pakistani Embassy:

> Pakistan in the past on most international issues sided with America. While China does not expect a great change in Pakistan's foreign policy, she would like to know the attitude of Pakistan as an Asian nation in this dispute [on Taiwan] between China and America invading Chinese territories.

In reply on October 1, 1958, Pakistan, pointing out that she had given neither de facto nor de jure recognition to the government in Taiwan, opined that no party should take action that would threaten world as well as regional peace. Most annoying to the Chinese was the following passage from the reply: "The juridical position of sovereignty over Formosa is not clear. The problem should therefore be settled by peaceful negotiations. The wishes of the local inhabitants should be given due consideration." This reply of October 1, I learned from reliable sources, was prepared in deference to the wishes of the U.S. government; noted for his devotion to the Americans, President Iskander Mirza himself ordered its drafting. It was a pity that in spite of China's flexible attitude on Kashmir, the Pakistan government adopted such a harsh and unbending stance on Taiwan. To the P.R.C., Taiwan is as clear and vital an issue as Kashmir is to Pakistan.

In 1958, when parliamentary democracy came to an end in Pakistan and the military regime of Ayub Khan emerged, Sino–Pakistani relations were at a low point, and they dipped even further the following year with the signing of the Pakistani–American bilateral military agreement and the Chinese protests this sparked. Ayub, who in the 1960s became the architect of friendship with China, earlier was highly critical of the policies of communist countries. He did not believe in hunting with the hounds and running

with the hare, he said forthrightly, assuring his Western allies that
Pakistan would follow a clear and unambiguous path.[57] Before he
realized the complexities of Pakistan's world situation, he unneces-
sarily and unwisely attacked China.

Dwelling again and again on "dangers of the North" at the time
of the Himalayan crisis that began in 1959,[58] he formulated a
scheme, presumably directed against the communist countries, for
joint defense with India. "I foresee China moving south through
Burma and Russia through Afghanistan and Iran, if there is no clash
between the two of them," Ayub declared on January 19, 1960.
"These moves need not necessarily be military: ideological penetration with communist-backed regimes would do." The Pakistani chief
told Nehru that an agreement on joint defense could be achieved
through good will and understanding on both sides; a formal pact
would not be needed. If differences between the two nations were
resolved, Ayub argued, Indian and Pakistani forces presently facing
each other could be released to defend against aggression from a
third party.[59]

Predictably, India scorned Ayub's proposal. In the first place,
Nehru did not share Ayub's belief in communist threats to the subcontinent: Nehru had nothing to fear from the U.S.S.R., and he was
still hopeful of a peaceful settlement of boundary disputes with
China on the basis of the five principles of coexistence. Moreover,
Nehru was not willing to sacrifice his policy of nonalignment through
a military arrangement with a member of SEATO and CENTO.[60]
Through the Indian High Commissioner in Pakistan, Nehru expressed on June 5, 1959 appreciation for the spirit of Ayub's gesture
but declined the offer. Read Nehru's message to Ayub:

> There can be no doubt that a full understanding between
> India and Pakistan about various issues will bring about a happy
> state of affairs and gradually our military burden may be lessened.
> But when the question of joint defence is raised, one has to think
> of wider policies and our relations with other countries. Our views
> about this are well known and we have refused to join any de-
> fence pact alliance.

Ridiculing the idea, Nehru rejected joint defense in less subtle
tones in a May 4 speech in Lok Sabha:

> I do not understand when people say "let us have a joint de-
> fence"—against whom? Are we to become members of the Bagh-
> dad pact or the SEATO or some other alliance? We do not want

to have a common defence policy; the whole policy we have pursued is opposed to this conception.[61]

By publicly criticizing the idea of any joint defense against the P.R.C., Nehru sought, in the days before the armed conflicts of late 1959, to retain the good will of China. The Indian Ambassador in Peking was reported to have pointed to Nehru's rejection of the Ayub plan as proof of India's continued friendship and adherence to the five principles.[62] In any case, Nehru's rejection neither forestalled warfare in the Himalayas nor prevented subsequent Pakistani–Chinese amity.

For its part, Pakistan, by suggesting common defense in the face of India's troubles in the north, tried to convince Western allies, particularly the United States, of its reasonableness toward India. In Washington, Ambassador Ahmad began to reemphasize his country's "peaceful gestures" and India's "intransigence." In a May 8, 1959, letter to President Ayub, the Ambassador, always a noted hawk, described grand success in "exposing India" and "projecting Pakistan's case." Ayub in his reply of May 23 thanked Ahmad and remarked: "I entirely agree with what you have been saying in America. . . . The Americans should also be made to realize that they have no stopping place in the East on the land mass of Asia except Pakistan."

In this letter, Ayub also made a noteworthy observation about Sino–Indian relations:

> Irrespective of what China did north of the Himalayas, Mr. Nehru will not willingly give up China, because of fear of them and because of the hope that he may be able to get them to agree to drawing a dividing line in South East Asia between their and his spheres of influence. He will certainly not move towards the West.

As we shall see, Ayub could hardly have been more incorrect.

NOTES

1. See Prime Minister Nehru's Sept. 30, 1954, speech in Lok Sabha in *Nehru's Speeches—Vol. III: 1953–1957, op. cit.*
2. Shao Chuan Leng, "India and China," *Far Eastern Review,* May 21, 1952, pp. 73–78.

3. *Ibid.*

4. *Nehru's Speeches—Vol. III: 1953–1957, op. cit.,* p. 275.

5. See Conrad Brandt *et al., A Documentary History of Chinese Communism* (Cambridge, Mass.: Harvard University Press, 1952).

6. A. Doak Barnett, *Communist China and Asia* (New York: Harper Brothers for the Council on Foreign Relations, 1960), p. 90.

7. Shao, *op. cit.*

8. A. N. Mukerjee, *Sino–Indian Relations and the Communists* (Calcutta: Institute of Political and Social Studies, 1960), p. 1.

9. *Nehru's Speeches—Vol. II: 1949–1953, op. cit.,* pp. 147–148.

10. Panikkar, *op. cit.,* pp. 80–81.

11. Sen Gupta, *op. cit.,* p. 99.

12. *The Statesman,* May 21, 1950.

13. *People's Daily* (Peking), Feb. 16, 1951, p. 79, cited in Shao, *op. cit.*

14. A. Appadorai, "Chinese Aggression and India," and K. S. Thimayya, "China's Aggression and After," *International Studies,* July–October 1963.

15. *People's Daily,* May 1, 1951, cited in Shao, *op. cit.*

16. *The Statesman,* Jan. 2, 1951, and May 28, 1952.

17. Panikkar, *op. cit.,* p. 71.

18. *Dawn,* Jan. 12, 1952.

19. See Sen Gupta, *op. cit.,* p. 344.

20. Mushtaq Ahmad, *The United Nations and Pakistan* (Karachi: The Times Press for the Pakistan Institute of International Affairs, 1955), pp. 88–94.

21. See *Official Record of the UN General Assembly,* Fifth Session, September 1950.

22. See Choudhury, *Relations with India, op. cit.,* pp. 146–155.

23. *People's Daily,* Jan. 2, 1950.

24. Alexandrowicz, "India's Himalayan Dependencies," in *Year Book of World Affairs* (1956), *op. cit.*

25. *Nehru's Speeches—Vol. II: 1949–1953, op. cit.,* p. 174.

26. *Ibid.,* pp. 174–175.

27. *Ibid.*

28. *People's Daily,* Oct. 31, 1950.

29. *The Statesman,* Nov. 1, 1950.

30. Panikkar, *op. cit.,* p. 102.

31. Alexandrowicz, *op. cit.*

32. For the text of the Sikkim treaty, see *Foreign Policy of India* (*Texts of Documents*), *1947–1964* (New Delhi: Lok Sabha Secretariat, 1966), pp. 169–173.

33. *Ibid.*, pp. 56–59.

34. *Nehru's Speeches—Vol. II: 1949–1953, op. cit.*, p. 177.

35. For the Government's pro-China views on the Korean War, see accounts of Nehru's July 7, 1950, press conference, in *The Statesman*, July 8, 1950.

36. See the Jan. 22, 1951, speech of Ambassador Sir Benegal Rao before the General Assembly, in *ibid.*, Jan. 22, 1951.

37. *Nehru's Speeches—Vol. II: 1949–1953, op. cit.*, p. 173.

38. Based on my research and personal interviews in Pakistan, 1967–1971.

39. Barnett, *op. cit.*, pp. 96–98.

40. *Ibid.*

41. For the text of the agreement, see *Policy of India, op. cit.*, pp. 198–205.

42. *Survey of International Affairs, 1954* (London: Oxford University Press for the Royal Institute of International Affairs, 1957), p. 3.

43. *Ibid.*, pp. 3–9.

44. See the text of the Chou–Nehru joint communiqué issued at the end of the visit, in *The Statesman*, June 29, 1954.

45. *Ibid.*, Oct. 20–25, 1954.

46. *Nehru's Speeches—Vol. III: 1953–1956, op. cit.*, pp. 273–279.

47. Barnett, *op. cit.*, p. 100.

48. Based on my research and personal interviews in Pakistan, 1967–1971.

49. *The Times* (London), Apr. 19, 1955.

50. *Ibid.*, Apr. 23, 1955.

51. Based on my research and personal interviews in Pakistan, 1967–1971.

52. *Register of World Events, 1955, op. cit.*, p. 165, and Barnett, *op. cit.*, pp. 103–105.

53. See *People's Daily* and *The Statesman*, Nov. 18, 1956–Jan. 2, 1957.

54. Based on a Dec. 15, 1956, report from the Pakistani Ambassador in Peking, uncovered in my research and personal interviews in Pakistan, 1967–1971.

55. Except where otherwise indicated, the remainder of this chapter is based on my research and personal interviews in Pakistan, 1967–1971.

56. *Dawn*, Dec. 25, 1956.

57. Mohammed Ayub Khan, *Pakistan Perspective: A Collection of Important Articles and Extracts from Major Speeches* (Washington: Embassy of Pakistan, n.d.), pp. 3–16.

58. See *Daily Telegraph,* Oct. 24, 1959.

59. See *Dawn,* May 11, 1959.

60. See *The Statesman,* May 5, 1959.

61. *Ibid.*

62. Based on the Pakistani Peking Ambassador's May 30, 1959, report—which related his talks with officials of the Chinese Foreign Ministry and diplomats of "friendly countries."

Chapter Eight

WAR AND WARMTH, 1959–1965

HONEYMOON'S END

THE STRAINS EVIDENT during Chou En-lai's visit to New Delhi in 1956 indicated that the days of *Hindi–Chini Bhai Bhai* and *panch sheel* were coming to an end. New clouds hovered over the Himalayas as the sphere of potential conflict grew to encompass the Sino–Indian frontier as well as Tibet. Relations between India and China deteriorated during the autumn of 1959 as a result of two serious incidents along their Himalayan borders—one in the North-East Frontier Agency (NEFA) and the other in the remote Ladakh area of northeast Kashmir.

The most serious development in early 1959 for Sino–Indian relations was the Tibetan uprising in early May. India expressed sympathy for the Tibetan people,[1] the Dalai Lama fled to India where he was given political asylum,[2] and the Chinese accused Nehru and India of interfering in China's internal problems. Interestingly, however, the Chinese press followed a line of "sorrow rather than anger." There was no return to the denunciation of Nehru as an "imperialist lackey," and the Chinese press continued to stress the value of Sino–Indian friendship and the hope that the Indians would be swayed by China's reasonable arguments.[3]

The Indian people and the world were startled by Nehru's August 28, 1959, claim in Lok Sabha that a Chinese detachment of 200 to 300 soldiers had crossed into Indian territory in the NEFA.[4] On September 7 Nehru submitted to Parliament a white paper that, citing notes, memoranda, and letters exchanged between the gov-

168

ernments of India and China, traced the border issue from 1954 to 1959. China presented its own account of the boundary disputes in *Documents on the Sino–Indian Boundary Question,* published in 1960.

Retrospective review of these documents reveals that the Sino–Indian relationship, having reached its peak in 1954, was now entering the phase of tension and conflict that culminated in the 1962 war. China did not recognize the McMahon line in India's northeast; Nehru firmly declared that the McMahon line, a legacy of British imperialism, was "our boundary." Disagreements also arose over such sectors of the frontier as that in the west between the Ladakh area of Kashmir and China's provinces of Sinkiang and Tibet. The Chinese contended that the entire boundary between the two countries was undefined and required negotiation, while India held that the boundary, based on treaty, administrative usage, and tradition, should be retained as it was. In his letter of December 14, 1958, to Chou En-lai, Nehru claimed that the Premier had given him the impression that Indo–Chinese boundaries "were quite clear and were not a matter of argument."[5] Chou, writing Nehru on September 8 of the following year, implied that he never imparted such an impression: "Using India as its base, Britain conducted extensive territorial expansion into China's Tibet region and even the Sinkiang region. All this constitutes the fundamental reason for the long-term disputes over and non-settlement of the Sino–Indian border question."[6]

THE OTHER IRRITANTS

In addition to the boundary dispute, such forces as the Sino–Soviet rift and President Kennedy's new policy toward South Asia were pulling apart the two giants that had once so joyously proclaimed *panch sheel* and the five principles of coexistence. Kennedy reinvigorated relations with India largely in the interest of the containment of China. Even more important, as their enmity deepened the Soviet Union and China took opposite sides in the subcontinent: the search for security against each other led India to rely heavily on the Kremlin and Pakistan on Peking. By the dawn of the 1960s, the original anti-American emphasis of Indo–Soviet ties seemed to have been superseded by the goal of Chinese containment. "There is not any country in the world which cares more for peace than the U.S.S.R. and none that cares less than China,"[7] Nehru told Lok Sabha on November 27. During Ayub's 1965 Peking visit Chou noted that when he went to New Delhi after the clash in 1959, Nehru was not accommodating; the Prime Minister had been assured of support from the Soviet Union—which, according to Chou, was to "encourage the movement of Indian troops in 1962."[8] Thus the Sino–Indian border dispute both affected and reflected bigger international developments in South Asia involving the three major powers and both subcontinent countries.

THE BORDER ARGUMENT

Differences over borders are not unusual between countries with common frontiers, as evidenced by China's problems with Afghanistan, Burma, Mongolia, Nepal, Pakistan, and of course the Soviet Union. But with every southern neighbor save India, China peacefully concluded border agreements. "A survey of these other Chinese boundaries," wrote Alastair Lamb, "shows that China *can* make a peaceful boundary settlement with her neighbors and can, as in the Sino–Burmese negotiations culminating in the treaty of January 1960, surrender claim to extensive tracts of territory."[9] Why could there be no such peaceful agreement between China and India, which had maintained such close ties in the preceding seven years? Was China's attitude more aggressive toward India? Or did India have special reasons to quarrel with China?[10]

The mountainous borders between China and its neighbors, including India, are a legacy of history; they are also a legacy of Western colonial rule in Asia, a point eloquently made by Nehru himself in *Glimpses of World History:*

> China did not enjoy parting with territories or granting concessions. She was forced to agree, on every occasion, by displays of naval force and threats of bombardment. What shall we call this scandalous behavior? Highway robbery? Brigandage? It is the way of imperialism.[11]

When Nehru became Prime Minister of India, he had to justify this "way of imperialism," or India's fruits from it, for the sake of national interests and security. Such is the irony of history.

The Sino–Indian border is divided into three sectors. The Western sector is the boundary between the Ladakh area of Indian-held Kashmir and China's provinces of Sinkiang and Tibet. The middle sector, much shorter in length, touches three Indian states—East Punjab, Himachal Pradesh, and Uttar Pradesh—and Tibet. The eastern sector separates Tibet from the Indian states of Assam and newly formed Nagaland. In 1959 the Indians, adhering to the McMahon line, controlled the disputed areas in the eastern sector, while in the western sector the Chinese were in possession of the strategically important disputed zone, Aksai Chin. In the middle sector, the total contested area was perhaps under 200 square miles.

It was over the eastern sector and Aksai Chin in the west that armed conflict flared in 1962. The eastern sector dispute concerned the validity of the McMahon line. The disagreement over the western sector, on the other hand, touched upon strategic and security considerations: through this largely wilderness area runs the sole reliable road, built by the Chinese during 1954–1957 along an ancient caravan route, from Sinkiang to Tibet. Because it is difficult to bring historical evidence to bear in quarrels over sparsely populated areas, the honorable and peaceful course here would have been to demarcate the frontiers by negotiation at the conference table. With the status quo established as the basis of negotiations, mutual adjustments could have been made, taking into account historical, geographic, and strategic factors and the interests of the parties concerned. Why was such a course not adopted?

Few international issues are examined without prejudice, and, at least in the West, the Sino–Indian clash was certainly not one of the few. The initial Western support for India, reflected in the writings of such authors as Guy Wint, was a function of political factors—of the relationship then existing between China and the West, particularly the United States. Only gradually has the real story been revealed. In congressional testimony, Maxwell D. Taylor, Chairman of the U.S. Joint Chiefs of Staff, was asked, "Did the Indians actually start this military operation?" Taylor replied, "Yes, sir, they were edging forward in this disputed area."[12] The remainder of his testimony along this line does not appear in the public transcript. Authors such as Alastair Lamb and Neville Maxwell have contributed to public understanding through their balanced accounts.

I cannot enter here into lengthy discussion on the events of 1959–1962, but merely point out some turning points and basic themes. On November 7, 1959, as the crisis deepened, China suggested that, to avoid further incidents, both sides immediately withdraw twenty kilometers from the "actual line of control" and that negotiations begin on the demarcation of the boundary. India demanded the Chinese evacuation of Aksai Chin as a prerequisite for negotiations. Facing tremendous pressure from Lok Sabha and other quarters to oust the Chinese from what India regarded as its territories, on February 15, 1960, Nehru placed before the Parliament a letter to Chou En-lai and the Indian government's reply to a note from the Chinese. In the letter Nehru said that he could not leave the country and suggested that he and Chou meet in New Delhi, rather than China or Rangoon as previously considered.[13] Chou received a cold but correct reception in New Delhi on April 19, 1960. The talks between the leaders lasted until April 25, when a joint communiqué indicated that they had not reached agreement.[14] Officials of the two countries continued to confer in New Delhi, Peking, and Rangoon from June to September, but no progress toward a settlement was recorded.

In these 1960 discussions China denounced the McMahon line as a "product of imperialism" but apparently was inclined to accept it. China recognized the line in its boundary agreement with Burma—provided India accepted China's de facto possession of Aksai Chin. China was in fact asking for recognition of the status quo and wanted to compromise; Chou reportedly told Pandit Sunder Lal, founder-president of the India–China Friendship Association, in New Delhi, "You keep what you hold, you take too anything that is in dispute and occupied by neither and we keep what we hold."[15] Indian public opinion, however, did not favor such give-and-take. "Nothing could be more thoroughly unacceptable to this country," wrote the Times of India, "than the suggestion that the status quo, which is a product of Chinese aggression, should be one of the guiding principles of a final solution." Nehru clearly discerned the public's mood: "If I give them that," he was reported to have said about a status quo solution, "I shall no longer be Prime Minister of India—I will not do it."[16]

It was at this point that India adopted in the western sector a "forward policy," which proved catastrophic. A technique that worked in Junagadh, Hyderabad, Kashmir, Goa, and, later, Bangladesh could not work against Asia's most powerful country.

In response, Chinese government and press organs began to interpret Nehru's inflexible attitude in terms of "ever-sharpening class contradictions, and social contradictions, and the deepening political crisis facing the Nehru Government."[17]

The crucial decision that the Chinese must be evicted "immediately and forcefully" was taken on September 19, 1962, at a meeting in the Defense Ministry under noted leftist Krishna Menon. Nehru was away attending the Commonwealth prime ministers' conference in London. In an October 3 note China reiterated its proposal that negotiations be held on the basis of the status quo, but by this time Nehru and his government were so committed to dealing decisively with the "Chinese aggression" that no talks were possible. On October 12 Nehru announced that he had ordered the Indian Army "to throw the Chinese out" of the disputed areas. *The Guardian* described Nehru's orders as an "ultimatum," while to the *New York Herald Tribune* of October 15, 1962, it was "tantamount to a formal declaration of war."[18] The *Sunday Telegraph* reported on October 21, "India made a secret high level approach to the West for support before launching her offensive against the Chinese on the Himalayan border. . . ." From all of this, one may conclude that the large-scale Chinese military operations in the NEFA and the western sector to oust the Indian border posts were largely a product of India's forward policy in the Ladakh area. The Chinese apparently concluded that the only possible response to India's forward policy was counter-offensive.

On October 20 the Chinese Army launched massive attacks in both eastern and western sectors. Overpowered by superior numbers and armaments, Indian forces fell back all along the fighting front, and India suffered its greatest military setback since independence. Broadcasting to a shocked nation on October 22, Nehru called on the people to face unitedly the greatest menace in the history of free India. Nehru also confirmed that India had been out of touch with the realities of the modern world.[19]

Meanwhile, world capitals wondered about Chinese objectives. How far south would China advance? British Foreign Secretary Lord Hume was pessimistic as he spoke before the House of Lords on November 1:

> I think that one can assess the Chinese objectives with some clarity: the first aim, I would think, is this: by the use of force to compel the Indians to make a frontier agreement which would put the Chinese in a better strategic position than they are today; and to leave them in a position with their military forces where they can isolate Bhutan and if necessary, Nepal and holding that

flank, debauch, if they so wish, into the Indian plain at a later date.[20]

The Chinese Foreign Minister, Chen Yi, replied heatedly, "Lord Hume's attitude proves exactly that the Indian reactionaries and the British imperialists are jackals of the same lair."[21]

In the Indian capital, the American Ambassador wrote in his diary that November 20 "was the day of ultimate panic in New Delhi, the first time I have ever witnessed the disintegration of public morale."[22] Late that night Nehru made an "urgent, open appeal for the intervention of the United States with bomber and fighter squadrons to go into action against the Chinese."[23] The world seemed to be lunging toward general war. But suddenly, on November 21, the Chinese announced, in a 2,000-word statement, a unilateral cease-fire along the entire front. China's forces would withdraw "20 kilometers behind the line of actual control which existed between India and China on 7 November 1959."[24]

The unilateral cease-fire and withdrawal raised great speculation. One interpretation, noted *The Times* (London), "is that they [the Chinese] have succeeded in the main aim of demonstrating to the Indian Government and to the world that they are able to make any border adjustment which they think necessary whenever they think fit and that they can now retire to conduct negotiations from strength." The Indians—although, like almost everyone else, confused by China's withdrawal—saw clearly that the Chinese were not going to let their gains in Ladakh be challenged. The war apparently reaffirmed the status quo of 1959, a fact that actually discomforted the Indians. As for China's interpretation, Chou told Ayub in 1965, "Chinese forces might have gone to Delhi [but the] Chinese had no such intention." They had been forced, Chou claimed, to "resort to arms and inflict a severe defeat on the Indians in order to make meaningful negotiations possible," and also to demonstrate that Indian "reactionary elements" could not rely on "imperialists" or "revisionists" for their "security and protection."[25]

WAR'S EFFECTS

The Sino–Indian war had great impact on the South Asian Triangle. It finished talk of "two thousand years of friendship" between China and India and led the latter to regard Westerners not

as enemies of Asian peoples, but rather as "appreciated friends."
With the war, China's quarrel with the Soviet Union no longer lay
beneath the surface. Pakistan's faith in the United States was badly
shaken, and Ayub introduced his policy of bilateralism—which resulted in closer links with China, normalized Pakistan's relations
with the U.S.S.R., and reduced commitments to the United States
and the West. India professed continued nonalignment, but Pakistanis, Chinese, and others ridiculed the assertion.

Another repercussion of the war was the strengthening of India
against Pakistan. The latter felt, rightly or wrongly, that India's arms
buildup was directed against not China but itself. Another attempt
at Kashmir mediation failed. Nehru died, and in 1964 new Prime
Minister Shastri found his nation weak and still smarting from the
shocks of 1962. Under Shastri, India took further steps to consolidate its position in Kashmir; Pakistan, whose foreign policy was now
mainly in the hands of the adventurous Bhutto, was toying with a
"forward policy" to "liberate" Kashmir.[26]

EMERGING ENTENTE

Not only a crucial year for Sino–Indian disenchantment, 1959
marked the lowest ebb in Sino–Pakistani relations. The Chinese
sneered at Ayub's proposal for joint defense with India—a rare departure from Pakistani preoccupation with defense *against* India—
as well as his harsh anticommunist speeches during this period. But
the Chinese perceived that Ayub's scheme of joint defense with
India was intended not merely to fend off China but also to please
America;[27] they knew that Ayub knew that Nehru would reject it.
Thus, if they protested the defense proposal, they did not attempt
to scuttle the relations with Rawalpindi that had been showing
some signs of improvement since the Bandung Conference.

In July 1963 Ayub told his Western allies that their new policy
in South Asia would lead the smaller powers of the region to look
to China for protection.[28] Wrote W. M. Dobell: "Such a statement
need not be interpreted as blackmailing or an extreme form of
sinophilism or anti-westernism. It was a plea for the maintenance
of a military balance in the subcontinent."[29] Still, in the 1960s many
Americans as well as Indians maligned China for its intentions in
moving toward Pakistan, intentions that were alleged to include the

undoing of CENTO and SEATO, the gradual integration of Pakistan into the "Chinese sphere of influence," and further humiliation of India by joint Chinese–Pakistani military actions.[30] Such allegations, based on prejudice, were erroneous. Michael Edwards wrote:

> This [China–Pakistan relationship] originated less as a political move against India than as a means of destroying Pakistan's image in the world as an American satellite. It also reflected President Ayub's appreciation of geopolitical realities in the Himalayas.[31]

Noted Klaus H. Pringsheim:

> If it is assumed that Pakistan's foreign policy is determined largely by her feelings of military insecurity vis-à-vis India . . . it is not difficult to understand how the policies followed by the Soviet Union and the United States may literally have driven Pakistan into the arms of the Peking regime. The relative caution with which the Pakistani Government pursued their cause indicates that there was by no means a uniformity of enthusiasm for the policy change and that the intent was not the achievement of a full-scale alliance with China but rather the obtaining of leverage which might dissuade the other powers from their Indian policies.[32]

Thus the Chinese acted in response to Pakistan's initiatives to its two major power neighbors, initiatives made at a time when, in the face of the shifting subcontinent power balance, it felt let down by the third major power. China was able to respond because it had kept open its options, had always been polite if not ardent in its contacts with Pakistan. In time, *Pakistani–Chini Bhai Bhai* superseded *Hindi–Chini Bhai Bhai,* and Pakistan claimed the unique distinction for a noncommunist country of enjoying a positive, intimate relationship with Communist China.

Into the 1960s, however, there persisted severe limitations of the relationship. If Pakistan had no complaints about the Chinese —attitude on Kashmir and military assistance to India being the two main criteria by which it evaluated the friendliness of a country—the Chinese were disturbed by Pakistan's stands on their entry into the UN, consideration of the Tibet question at the UN, the status of Formosa, and a few other issues.

One of the relationship's limiting factors was removed as Pakistan began the process of disengagement from military pacts. The

Chinese were delighted. A congenial Liu Shao-chi told Foreign Minister Bhutto on a 1963 visit to China:

> Our mutual understanding has been strengthened greatly and we feel that you understand us. So we shall speak the truth. When you joined SEATO, we doubted your intentions. At that time, we protested that your participation in SEATO was directed against China. You replied that it was not so. Later on, your Prime Minister, Mr. Suhrawardy, came to China and told us that your participation in SEATO was for defence against big nation chauvinism. At that time, we developed some belief about this position but were not so deeply convinced as we are now. We are now convinced that your participation in SEATO is only against India and not against China at all. At the same time, we admired your bravery against pressure tactics."[33]

When Peking Ambassador Sultan Khan presented his credentials in 1966, Liu said that his country had once been "suspicious of Pakistan's membership in SEATO—[but] China was wrong in suspecting Pakistan and trusting India." Along the same line, in 1969 Foreign Minister Chen noted the "opposition from countries like Pakistan" to "U.S. imperialism" within SEATO.[34] That Pakistan was singled out for praise even though France had gone to greater lengths to stymie U.S. SEATO moves clearly demonstrated the growing favor with which Peking regarded Pakistan.

Pakistan increased that favor by gradually switching sides on the UN entry issue. After acceding since the mid-1950s to America, Pakistan drew sharp Chinese protest in 1960 for its continued support of the U.S. resolution to postpone action on P.R.C. membership. Also in 1960, Pakistan voted in the General Assembly for inclusion on the agenda of the Tibet question, an inclusion that China considered "crude interference in internal affairs." The Ministry of Foreign Affairs expressed to Pakistan's Ambassador in Peking "extreme regret" over Pakistani voting on the membership and Tibet issues. "This cannot but be regarded," warned China's Vice-Foreign Minister "as an unfriendly act."[35]

Embarrassed by votes registered in deference to American wishes, the Pakistani government did its best to explain away to the P.R.C. its membership and Tibet positions in the UN. Pakistan would have liked to vote for UN membership for the People's Republic, Rawalpindi claimed; it was just that the time was not right, the world was not ready. "In the matter of molding world opinion to create a favorable atmosphere in which this question may safely be put, Pakistan has been playing and will play an effective role." As for the other matter, Pakistan claimed that "respect for the principles of the UN Charter and of the Universal Declaration of Human Rights" dictated its action. "Only in so far as the Tibetan question affects human rights," Peking was assured, "is Pakistan interested in it."[36]

In 1961 Pakistan finally broke with the Americans on the membership question. When the United States moved that any change in the representation of China be considered as "an important question" within the meaning of Article 18 of the UN Charter, Pakistan abstained from voting. Two years later, Pakistan voted for the P.R.C.'s entry, and from 1965 through 1971, when the place of the People's Republic was secured, Pakistan cosponsored the pro-P.R.C. resolution.

As for the last major roadblock to the most cordial Sino–Pakistani relations, in 1965 Pakistan's delegate declared in unambiguous terms before the General Assembly, "Taiwan is an integral part of China." Subsequently Pakistan decided to shun international conferences and meetings held in Formosa and to host no conference that Taiwanese representatives might attend.[37]

A PEACEFUL WAY TO SETTLE ON BORDERS

Highly significant to the emerging Sino–Pakistani entente was the 1963 border agreement. China's refusal to discuss boundary lines between Pakistani-held Kashmir and the Chinese province of Sinkiang during the 1960 talks with the Indians goaded Pakistan to suggest in a diplomatic note on March 28, 1961, that China conclude with it a formal treaty on boundaries.

The cease-fire line in Kashmir, enforced by the United Nations in 1949, entrusts to Pakistan responsibility for areas contiguous with Sinkiang from the Karakoram Pass in the northeast to Kashmir's northwestern extremity. Comprising two distinct areas, Baltistan and Hunza, the border region contains one of the world's greatest mountain complexes, the Muztagh/Karakoram range. No accurate map of this region existed as late as 1924; no Pakistani definition of the 300-mile boundary had ever been made.[38]

Pakistan's desire to determine the boundary line with Sinkiang was first publicly voiced at an October 28, 1959, news conference at which President Ayub said that Pakistan would approach China for a peaceful settlement.[39] Following the Pakistani Foreign Office's discovery of a Chinese map that showed certain areas claimed by Pakistan as part of China, and following reports in Indian newspapers of Chinese claims on Pakistani territory (reports denied by the Chinese as "pure fabrication"), the government of Pakistan sent its March 28, 1961, note through the Embassy in Peking. On February 27, 1962, the Chinese government indicated in a note delivered to the Pakistani Embassy its readiness to reach "an agreed apprehension of the location and alignment of this boundary so as to prevent the tranquility on the border from being adversely affected on account of misunderstanding."[40]

Subsequently, on May 3, 1962, a joint statement confirmed that "the two sides have agreed to conduct negotiations so as to attain an agreed understanding of the location and alignment of this boundary."[41] China and Pakistan made clear in the statement that the understanding would be provisional: after settlement of the Indo–Pakistani Kashmir dispute the sovereign authorities concerned would negotiate a formal treaty. This stress on the "provisional" nature of the understanding was designed to deflect Indian insistence that no Sino–Pakistani agreements be reached on an area that was, according to New Delhi, illegally possessed. More important, the agreement was provisional because both Pakistan and China, as we have seen, considered the Kashmir issue unsettled.

Negotiations started in September 1962, and—in an atmosphere of cordiality, mutual understanding, and accommodation—the two sides reached complete agreement in principle by December. Following the working out of technical details, Foreign Minister Bhutto signed the agreement in Peking on March 2, 1963, and both countries rejoiced.

Of the 3,000 to 4,000 square miles of territory in contention, China agreed to vacate 1,350 square miles in the Khunjerab area, the Oprang Valley, and the Darwaza Darband pockets to the east of the Shimshal Pass—in some of this territory China had built army barracks and outposts, roads, and salt mines that were now of economic value to Pakistan. The agreement did not require Pakistan to relinquish any territory it held. Immediately after the signing, India contended that Pakistan had "surrendered" 13,000 square miles. In response, the Ayub government pointed out that it was China rather than Pakistan which had given up de facto control of territory and that, moreover, the question of "surrender" could not have applied since no Pakistani map had ever shown a defined frontier in this area.[42] When the Indian government and media pressed their allegations of lost Kashmiri—and, to New Delhi, rightfully Indiancontrolled—lands, the Pakistani government threatened to publish a map, which Nehru had given Ayub during their 1960 meeting, that indicates India had *not* claimed the 13,000 square miles it now castigated Pakistan for ceding.

Impartial foreign authors agree that Pakistan was the gainer in the 1963 border agreement.[43] With the guns still hot from its war with India, China signed the agreement not for land, but for proof of its willingness to settle boundary questions peacefully. If New Delhi was embarrassed and annoyed, Peking scored with the agreement a diplomatic triumph, particularly among the Afro–Asian countries.

The agreement was signed, despite Washington's reported pleas for delay until a more tactful moment, while the Indo–Pakistani talks on Kashmir were going on at the initiative of the United States and Britain. Pakistan contended that the negotiations with China had progressed far by the time the Kashmir talks began and that India, well aware of these other negotiations, should not regard them as a jeopardizing factor in its talks with Pakistan. In fact, Pakistan had never harbored serious hope of a Kashmir settlement; unhappy and bitter, it knew that Nehru had agreed to talk about Kashmir only reluctantly, only under heavy pressure from arms-supplying Washington and London. As indicated by a study of the minutes of the Sino–Pakistani discussions, China did not resort to pressure tactics to induce Pakistan to sign the border agreement at the time of the Kashmir talks. It did not need to: with the Indian delegation at the bilateral talks offering no more than the status quo in Kashmir, Pakistan would not sacrifice an important agreement with China to sustain the empty hope of reaching a settlement with India. *The Guardian* pointed out:

> Pakistanis may be excused for thinking that a bird in hand is worth two in the bush. They have got very little from talks with India over the past decade or so, and the results of the present round are entirely speculative. There is still no evidence that India is ready to concede their minimum demand. Certainly the agreement with China may be used by India as justification if the negotiations fail but the Indian Government has never been at a loss for such justifications in the past.[44]

The 1963 border agreement not only worsened Indo–Pakistani relations but also worried Washington and Moscow. The Americans resented not so much the agreement's contents as its implications of new, Peking-oriented trends in Pakistan's foreign policy. Stories circulated about a secret military pact between China and Pakistan. Partly responsible for such stories was Bhutto's statement in the National Assembly that Pakistan, if attacked by India, would be aided by the largest Asian power.[45] Ayub spoke in a similar vein: "If we are attacked by India then that means that India is on the move and wants to expand. We assume that other Asiatic powers especially China would take notice of that."[46] Despite this, during my research at the Ministry of Foreign Affairs I could not find any evidence of a secret military pact with China.

(It is interesting to note, by the way, that the preamble to the border agreement referred to the ten principles enunciated at the 1955 Bandung Conference. These, unlike the now defunct five principles of coexistence between India and China, included the right of self-determination.)

The suspicions and misgivings that the 1963 agreement aroused in world capitals were regretted in Rawalpindi, which made public the text and maps of the agreement so that all could see what it was—and what it was not. President Ayub, Foreign Minister Bhutto, and other policy makers repeatedly stressed that the sole reason for demarcating the boundary was to avoid conflict. Pakistanis felt that had India acted similarly, the unfortunate armed conflict of 1962 might have been avoided.

MORE AGREEMENTS

Another agreement with Peking that gave rise to much speculation outside the country but earned popularity within was the civil aviation agreement signed on August 29, 1963. This was a commercial treaty that expanded Pakistan International Airlines' business and foreign exchange earnings. With plans to extend international services to Tokyo, the airline was refused landing rights in Hong Kong; subsequently, PIA approached Chinese aviation authorities and secured rights and facilities in Canton and Shanghai.

Despite the purely commercial nature of the agreement, New Delhi and Washington were furious. Pakistan was threatened with a stoppage of spares in maintenance parts for PIA's Boeings, and as a further sign of displeasure the United States cut off aid for the development and modernization of an airport at Dacca.[47] According to U.S. officials, the Soviet Union and China were eager to open routes to "crucial" and "sensitive" areas in the Middle East and Africa, and the air agreement, which the State Department termed "an unfortunate breach of free world solidarity,"[48] made Pakistan a Chinese stepping-stone. State Department officials warned of the negative impact the agreement would have on the general relationship between Pakistan and the United States. But in pursuit of its new policy, Pakistan ignored the American threats and tapped its own resources for the development of the Dacca airport. The Chinese press was exuberant: "When the choice had to be made between national prestige and the American dole with all its accompanying insolence and insult, Pakistan preferred to uphold the honor of its people."[49]

The air agreement allowed the airlines of each country to operate in the other's air space and provided all facilities necessary for the smooth flow of traffic; a weekly service from Dacca to Shanghai via Canton was inaugurated by Pakistan International Airlines on April 29, 1964. PIA Chief Nur Khan remarked that the negotiations were carried out in a spirit of mutual understanding and cooperation and that the interests of the two countries' airlines were advanced.[50]

Further treaties included the trade agreement of January 1963 and the barter agreement of September. The former granted each country most-favored-nation status in bilateral trade and commerce, including shipping. As a result, China, formerly an insignificant trade partner, became in 1963 the biggest buyer of Pakistani cotton and increased thereafter its importation of Pakistani cotton, jute, jute manufactures, leather, textiles, surgical instruments, and chromeware; Pakistan imports Chinese metals and steel products, coal, cement, machinery, chemicals, raw materials, and cereals. In July 1964, China offered an interest-free $60 million loan, and an agreement for economic and technical cooperation was concluded in February 1965. As for projects, in 1966 China assisted Pakistan in setting up a heavy mechanical complex at Taxila. The National Shipping Corporation of Pakistan commenced service in 1965, and the first maritime transport agreement was signed in October 1966. In 1967 Pakistan received two loans totaling $47 million for purchasing wheat and rice urgently required in East Bengal. A Sino–Pakistan cultural exchange program was inaugurated.

It is evident from this list of agreements that wide cooperation in the economic, technical, and cultural spheres both reflected and furthered Pakistan's turn to the East.

CHOU TO PAKISTAN AND AYUB TO CHINA

Chou En-lai came to Pakistan in 1964 and declared support for Pakistan's Kashmir position. If in the past China had not recognized India's claim on Kashmir, this represented the first time that it endorsed the idea of a settlement in accordance with the wishes of the Kashmiri people. "It would be to no avail," according to the joint communiqué issued at the end of Chou's visit, "to deny the existence of this dispute and to adopt a national chauvinistic attitude of imposing one's will on others."[51] Regarded by *The Economist* as a "striking success for President Ayub Khan," the visit and the communiqué were hailed by Pakistanis as a diplomatic coup. In addition to its warm words on Kashmir, the joint communiqué expressed the desirability of holding another Afro–Asian Conference on the lines of the Bandung Conference of 1955 and of resolving the Sino–Indian border conflict peacefully through negotiations. At a well-attended February 18 civic reception in Karachi, Chou declared that the development of friendly relations between China and Pakistan was "an important contribution" to peace in Asia and the world.[52] New Delhi, Washington and probably Moscow disagreed. "In India Chou En-lai's visit to Pakistan signified another proof of a common desire to weaken and browbeat India," Sisir Gupta said. "The Sino–Pakistan alliance . . . spelled danger for India."[53]

In March 1965 Ayub garnered a most enthusiastic welcome in China.[54] Meeting with Chou and President Liu Shao-chi on March 3, Ayub entered into discussions on Sino–Pakistani, Sino–American, and Sino–Soviet relations; India's strengthening of its military; Vietnam; Formosa; and many other issues. First, Ayub gave a résumé of his country's relations with the United States and its concern over the U.S. and Soviet military shipments to India. Ayub said that while Pakistan was grateful for America's help, he could not tolerate its "policy of internal interference in other countries." The United States, Ayub added, wanted "to make India into a counterforce to

China, both economically and militarily," and to press Pakistan, which had proved an obstruction in U.S. strategy. Ayub assured the Chinese leaders that Pakistan would stand up against pressure and remain true to its Chinese friendship.

Pointing to the Soviet and American military aid to India and its implications for "the birth of neo-colonialism," the Chinese leaders assured Ayub, "If India commits aggression into Pakistan territory, China would definitely support Pakistan." Chou added:

> Neither the U.S. nor Britain wants to see India and Pakistan fight one another, because of the existence of China. Furthermore, the U.S., UK and USSR have to consider that if they help India, China would support Pakistan. This is a big point which has to be considered by their policymakers. India could not *really* become strong by military assistance from the U.S. or USSR. The U.S. was giving aid to Thailand and Taiwan, but this did not make them strong and the morale of their people was very low.

Chou disclosed that the Soviets had explained to China that if they did not help India, the United States would dominate it—just as each of the two superpowers told the Pakistanis that if it did not help India, the other would dominate. Receiving a message through Ayub from Prime Minister Wilson, Chou asked Ayub to tell Washington—which the President was scheduled to visit within a few weeks—of China's "desire to live in peace" and its determination to "abide by its obligations."

Pakistan's new, friendly relations with China were dramatized by Ayub's meeting with Mao Tse-tung, which was held March 4 in an atmosphere of extreme cordiality. "China and Pakistan could trust each other," said Mao, initiating the dialogue, "as neither has the intention of pulling the rug under the feet of the other." Ayub replied that "both countries want peace and friendship and are against foreign domination," and Mao agreed. After Ayub paid tribute to Mao's military acumen, pointing out that his writings were studied carefully at Pakistan's military academies, Mao gave China's version of the border conflicts with India: "China does not look upon India as an enemy; China had very few troops on the Indian border, yet Nehru went back and published a document as a white paper containing all sorts of untrue things." The two leaders then talked about the road connections between Pakistan and China and between Nepal and China—connections that unsettled New Delhi. To Ayub's query about Sino–Soviet relations, Mao said that

Khrushchev's successors "had not tried to improve relations with China. The U.S. and U.S.S.R. are now trying to have some sort of understanding so as to follow a policy of containment against China." Mao concluded his talks with Ayub with the words, "We agree with you and we are not with Shastri." Nothing could have been more pleasing to the President.

At the end of Ayub's first state visit to China—which saw the conclusion of a cultural agreement providing for the exchange of educators, scientists, scholars, and other experts—the joint communiqué of March 9, 1965, reflected Pakistan's changing external relations. Joining with China, Pakistan spoke more clearly than ever before on "liquidation" of imperialism and colonialism, in opposition to the presence of Americans in the Indian Ocean, and in support of the P.R.C.'s entry into the UN.[55]

NOTES

1. See *Prime Minister on Sino–India Relations, Vol. I: March 17, 1959 to April 3, 1961* (New Delhi: Ministry of External Affairs, Government of India, n.d.), pp. 31–48.

2. *Ibid.*, pp. 28–30.

3. See Lord Lindsay of Birker, "Chinese Foreign Policy: Recent Developments," in *Year Book of World Affairs (1961), op. cit.*, p. 85.

4. *Ibid.*, pp. 80–92.

5. See *Notes, Memoranda and Letters Exchanged and Agreements Signed Between the Governments of India and China, White Papers I–IV* (New Delhi: Ministry of External Affairs, Government of India, 1959), p. 49.

6. *Documents on the Sino–Indian Boundary Question* (Peking: Foreign Language Press, 1960), p. 2.

7. *The Statesman*, Nov. 28, 1959.

8. Based on my research and personal interviews in Pakistan, 1967–1971.

9. Alastair Lamb, *The China–India Border* (London: Royal Institute of International Affairs, 1964), p. 5.

10. For original sources, one may consult the following:
Official Indian Publications

   a. *Notes, Memoranda, White Papers I–XXV, op. cit.*
   b. *Report of the Officials of the Government of India and the Peo-*

   ple's Republic of China on the Boundary Question (New Delhi: Ministry of External Affairs, Government of India, 1961).

   c. *Atlas of the Northern Frontier of India* (New Delhi: Government of India, 1960).

   d. *Prime Minister, op. cit.*

   e. *Indo–China Border Problem* (New Delhi: Government of India, 1969).

People's Republic of China Publications

   a. *Sino–Indian Boundary Question, op. cit.;* enlarged ed., 1962.
   b. *The Question of Tibet* (Peking: Foreign Language Press, 1959).
   c. *Peking Review,* Nov. 30, 1962.

11. J. Nehru, *Glimpses of World History* (New York: Asia Publishing House, Inc.), p. 474.

12. See "Pakistan: India Unreconciled," *Round Table,* June 1963, p. 289.

13. *The Statesman,* Feb. 16, 1960.

14. *Ibid.,* Apr. 20 and 26, 1960.

15. Cited in Maxwell, *op. cit.,* p. 160.

16. Cited in *ibid.,* p. 161.

17. *Peking Review,* Nov. 2, 1962, cited in *ibid.*

18. Cited in Felix Greene, *The Wall Has Two Sides,* revised ed. (London: Jonathan Cape, Ltd., 1963), p. 414.

19. *The Statesman,* October 23, 1962.

20. Cited in *International Affairs* (1962), *op. cit.*

21. *Ibid.*

22. Cited in Maxwell, *op. cit.,* p. 410.

23. *Ibid.*

24. *People's Daily* and *The Statesman,* Nov. 22, 1962.

25. Based on my research and personal interviews in Pakistan, 1967–1971.

26. See Choudhury, *Relations with India, op. cit.,* pp. 131–140, 283–288.

27. Based on my research and personal interviews in Pakistan, 1967–1971.

28. See "Pakistan's Bitterness Inclines Her towards China," *Observer Foreign News Service,* July 22, 1963, and *Sunday Times,* Oct. 20, 1963.

29. W. M. Dobell, "Ramifications of the China–Pakistan Border Treaty," *Pacific Affairs,* Fall 1964, p. 203.

30. House Committee on Foreign Affairs, "U.S. Policy towards Asia," in *The Report of the Subcommittee on the Far East and Pacific* (Washington: Government Printing Office, 1966).

31. Michael Edwards, "Tashkent and After," *International Affairs* (London), July 1966, pp. 381–389.
32. Klaus H. Pringsheim, "China's Role in Indo–Pakistani Conflict," *China Quarterly*, October–December 1965, pp. 170–175.
33. Based on my research and personal interviews in Pakistan, 1967–1971.
34. *Ibid.*
35. *Ibid.*
36. *Ibid.*
37. *Ibid.*
38. Alastair Lamb, *Asian Frontiers* (London: Pall Mall Press, Ltd., 1968), pp. 94–110.
39. *Dawn*, Oct. 29, 1959.
40. Except where otherwise indicated, the remainder of this section is based on my research and personal interviews in Pakistan, 1967–1971.
41. *Dawn*, May 4, 1962.
42. See Foreign Minister Bhutto's press statement of Mar. 26, 1963, in *Dawn*, Mar. 27, 1963.
43. See Maxwell, *op. cit.*, p. 217.
44. *The Guardian*, Mar. 5, 1963.
45. *Dawn*, July 18, 1963.
46. *Washington Post*, Sept. 12, 1963.
47. "Pakistan: A Step-Child of the West," *Round Table*, September 1973, pp. 393–398.
48. *New York Times*, Sept. 1, 1963.
49. *Peking Review*, July 3, 1964.
50. Except where otherwise indicated, the remainder of this chapter is based on my research and personal interviews in Pakistan, 1967–1971.
51. *Dawn*, Feb. 25, 1964.
52. *Ibid.*, Feb. 19, 1965.
53. Swivaji Ganguly, "Chou En-lai in Pakistan," *Foreign Affairs Reports*, April 1964.
54. *Dawn*, Mar. 2, 1965.
55. *Ibid.*, Mar. 11, 1965.

Chapter Nine

ALLIANCE, 1965-1970

A GREAT ENIGMA or a contemporary miracle depending upon one's point of view, the close, special relationship between Communist China and Muslim Pakistan has shaken the South Asian Triangle. In New Delhi, it has been interpreted as anti-Indian and has given rise to further bitterness toward both China and Pakistan. In Washington, it was originally considered anti-American and led to President Johnson's discourteous cancellation of Ayub's spring 1965 visit and the withholding of U.S. economic aid in the same year; later, President Nixon smiled upon the relationship. In Moscow, it was thought anti-Soviet and helped lead to a period of greater Soviet flexibility, which was shown, in part, to wean Pakistan away from China; later, the Soviets demanded the end of the relationship.

If India believed the Chinese and Pakistanis found only in antipathy to itself a firm basis for cooperation,[1] they denied it. China claimed to ground relations with Pakistan during the 1960s in the same five principles of co-existence that had guided Sino–Indian affairs during the 1950s,[2] while Pakistan held that the Pakistan–China friendship mixed realism with mutual advantage and also served notice on the Western allies, which allegedly had upset the balance of power in the subcontinent.

The quest for security has always been dominant among Pakistani foreign policy objectives. To ward off India, Pakistan turned to the Commonwealth and to the Muslim countries in the early years of its independence (1947–1953); next it relied upon the United States through bilateral and multilateral defense pacts. When Western arms joined Soviet arms in India's buildup following the Himalayan debacle, Pakistan looked to China. Not only did China,

of the three major powers, show the most sympathy in regard to
Pakistan's anxiety over India; also it did not exhibit the coolness
toward Pakistan then flowing from Washington, and it did not as-
sign priority to a friendly India as did both powers in their containment mania. At no time was this more evident than during the
bloody, tragic months of mid-1965.

THE 1965 WAR

China backed Pakistan from the outset.[3] On the eve of the Indian
attack across the international frontier, Chinese Foreign Minister
Chen Yi assured Bhutto during a long meeting on September 4 in
Karachi that China would go to any length in supporting Pakistan.
On September 7, Peking assailed the thrust across the international
border: "The Indian armed attack on Pakistan is an act of naked
aggression." On the same day, Premier Chou told the Pakistani
Ambassador during a long interview that "China would await further developments and would consider further steps as and when
necessary." Chou sought two assurances from Ayub: that Pakistan
would not submit to any Kashmiri solution favorable to India, and
that Pakistan would not submit to U.S., Soviet, or UN pressures
for such a solution; Ayub cabled these assurances. In a September
8 letter to Ayub, President Liu reaffirmed China's support, making
it clear that China would respond to an Indian attack on East Pakistan not only there but also in the north. On September 12, Pakistani Air Marshal Asghar Khan was instructed to inform the Chinese
government of the "type of military intervention" that might be
required if the war developed further.[4]

On September 8, Peking Radio announced that Chinese forces
on the Indian border had been put on the alert, and the Chinese
government sent a note to India stating that unless it took down all
its military structures on the Sikkim border and ended its "frenzied
provocative activities," the responsibility for all consequences would
be its own.[5] The Indian government denied the Chinese allegations
in a September 12 note. At midnight on September 16, a Deputy
Director in the Chinese Foreign Office summoned the Indian chargé
d'affaires to give him a communication: unless the Indian government dismantled within three days all military facilities on the
Chinese side of the China–Sikkim border and on the border itself,

read the note, it must "bear full responsibility for all the grave consequences."[6] Indian diplomats consulted feverishly with the British, American, and Soviet governments about what appeared the probability of Chinese intervention in the Indo–Pakistani war; both the United States and the Soviet Union assured India of military help in the event of Chinese intervention, and both reinforced their efforts to bring about a quick end to the Indo–Pakistani fighting.[7] Declared Prime Minister Shastri on September 20 before Parliament, "It is clear . . . that China is not looking for a redress of grievances, real or imaginary, but some excuse to start its aggressive activities again, this time acting in collusion with its ally, Pakistan."[8] Pakistani officials denied any connection between the Chinese ultimatum to India and the Indo–Pakistani war, but they knew better: China's aim was to help Pakistan.

I do not know whether China concurred in it, but by this critical juncture Pakistan's top military men had formulated the following contingency plan for a joint blitz on India: Seeking to gain for Pakistan a superior position at postwar negotiations by grabbing territories and inflicting humiliation on India, China would occupy a big chunk of Indian land in the North-East Frontier Agency, while Pakistan, with much of the pressure thus siphoned off from the West, would drive from the West Pakistan frontier.

Such a plan, in the opinion of the Pakistani military chiefs, entailed little risk of immediate general war. India and the Soviet Union were not yet linked by a defense pact (that was to come in time for the next war, however), and Sino–Soviet relations had not yet soured to the point that Moscow would relish *direct* action against China. Besides, even if they were determined to go to war with China and Pakistan, it would take the Soviet Union and the United States several days to react forcefully to the blitz. By the time sizable Soviet or American contingents reached the subcontinent, they might find Indonesians as well as Chinese and Pakistanis arrayed against them: President Sukarno was ready to extend full support to Pakistan, including fighter and bomber squadrons and the powerful Indonesian Navy patroling the Bay of Bengal and the Indian Ocean. Pakistan would urge fellow CENTO members Iran and Turkey to use their good offices to restrain Washington from direct involvement. With this contingency plan in mind, some Pakistani generals urged Ayub to opt for a prolonged and expanded war.[9]

The Chinese ultimatum of September 16 was not a paper threat.

For five days the world wondered and worried whether the war would escalate into a wider, longer, and graver conflict, involving not just India and Pakistan but China as well—and perhaps either or both of the superpowers. It was during this crucial period that Ayub, in an act of courage and statesmanship, slipped into China for intensive discussions. By this time, Ayub—determined to avoid a prolonged war—concluded that he must accede to the pressure of the Soviet Union, the United States, and the UN and accept the proposed cease-fire. But he was very anxious that before his acceptance was announced, "the Chinese friends be taken into full confidence": and their reaction be given the "fullest consideration." China's leaders welcomed Ayub's acceptance, but they would have stood by Pakistan in any case. Apparently ready to come to Pakistan's rescue *provided* Pakistan wanted such assistance, the Chinese had given Pakistan full freedom to make its own decision—even though they knew that China's cost, if Pakistan sought a wider war, would be high: "Mr. President," Mao told Ayub, according to a Pakistani aide present on the China trip, "if there is nuclear war, it is Peking and not Rawalpindi that will be the target." There was no pressure; China acted as a true friend in a time of need. Ayub returned home fully satisfied, and he accepted the cease-fire without damaging relations with China.[10]

INDIAN RELATIONS TO 1969

If they had not been already, with the second Pakistani war Sino–Indian relations appeared hopelessly estranged.

India developed deep suspicion of what it termed the "Peking–Rawalpindi axis" and in 1968–1969 claimed to have evidence of Chinese subversion in Nagaland and among the Mizos and other tribal groups in Assam. India has been sensitive to the Chinese "presence" in Bhutan and Sikkim and any Chinese overtures to Nepal. It has been particularly worried over China's construction of a road linking Katmandu and Tibet;[11] suspect was King Mahendra's desire to avoid complete Indian domination and to widen Nepal's diplomatic options by cultivating amicable relations with China.

China, like any other country, considers both ideological and national interests in the pursuit of external policy. Supporting national liberation movements in accordance with its ideology, China

—after the *Hindi–Chini Bhai Bhai* period as before it—refutes the Indian "myth" of a peaceful transition to socialism by the parliamentary road and encourages revolutionary upsurges in India. The Indian revolution, wrote *People's Daily* after the 1965 war, "must take the road of relying on the peasants—establishing base areas in the countryside, persisting in protracted armed struggle and using the countryside to encircle and finally capture the cities."[12]

From the standpoint of national interests, on the other hand, China sees India as a crucial feature in the U.S.S.R.'s containment design. And not without reason: as noted earlier, the Soviets' immense contribution to India's post-1962 military buildup was largely directed against China—as evidenced, in the context of the Sino–Soviet border clashes of 1969, by the Soviet moves of the late 1960s to enlist in the anti-China cause South and Southeast Asia. If India could not, or would not, take any initiative at improving relations with Peking that might jeopardize its much stronger ties with Moscow, Peking, in dealing with New Delhi, would not rip apart understandings with Islamabad or, more important, forget to take a backward glance at the bear to the north.

WORRY AND REASSURANCE

China seemed to agree Pakistan had no option other than to accept the 1965 cease-fire, but it resented Pakistani acquiescence to the Tashkent declaration. When Liu Shao-chi visited in March 1966, Ayub tried to convince him of the value of the Tashkent declaration in response to Liu's warnings about the U.S.S.R.'s "so-called friendship" toward Pakistan. During a lengthy meeting alone on March 26 Liu and Ayub touched upon Pakistan's relations with the Soviet Union in general and the Tashkent Conference in particular.[13] In June 1966 Chou followed Liu to Pakistan, and he discussed most of the same subjects, including not only Soviet–Pakistani relations but Sino–American relations as well. The Premier's most important conversations in Pakistan concerned the extent and type of Chinese assistance, including military aid and indirect intervention, in the event of a new war with India.

In the face of the Soviet-aided expansion of Indian military capabilities and the limitations imposed on Pakistan's defense apparatus by Washington's aid cutoff, China not only promised support in future wars but also became Pakistan's chief armorer. Chou En-lai told the Pakistanis, "Unlike imperialist or Soviet revisionist, Chinese military aid would not be of such a nature as would become useless after three months—and this will also apply to aircraft." He promised that China would provide not only aircraft but also spare parts, including engines. In short, China would like "to see the aircraft maintained as long as possible unless they are destroyed in battle." Ayub was disturbed by the news of internal upheaval during the cultural revolution, thinking that a leadership change in China might affect his country's special links. Relations with Pakistan, however, remained unscathed. The flow of military supplies and the setting up of the Dacca ordnance factory continued strictly according to schedule. After 1966 the upheaval prevented top Chinese dignitaries from visiting Pakistan, but Pakistanis continued to venture to China regularly.

Pakistan's new Foreign Minister, Arshad Husain, went to Peking in August 1968, meeting with Chou and other Chinese leaders; Mao himself received him for about one and a half hours. Ayub had worried about the Chinese reaction to the dismissal of the previous Foreign Minister, the obstreperous Bhutto. The Chinese made it clear to Husain that the dismissal suited them; Chen criticized Bhutto for his claim that he was the architect of Pakistan–China friendship. Reaffirming their friendship and their pledge to continue to supply military wares, the Chinese repeated their promise to "intervene to help Pakistan" in the event of Indian attack—already, certain troop dispositions had accordingly been made in Tibet and Sinkiang. China added that there was no possibility of Sino–Indian rapprochement: India wanted to send one of its senior diplomats, B. K. Nehru, in an attempt at reconciliation, but the Chinese had shown no enthusiasm. Foreign Minister Husain returned home fully pleased. As chief of the Pakistani Army, General Yahya Khan visited China in 1968 mainly to discuss military supplies to Pakistan, and he was received warmly.

But before the fall of Ayub in March 1969, China seemed to harbor reservations about Pakistan, and for this the Pakistani ruling elite was responsible. During his dialogues with Liu and Chou in 1966, Ayub gave categorical assurances that as long as he was at the helm Pakistan would remain China's sincere friend. Yet Ayub's moves in the direction of the Soviet Union, apparent during his visit to Moscow in 1967 and Kosygin's arms-bearing visit to Pakistan in early 1968, raised suspicions in Peking. Ayub blundered in over-

rating Russia's dubious devotion and thus endangering China's unqualified friendship.

YAHYA IN POWER

Soon after the change in government, Chou sent a message to
President Yahya assuring him of China's continued support.[14] Shortly
thereafter, Kosygin made his second trip to Pakistan, and the Soviet
Union began to pressure Pakistan to join its regional economic and
military organizations. Naturally, the Chinese were anxious to gauge
Pakistan's reaction to the Soviet pressures.

After a lapse of about two years during the cultural revolution,
in 1969 China filled the post of Ambassador to Pakistan with senior
diplomat Chang Tung—Pakistan was one of only three countries to
which China sent ambassadors immediately after the cultural revolution. Formerly at the Asian desk of the Chinese Foreign Office
and during 1956–1959 Ambassador to India, Chang called on the
Pakistani Foreign Ministry on July 3, 1969, receiving a promise that
"Pakistan will not be a party to any arrangement, economic or
military, which will be aimed against China." On July 13 Yahya
dispatched to Peking one of his top military colleagues, Marshal
Nur Khan, chief of the Pakistani Air Force. Nur Khan reaffirmed
Pakistan's firm determination not to collaborate, no matter what the
Soviet pressure, in any scheme that would be directed against China,
and the Chinese leaders believed him; the wisp of coolness that
had developed during the last days of the Ayub era was removed.

During the first two years of his rule Yahya concerned himself
mostly with the country's internal problems, particularly the growing tensions between East and West Pakistan. During this period
Pakistan had hardly any foreign policy. With no Foreign Minister,
Pakistan's external affairs were looked after by the Rasputin of
Yahya's regime, Lieut. General Peerzada, who possessed almost no
qualifications for the practice of diplomacy. The only diplomatic
coup of this period for Pakistan—and perhaps it is stretching a
point to call the coup Pakistan's—came through Yahya's courier role
between Washington and Peking in the context of President Nixon's
new China policy. Pakistan forged still stronger links with China
and repaired its U.S. ties.

As prospects for better understanding between China and the

United States gradually brightened, in November 1970 Yahya traveled to China, where he was received with the same warmth accorded Ayub Khan during his first state visit to China. I personally was struck by the difference between Yahya's spontaneous and unqualified welcome and the cool, almost indifferent treatment I remembered from Ayub's 1965 U.S.S.R. trip. The contrast to that Russian sojourn extended into the conference sessions; friendliness and frankness were the keynotes in Peking. The two nations spoke as intimate friends if not allies: the tone of this dialogue between China and Pakistan was strikingly similar to that of the dialogues prime ministers Mohammad Ali and Suhrawardy engaged in when they visited Washington in 1954 and 1957.

The crucial talks ensued not in the conference room but at the suite of the Peking Guest House, where Yahya was staying. Chou and Yahya conversed for at least fifteen to eighteen hours, covering a range of subjects including the "foreign influences" that Chou warned Yahya were subverting his authority in East Pakistan. During his sessions with Chinese leaders, which included an interview with Mao, Yahya secured a Chinese promise to provide substantial economic aid for Pakistan's fourth five-year plan and continued military assistance. Peking's top men indicated pleasure at Pakistan's unqualified support for P.R.C. entry into the UN, support voiced by Yahya at the twenty-fifth anniversary of the organization in October 1970; Yahya repeated what he had declared at the UN: that friendship with China was the cardinal feature of Pakistan's foreign policy. The straightforward Yahya seemed to create a good impression in China.

But this was a period of change and uncertainty for Pakistan, and China saw the impending crisis. The junta's unwise handling of East–West tensions—as well as the hardening, uncompromising attitudes of the two principal political leaders of East and West Pakistan, Sheikh Mujibur Rahman and Bhutto—cast ominous shadows.[15] In such an unsettled situation, no decisive development in China–Pakistan relations could be expected; like many other countries, China wanted to see which way the national winds blew before making any further political or military commitments. But from China there was no dearth of good will, understanding, or sympathy for the peoples of Pakistan, both East and West.

Indicative of that good will was the building of the "Highway of Friendship." The first road linking the two countries, it is an all-weather route 3 miles high through the Himalayas that traces the path of an ancient mule track—the "Silk Road," used more than a thousand years ago. The Highway of Friendship runs from remote Kashgar in Sinkiang province to the Mintaka Pass (15,450 feet above sea level) on the Pakistani side and through 80 miles of Pakistani-held Kashmir to Gilgit. (The highway was inaugurated in February 1971, and one of my last assignments as Communications Minister was to receive my Chinese counterpart at the ceremony.) The new road is regarded as having far more political than military or economic significance, but India was concerned over its construction. In summer 1969 India charged that "12,000 Chinese troops had been brought into the territory in Kashmir 'illegally occupied' by Pakistan and were secretly helping Pakistan to construct . . . the Sinkiang–Tibet road via the Khunjerab Pass."[16]

China's special relationship with Pakistan from 1960 through 1970 was based on mutual advantage and pragmatic reality. No formal pact or alliance existed between the two countries, but their relationship was of the same intensity as that between the United States and Pakistan in the mid-1950s or that between the U.S.S.R. and India in 1971.

PEACE?

As the 1960s waned, there were glimmerings of possible détente between China and India.

At a press conference on New Year's Day 1969 Mrs. Gandhi hinted at Indian interest in establishing a dialogue. The Prime Minister confessed that she did not know how "to solve our problems with China," but she said that she was not happy about the continuing rigidity in relations.[17] Even earlier, when the U.S.S.R. announced its 1968 decision to arm Pakistan, voices rose in both Parliament and press over whether India should broaden its diplomatic options by improving relations with China—just as the Russians had toed a new path in approaching Pakistan.[18] If this suggestion was not serious in 1968, Mrs. Gandhi was reported to have told the Committee on External Affairs of the Congress parliamentary party in December 1968 that she was willing to take some initiative in improving relations with China. Rejecting demands to break off diplomatic relations with China, she insinuated that it would be worthwhile to conduct periodic exchanges "on the mode of the Warsaw meetings between the U.S. and China."[19]

Peking did not respond immediately to India's hints, concentrating instead on the growing Soviet–Indian collaboration in various fields, particularly the military sphere. As late as November 5, 1971, while Yahya Khan was visiting Peking, Peking Radio announced that continued Indian support of Tibetan dissidents showed unchanging hostility toward the P.R.C. But in May 1970 Mao Tse-tung reportedly observed to the Indian chargé d'affaires in Peking that India, "a great country," had been a friend of China and the two should renew their friendship. The Chinese Foreign Office asked the chargé for Indian reaction to Mao's remarks, which caused speculation in many capitals and concern in Islamabad. India reportedly replied that "it was for the Chinese Government to take the initiative" toward relaxed relations; the Chinese shot back that Mao's remarks had indicated China's desire for improved relations, and "it was for the Indian Government to respond with concrete proposals."[20] In October 1970 the Indian and Chinese ambassadors in Cairo passed a friendly and cordial seventy-five minutes in the first such ambassadorial meeting in a third country in several years. Subsequently, Indian Foreign Minister Singh told the Parliament's upper house, Rajya Sabha, "We do notice a slight change in the attitude of China towards, and propaganda against, India, of late; but we have not yet seen any change in the substantive matters so far as the Chinese stand towards India is concerned."[21]

Two years later, on November 25, 1972, Mrs. Gandhi summed it up: "There seemed to have been a softening of the [Chinese] attitude after the Cultural Revolution. Then came Bangladesh and we were back where we were."[22]

NOTES

1. Mohammed Ayoob, "India as a Factor in Sino–Pakistani Relations," *International Studies,* January 1968, pp. 279–300.
2. See Chou En-Lai's speech in Karachi on Feb. 18, 1964, cited in *Dawn,* Feb. 19, 1964.
3. Based on my research and personal interviews in Pakistan, 1967–1971. Despite the perceptive studies of C. P. Fitzgerald and others, up to the present the Chinese role in the 1965 Indo–Pakistani war has not been fully described to the world—a lapse reflected in those works that have suggested China suffered a considerable diplomatic defeat. Here, finally, is the whole story. In preparing this account, I read, most carefully, minutes of the wartime discussions between

Ayub and Bhutto and the Chinese Ambassador to Pakistan; between Chou and Liu and the Pakistani Ambassador to China; between Ashgar Khan and Chinese leaders; and between Ayub—who, like Ashgar, flew to Peking in the heat of crisis—and Mao, Chou, Liu, and Chinese military chiefs. After his retirement in 1969, I questioned Ayub at length about his secret mission to China. I read the diplomatic cipher messages exchanged daily between Peking and Rawalpindi during the war. As a member of the Cabinet (1969–1971), I conducted lengthy interviews with the top Pakistani military and civilian leaders who made the war's crucial decisions.

4. Based on my research and personal interviews in Pakistan, 1967–1971.

5. *The Guardian*, Sept. 9, 1965.

6. *Peking Review*, September 1965.

7. Based on Pakistani ambassadors' reports, uncovered in my research and personal interviews in Pakistan, 1967–1971.

8. *The Statesman*, Sept. 21, 1965.

9. Based on my research and personal interviews in Pakistan, 1967–1971.

10. *Ibid.*

11. Palmer, *Recent Soviet and Chinese Penetration, op. cit.*, pp. 48–53.

12. Reprinted in *Peking Review*, July 14, 1967. For a fuller account of the "Maoist Line for India," see Bhabani Sen Gupta's article in *China Quarterly*, January–March 1968.

13. Except where otherwise indicated, this section is based on my research and personal interviews in Pakistan, 1967–1971.

14. Except where otherwise indicated, this section is based on my research and personal interviews in Pakistan, 1967–1971.

15. See G. W. Choudhury, *The Last Days of United Pakistan* (Bloomington: Indiana University Press, 1974).

16. See Palmer, *Recent Soviet and Chinese Penetration, op. cit.*, p. 61, and *Dawn*, Feb. 10 and 11, 1968.

17. Palmer, *Recent Soviet and Chinese Penetration, op. cit.*, pp. 53–54.

18. See *The Statesman, Times of India*, and other publications, July 10–12, 1968.

19. Palmer, *Recent Soviet and Chinese Penetration, op. cit.*, p. 55.

20. See T. Karki Hussain, "Sino–Indian Relations," *Economic and Political Weekly*, Sept. 18, 1970, pp. 2017–2021.

21. Cited in *ibid.*

22. "Need for Closer Ties with U.S.A., China and Pakistan," *Indian and Foreign Review* (New Delhi), Dec. 15, 1972, pp. 6–7.

Part Four

Bangladesh and Continuing Tensions

Chapter Ten

BANGLADESH

ALTHOUGH THE RISE of Bengali nationalism and the birth of Bangladesh were largely the fruits of Pakistani political instability and ruling elite irresponsibility,[1] the great, tragic events of 1971 directly or indirectly involved the three major powers and India and resulted in a transformation in the patterns of alignment in the subcontinent. The Soviet Union, along with its victorious Indian partner, gained considerably; the United States and China, whose policies during the crisis were not free of dichotomies and complications, suffered big diplomatic setbacks, at least initially.

The emergence of Bangladesh is not likely to erase tensions or obliterate regional and international conflicts, as Premier Chou En-lai intimated after the December 16, 1971, Indian capture of Dacca, which became the new nation's capital. That the United States, like China, would refuse to pull out of the subcontinent was made clear months before. America would accede to legitimate Chinese and Soviet interests in South Asia, President Nixon declared in his February 1971 "State of the World" message, but it would not allow any outside power to attain predominant influence and make the area a focus of great power conflict.[2] As James Reston put it, the Bangladesh crisis represented

> not only another phase in the long religious conflict between the Muslims and the Hindus, not only a moral conflict between Pakistan's vicious suppression of the Bangladesh rebels and India's calculated military aggression to dismember the Pakistani state. Back of all this, there was a power struggle between China and

the Soviet Union and a strategic struggle between Moscow and Washington.[3]

The struggle continues today.

THE SOUTH ASIAN TRIANGLE ON THE EVE OF THE CRISIS

At the outbreak of the civil war in Bangladesh, Indo–American relations could be described as diplomatically correct at best. American dealings with Pakistan, on the other hand, were spirited.

In October 1970 the Nixon administration announced that it would supply Pakistan with six modern fighters, seven B-57 bombers, and 200 armored personnel carriers—the first U.S. arms to the subcontinent since 1965. The official explanation for the policy change was that the withholding of military supplies had not brought peace.[4] Weighing more on Washington policy makers' minds, however, were the Soviet Union's continued massive military shipments to India and the frantic Pakistani appeals for a redress in the balance of power. President Nixon showed greater sympathy to Pakistani appeals—and they had been constant since Yahya met the President in August 1969—than had his Democratic predecessors; in talks with Yahya, Nixon recalled his Vice-Presidential role in establishing a "special relationship with Pakistan," adding that "Pakistan's friendship with the U.S. will be dearer" to him as President.[5] Also leading to the U.S. arms policy shift was Nixon's China initiative, for which Pakistan deserved favors, or at least improved relations, for services rendered. It is ironic that as the Nixon Doctrine called for limited disengagement from Asia, the United States and Pakistan revived, to some extent, their old alliance—almost as ironic as the fact that détente with China contributed to the revival of an alliance initiated to further containment of China.

While the Western giant was disengaging in at least some parts of Asia, the two communist giants were competing more fiercely in Asia, particularly in Southeast Asia. In the aftermath of the cultural revolution, China's new, outward-looking foreign policy clearly aimed to secure Peking's place as both an ideological fountainhead within the communist world and a determining force within the developing world. As it does today, China in the days before the Bangladesh dam burst perceived Asia as its national cultural domain, an area in which it must and eventually would predominate. Peking believes it is entitled to the leadership of the global process of revolutionary change. The Soviet Union was and is the problem. China long has interpreted Soviet activities in Asia as designed to encircle it with states under Moscow's strong influence, India being the most important of these states and the U.S.S.R.'s biggest asset in its diplomatic offensive. (That the U.S.S.R. had already ascended to "the first rank of China's enemies" was gleefully noted by U.S. Secretary of State William P. Rogers in conversation with Yahya in May 1969.)[6] Peking's cordiality toward the bourgeois, military-run government in Pakistan—the outstanding example of its willingness to overlook ideological considerations when occasion demands—was partly explained by this competition with Moscow, partly by the yearning to maintain a friend, and an enemy of India, on China's frontier.

Attempting to discredit China and its policies, stressing "China's great power chauvinism," the Soviets contend that Asia, the developing nations, and the world require a single variety of communism, a single nation to lead—and that variety and that nation are not Chinese.[7] With the dawn of the 1970s the U.S.S.R. strengthened its bonds with New Delhi, applauding Prime Minister Gandhi as she surpassed her father in the domestic application of socialist principles, and as she triumphed in the 1971 elections. The Kremlin and Islamabad got along considerably less well.

BANGLADESH

The crisis in East Pakistan started on the night of March 25, 1971, when negotiations between Yahya Khan and Mujibur Rahman broke down after failing to produce a compromise to resolve the constitutional crisis. The talks were complicated by Bhutto, who objected strenuously to the various concessions Yahya put forth in bids to preserve the unity of Pakistan. It is most tragic that the Pakistani Army, instead of penalizing the person who eliminated all chances of settlement, plunged into ruthless and unprecedented atrocities on the unarmed Bengali population—a vile campaign in which thousands of innocents, including women, old people, sick people, and children, were brutally murdered; millions fled their homes to take shelter in India.

While most governments refrained from immediate condemnation of the massacre, the press, particularly in Britain and the United States, rendered a service to humanity by publicizing the horrors in East Pakistan. This publicity, which contrasted to apparent indifference in the world press to other tragedies in Afro–Asian countries, went a long way in rousing support and sympathy for the suffering Bangalis. The pro-Moscow elements in Bangladesh, which today are trying to magnify the role of the Soviet Union in the liberation, conveniently overlook the moral and material support given by the people of the West as a result of the vigorous Western press campaign in the Bengali cause.[8]

BANGLADESH: THE SOVIET ROLE

The Soviet Union was the first among the major powers to condemn Pakistan's army action in East Bengal, but it is naïve to assume that the Kremlin leaders were moved only by the suffering humanity in Bangladesh or were interested in "restoring the democratic rights" of the Bengalis.[9] Far more important motivations were annoyance with Pakistan for its continued links to China, and close and growing Soviet friendship with India.

India's prompt reaction to the events in East Pakistan was a function of a number of factors. Many Indians still regret the "tragic mistake" of partition of their motherland in 1947; even more Indians regret the security problem posed by the Muslim fruit of that partition. New Delhi smiled and nodded at Mujibur Rahman's pro-Indianism and his denunciations of what he termed Pakistan's "provocative friendship" with China.[10] For these reasons, it was quite natural that India lent all-out support to the Bengalis *even before the refugees began to flow into India*. Two days after the onset of the crisis Mrs. Gandhi declared in Parliament that India would help the majority in East Pakistan,[11] and in the same month an exile Bangladeshi government was formed on Indian soil. The influx of refugees, most of them Hindus, provided India with an excuse to train and equip the Bengali liberation forces and finally to resort to war.[12]

The Soviets were well aware of India's sympathy, and they acted in conjunction with it. For them it was an easy choice between a tottering, China- and U.S.-supported Pakistan and a stable, strong, friendly India. As the armed uprising in East Pakistan was nursed by New Delhi, New Delhi was bolstered by the Kremlin. The Soviet stand in the deepening crisis was made clear in President Podgorny's April 2 letter to Yahya, which demanded a stop to "the bloodshed and repression" in East Bengal. Yahya's reply was equally sharp: Pakistan was determined not to allow any country to interfere in its internal affairs.[13] More acrimonious were unpublished diplomatic notes between the two countries, Yahya's communications with the Soviet Ambassador in Islamabad, and the Moscow talks of Yahya's special emissary, former Foreign Minister Arshad Husian. Yahya, in his fury, reminded the Soviet Ambassador of atrocities in Czechoslovakia and the U.S.S.R.'s Central Asian Republics; Arshad Hosian had the worst experience of his life trying to justify the military actions in East Bengal.

Podgorny's letter to Yahya indicated a major change in Soviet South Asia policy. Eventually convinced, with India, that "an independent East Bengal was not only inevitable but the best way to preserve stability in the region,"[14] the Kremlin leaders were now willing to reconsider their policy of satisfactory relations with *both* subcontinent powers. As one Western news source observed, "For the time being, Moscow has written off Pakistan as a factor in Asian affairs."[15] Still, the U.S.S.R. only edged into a publicly anti-Pakistan stance, and for good reason—China's eventual role in the crisis was an important consideration for the Kremlin. Also not to be overlooked was the attitude of the Muslim Middle East, with which Moscow had developed closer ties and which supported Pakistan strongly. Thus the Soviets long avoided (at least officially) discussion of an independent Bengali state, talking instead of a political settlement acceptable to the whole of Pakistan; during his Algerian visit in the summer of 1971, Kosygin referred to Pakistan's "territorial integrity."[16] Moreover, the Soviet press was slow to condemn the Pakistani Army massacres.

By the time the treaty of friendship with India was signed in August, however, Soviet good will for Pakistan had evaporated. In the meantime Henry Kissinger had dramatically traveled to Peking via Rawalpindi in July, and Nixon had announced his intention to visit China. As pointed out earlier, Pakistan's role in arranging the Sino–American dialogue was greatly resented in Moscow, which, like New Delhi, engaged in what President Nixon termed "fanciful speculation of a U.S.–Chinese alignment."[17] The Soviets largely agreed with Professor Sisir Gupta of Jawalarlal Nehru University, New Delhi:

> However great the reluctance of the Indian optimists to admit it, the fact is that Sino–U.S. rapprochement has altered the international context in which India has to conduct its local struggles and that on the specific issue of Bangladesh, the entire weight of this development can be thrown against our country.[18]

After a ten-day silence, *Pravda* came out on July 25 with a lengthy article on Nixon's overtures to Peking; earlier the press in Bulgaria, Czechoslovakia, Poland, and Hungary questioned China's motives in terms similar to those used by Moscow.

Nixon's China policy had an immediate impact on the crisis in Bangladesh. After his Peking trip Kissinger reportedly told the Indian Ambassador in Washington that China would intervene if India attacked Pakistan—and the United States might not come to India's help, as it had in 1962 and in 1965 when it warned China against intervention.[19] According to the Pakistani ambassadors in New Delhi, Moscow, and Washington, this Kissinger threat made the Indians hasten to sign with the Soviet Union the treaty of friendship, which had been in preparation ever since Brezhnev proposed his security system two years before.[20] Because of India's long tradition of eschewing all military pacts, the treaty was called an agreement of "peace, friendship and cooperation." But close scrutiny of the text of the treaty leaves no doubt that, whatever the disguise, it is a military pact.

Only with the signing of the treaty—and on the eve of Mrs. Gandhi's visit to Moscow in September 1971—did the Soviet press, in tune with official policy, launch into condemnation of Pakistan. Neither the Kremlin nor the Soviet press had chuckled over the human suffering in East Bengal, but it was only after the Soviet Union had consolidated its national interests in South Asia by drawing India into the treaty of friendship that concern for Bangladesh became vocal and unqualified.

These are some of the basic facts that the leaders and people of the new state of Bangladesh should not forget as pro-Moscow elements seek to capture power through repeated reference to "generous Soviet help" during the independence struggle.[21] The *raison d'être* of Soviet activities during the crisis was not humanitarianism or even ideology, but the traditional Russian ambition to establish hegemony in the subcontinent and in the Indian Ocean through control of, or (as in this case) close relations with, India, the dominant power in the area.

BANGLADESH: THE AMERICAN ROLE

"Few if any postwar American policy ventures," recorded William J. Barnds, "have brought forth as immediate and widespread opposition as the Nixon Administration's policy toward the Indian sub-continent during 1971."[22] True enough, yet the United States has shown more consistent and sincere concern for the welfare of the people of East Bengal than either of the other great powers.

It is ironic that, in the months and years before the crisis, the Pakistani intelligence services, both civilian and military, never tired of "discovering" the "grand American designs" to encourage secession in East Pakistan.[23] Almost all American visitors, including intellectuals, were harassed, sometimes humiliated, as "agents of the Central Intelligence Agency"; and almost all Bengalis, intellectuals not excepted, were haunted and harangued if they had innocent dialogue with visiting Americans. The American economists associated with the Pakistan Planning Commission were constantly watched and suspected because of their objective and honest concern about economic conditions in East Pakistan; if their recommendations to remove the economic grievances of the Bengalis had been followed, the tragedy of 1971 might have been averted. (It must be said here, however, that some of the economists earned the suspicion cast their way, passing out political as well as economic advice to the Bengalis.) On March 26, 1971, the *New York Times* reported from Rawalpindi that "in Pakistan, the United States is a villain"; American Ambassador Farland, the *Times* reported, "is regularly portrayed as a CIA agent subverting Pakistan's interests—often in favor of India." Even Farland's predecessor, Benjamin H. Oehlert, Jr.—who was to advocate military support for Pakistan in December 1971—was vilified by the Pakistani press.[24]

Despite the criticism and disappointment both within the United States and abroad over American policy during the Bangladesh crisis, neither the American government in general nor Richard Nixon in particular condoned Pakistan's military atrocities in East

Bengal and opposed the aspirations of the Bengali nationalists. It was Nixon's intervention that saved the life of Mujib, whom the hawkish Pakistani generals, backed by Bhutto, were planning in August and September 1971 to execute; Bhutto told me in September that Yahya should execute Mujib before departing the following month for Tehran, where President Nixon would also be in attendance at the two thousandth anniversary of the Iranian monarchy. Yahya withstood the severe pressure to do away with the Awami League leader only because of Nixon's strong pleas to refrain from such a course. Similarly, President Nixon pressed Yahya to make a political settlement with the Awami League leaders exiled in India, and Yahya agreed. It is not certain that even if all parties had fully cooperated Nixon's efforts for a political settlement would have been successful, but those who know the inside story, as I do as a result of my private visit to Rawalpindi in September 1971, realize that the Nixon administration was doing its best both to avert Indo–Pakistani war and to achieve in the shortest possible time the goal of the Bengali nationalists. President Nixon's personal sympathy for Pakistan, his cherished China policy, and the unpleasant image of Pakistan's dismemberment under the guns of Soviet-backed Indian forces motivated him and his government to work diligently toward an honorable settlement suitable to both the Bengalis and the West Pakistanis.

Islamabad and Calcutta, where the exiled Bangladesh government was functioning, but unfortunately not New Delhi, were responsive to the American campaign for a peaceful solution. By September–October 1971, Yahya—only slowly getting over his happy delusion that because of his "grand role" as a liaison between them the Chinese and Americans would bail him out of any problem he stumbled into—finally realized that his bankrupt government could not afford much longer the costly military operations in East Pakistan. "If the Americans cannot continue the Vietnam war," the Pakistani President told me during my exclusive September 6 interview, "how can Pakistan, whose exchequer is empty, carry on this costly operation?" He bitterly attacked India for not allowing time to reach a political settlement arranged by Nixon and the Shah of Iran, and he took an unscheduled trip to Tehran to discuss such a settlement with the Shah, who was acting in perfect understanding with Washington. Contrary to Yahya's fears, when Mrs. Gandhi visited Washington in November, she seemed to accede to President Nixon's request for more time to achieve the objective of the Bengali nationalists without war. It appeared that Washington's mediation was working.

But within a week of the Prime Minister's return to India its troops began to cross the borders of East Pakistan in the name of "self-defense." "Self-defense" is a dangerous enough doctrine when confined to the realm of domestic quarrels. If it is applied to international relations and accepted as just cause for starting a war, then the territorial integrity of any smaller country is unsafe and the principles and premises of the UN Charter are negated. India bolstered its self-defense claim by pointing to the millions of East Bengali refugees who were creating an explosive situation in its turbulent state of West Bengal, but its justification in resorting to war was still debatable in terms of international law and UN Charter obligations—particularly because it rejected not only Washington's proposals for a political settlement but also the UN Secretary General's suggestions for stopping or reversing the flow of Bengali refugees. Some say India was justified on humanitarian grounds,[25] but when the issue was brought before the UN General Assembly, the overwhelming majority urged India to accept a cease-fire. India refused and, with the Soviet Union behind it, pressed its operations until Dacca fell.[26]

In an account of America's role during the Bangladesh crisis in his report to the U.S. Congress on February 9, 1972, President Nixon stressed that "the United States did not support or condone" Islamabad's harsh repression of the East.

> Immediately in early April, we ceased issuing and renewing licenses for military shipment to Pakistan, we put a hold on arms that had been committed the year before and we ceased new commitments for economic development loans. This shut off $35 million worth of arms. Less than $5 million worth of spare parts, already in the pipeline under earlier licenses, was shipped before the pipeline dried up completely by the beginning of November.[27]

The Nixon administration claimed after March 25, 1971, that total stoppage of aid to Pakistan would leave the United States without influence on Yahya, but in loud protests India and large segments of the Western press decried the policy.

Indeed Nixon's policy, overoptimistic about the amount of American leverage, was in some ways misguided. Washington did not realize the extent to which the military junta would fight against complete independence for East Bengal or the extent to which the

Bengalis, furious at what had happened to their homeland since March 25, would fight for it;[28] and in any case, continued military shipments to Yahya's regime were hardly justified. In an April 15 statement, the State Department gave the impression that an air-flight embargo on arms supplies to Pakistan had been imposed, yet in June it was found that U.S. arms were bound for Pakistan by sea.[29] Indignation was great both in the United States and abroad. But if the United States was not serving the cause of humanity with the arms shipments, at least for better or worse it was ful-filling its commitments to defend the government of Pakistan.

When President Nixon labeled the Indian military action "ag-gression," he reflected a sense of betrayal; had Mrs. Gandhi delayed the invasion, Nixon felt, his efforts toward a peaceful solution might have made the invasion unnecessary.[30] But a U.S.-orchestrated "Tashkent type" solution would have represented a diplomatic coup for Nixon that neither the U.S.S.R. nor India was prepared to give. On the contrary, through Indian force of arms, India and the Soviet Union were the diplomatic winners, taking the title of "liberators" of 75 million Bengalis.

The tone and content of U.S. policy during the Bangladesh crisis offended many liberals and friends of democracy, and many believed that the United States stood with the forces of militarism against democracy. Democratic Senator Edward Kennedy of Massa-chusetts charged that President Nixon "watched this crisis in si-lence,"[31] and a Louis Harris survey found that the American people, who had never shown much interest in South Asia, disapproved by a two-to-one margin Nixon's handling of the crisis.[32] But Nixon's policy was not basically wrong or unjustified. If Washington's at-tempts at mediation had succeeded, enormous loss—human, physi-cal, social—would have been avoided in Bangladesh. Full-scale war would have been avoided but independence secured.

BANGLADESH: THE CHINESE ROLE

China faced a dilemma.[33] True to its traditional sympathy for national liberation movements, Peking might have been expected to extend support to the movement for Bangladesh. But in the context of friendship with Pakistan and hostility toward the U.S.S.R. and India, Peking could hardly support a New Delhi– and Moscow–

backed independence movement for the East Bengalis. Thus China chose pragmatism over ideology—or so it is said.

Peking claims that the choice was not as clear-cut as it might have seemed because the rebels in East Pakistan were not of the proper ideological ilk—their fight, went Mao's line, was not a genuine national liberation movement, but a bourgeois movement sustained by "reactionary" India and "socialist imperalist" Russia. The Chinese were confirmed in—one is tempted to say driven to—their assessment by Mujib's rabid anti-China sentiments. There was little question as to whom a new nation under his leadership would turn for allies—and to whom it would not.

Moreover, if China did not really forsake ideology in opposing the Bengali movement, it did not always please Yahya's regime in pursuing a policy containing large doses of pragmatism. When the President visited Peking in November 1970, Chou urged him, as Nixon would urge him, to find a fair answer to the growing East–West problems. After the December elections Chou wrote both Mujib and Bhutto to ask them to come to a satisfactory settlement. Neither leader was in a mood to listen, and Yahya himself was totally incapable of taking friendly advice.[34]

When the crisis finally erupted in March 1971, neither Government nor press in China made any hasty comment. The first reaction, expressed in *People's Daily* on April 11, did not defend or assail either side in the Pakistani quarrel, attacking instead "open interference in the internal matters of Pakistan" by the Indian government; the Russian role, particularly Podgorny's letter to Yahya, was also criticized as interference in Pakistani affairs.

After Podgorny's letter, Yahya appealed to Peking to counterbalance Moscow's backing of India, and China, after initial hesitancy, sent a message of support. In an April 11 message, Chou expressed to Yahya the hope that Pakistan's crisis would soon end. "In our opinion," the Premier added, "unification of Pakistan and unity of the peoples of East and West Pakistan are basic guarantees for Pakistan to attain prosperity and strength."[35]

Chou En-lai's letter, which was not published in China, notably lacked criticism of Mujib or his Awami League, but, because it was meant for public consumption in the subcontinent, it did not hint of Peking's growing concern about Yahya's course. The Chinese left little unsaid, however, as Foreign Secretary Sultan Khan and Lieut. General Gul Hasan (a top member of the military junta), secretly sent by Yahya to secure Chinese support, found it difficult to explain to Peking the military atrocities in East Bengal. Chou warned of "grave consequences" if a political solution was not quickly found. Unfortunately, the two-member mission failed, upon returning home, to give Yahya an honest assessment of China's attitude. After the dissolution of his Cabinet in February, Yahya had become completely dependent upon bureaucrats and generals who provided only those reports and assessments that were pleasing to the ears of their boss. Yahya, like Ayub before him, demonstrated the military dictator's paucity of sources for honest, independent, and accurate advice. This lack of good advice was largely responsible for Yahya's incredible errors during the crisis, and for the immense suffering that resulted.

China, like the United States, was not happy at the prospect of supporting a military regime against Mujib and the other popularly elected East Pakistani representatives. For China as for America it was the diplomatic realities in South Asia—for Peking the Sino–Soviet rivalry loomed most important—that led to grudging support of Yahya's bloody regime. But if the open support was there, behind the scenes the Chinese, like such other friends of Pakistan as Britain and the United States, pressed Yahya to end the violence.

Things grew worse within the West Pakistani ruling clique. Referring to himself, in the course of my discussions with him, as the helpless prisoner of an unfortunate environment, Yahya did not possess sufficient imagination to take the bold initiatives required to extricate Pakistan from its tragedy. Within the military junta a group headed by General Peerzada—who was once described by the *Sunday Times* as a de facto Prime Minister and who colluded with Bhutto—was determined to sabotage any meaningful dialogue with the elected representatives of East Pakistan.

The Chinese Ambassador, with whom I had lengthy talks on my two visits to Pakistan during the crisis, evidenced China's distress, its perception of the mounting disaster. The support became purely formal—Peking could tell a lost cause when it saw one and was losing face in it. Indeed, the British China expert John Gittings, writing in *The Guardian*, went so far as to contend that Peking was no longer supporting Yahya at all. According to Gittings, China had adopted a "policy of strict non-intervention." Even Chou's letter to Yahya of April 11, "if one reads between the lines," could be construed "as a plea for negotiation instead of bloodshed." Gittings also pointed to a pamphlet entitled *The People's War*, issued by the Maoist Communist party of Bangladesh, that claimed, perhaps correctly, "The Chinese have never opposed the right of the people of Bangladesh to self-determination." The Bangladeshi Maoist groups led by Mohammed Toha had joined the liberation movement, while Mauiana Bashani, leader of the pro-Peking group of the National Awami party (which worked for the banned Communist party) had appealed to Mao Tse-tung for recognition of Bangladesh.[36]

In November 1971, on the eve of war, Bhutto went to Peking as Yahya's special emissary and returned practically empty-handed. China again demanded, publicly this time, that a "rational solution" be found for East Bengal, clearly indicating disapproval of the atrocities. The vital assurance sought by Pakistan was that in the event of war China would be willing, as it had been in 1965, to hold down Indian divisions by diversionary action on India's northern frontier; China offered no such assurance. Aiming directly at the hawkish elements of West Pakistan's junta, the Chinese apparently advised the negotiation of a political settlement.[37] Pakistan extracted a "declaration of support" from Peking, but no specific commitments or assurances. Acting Foreign Minister Chi, speaking on November 7 at a banquet in honor of the delegation headed by Bhutto, offered vague "support" to Pakistan against "foreign aggression." His statement, however, did not go "beyond the ambiguously worded promise that Mr. Chou En-lai, the Chinese Prime Minister, made to President Yahya Khan in a letter on April 11."[38]

Bhutto, like the April mission before him, did not report faithfully to Yahya.[39] Home from Peking, Bhutto loudly proclaimed that China would give all-out support if war broke out with India; he and his followers paraded the streets with the cry "Crush India."[40]

After the war finally erupted on December 3 with Indian military intervention to "liberate" Bangladesh, China supported Pakistan in the UN Security Council, but Peking appeared more against the Soviet Union than in favor of West Pakistan. Although neither communist power seemed ready to step up its material support to the contestants or to enter the fighting, the sharpness of the polemics exchanged between the two might have led one to believe otherwise. Less than a month after taking its seat in the Security Council, China used its first veto to kill a Soviet draft resolution that called for a political settlement in East Pakistan involving a "cessation of hostilities" and an end to "all acts of violence by Pakistani forces." Peking's own view—that India should be condemned for creating a "so-called Bangladesh," that it should recall its forces from Pakistan, and that both sides should cease fire and withdraw from the border—was contained in a draft resolution that was retracted before reaching a vote. The Chinese retraction made little practical difference: until the fall of Dacca Moscow was as willing as Peking to veto any resolution that impugned its patron.[41]

The Soviets and Chinese fought their battles in the press as well as in the Security Council. Moscow accused China of a *volte-face* in backing the Pakistani government's aims in the east after it had earlier prodded extremists there into "adventurous actions"—apparently a reference to Peking encouragement of Mohammed Toha's Maoists. China was also accused of promoting in Asia "chauvinist great-power aims." Peking saw Soviet support for India as an example of "social imperialism."[42] A *People's Daily* editorial on December 7 asked whether the Soviets intended to take action in Pakistan similar to their armed occupation in Czechoslovakia, since they had described the situations in both countries as threats to the U.S.S.R.'s security. The article drew an analogy between the Soviet endorsement for India's attempts to create a "puppet Bangladesh" and the German and Italian fascists' support for the 1930s Japanese construct of Manchukuo in northeast China.

A MATTER OF *REALPOLITIK*

Above all else, Washington and Peking acted as they did because of *realpolitik* imperatives: the Soviet Union, bent on expanding its influence and power no matter what the cost in human lives and suffering, found in the Bangladesh crisis a unique opportunity to weaken and humiliate China and also to further its own global interests vis-à-vis the United States. The Soviets did not act out of love and righteousness any more than the Americans and Chinese backed Yahya because they enjoyed the butchering of babies; but for the Soviet Union's direct encouragement of regional tensions between India and Pakistan, the dreadful war over Bangladesh might have been avoided. When the full story of the disintegration of Pakistan and the role of the three major powers and India is fully examined in proper perspective, the world will see that the United States and China were considerably less than devils, the Soviet Union and India considerably less than gods. Said Richard

Nixon, "Soviet policy, I regret to say, seemed to show the same tendency we have witnessed before in the 1967 Middle East War and the 1970 Jordanian crisis—to allow events to boil up toward crisis in the hope of political gain."[43]

NOTES

1. See G. W. Choudhury, "Bangladesh: Why It Happened," *International Affairs* (London), April 1972.

2. See *U.S. Foreign Policy for the 1970's: The Emerging Structure of Peace*, A Report to the Congress by Richard Nixon, President of the United States, Feb. 9, 1972 (Washington: Government Printing Office, 1972).

3. James Reston, "Who Won in India?" *New York Times*, Dec. 17, 1971.

4. *Dawn* and *New York Times*, Oct. 7 and 8, 1970.

5. Based on unpublished records of the Nixon–Yahya talks, Lahore, August 1969, uncovered in my research and personal interviews in Pakistan, 1967–1971.

6. Based on unpublished records of the Yahya–Rogers talks, Lahore, August 1969, uncovered in my research and personal interviews in Pakistan, 1967–1971.

7. Moscow Radio, Mar. 21, 1970.

8. See Choudhury, *Last Days, op. cit.*

9. Except where otherwise noted, this section is based on my research and personal interviews in Pakistan, 1967–1971.

10. Mujib made the "provocative friendship" reference during my Dec. 3, 1969, visit with him and on other occasions.

11. Indira Gandhi, *India and Bangladesh: Selected Speeches and Statements—March to December 1971* (New Delhi: Orient Longmans, Ltd., 1972), pp. 9–19.

12. See Nirad Chaudhuri, "The Vicious Spiral of Hindu–Muslim Hatred," *The Times* (London), Dec. 21, 1971.

13. For the text of Podgorny's letter and Yahya's reply, see *Pravda*, Apr. 4, 1971, and *Dawn*, Apr. 7, 1971.

14. Dev Murarka, "Podgorny's Appeal Aligns Russia with Pakistan Rebels," *Observer Foreign News Service*, Apr. 5, 1971.

15. *Ibid.*

16. *Dawn*, Aug. 8, 1971.

17. Nixon, *Emerging Structure, op. cit.*

18. Sisir Gupta, "Sino–U.S. Detente and India," *India Quarterly,* July–September 1971.

19. Reported by Yahya's economic adviser, M. M. Ahmad, after he met with Nixon and Kissinger and by the Pakistani Ambassador in Washington; uncovered in my research and personal interviews in Pakistan, 1967–1971.

20. Robert H. Donaldson, "Soviet Political Aims in South Asia," a paper delivered at the Twenty-fifth Annual Meeting of the Association for Asian Studies, Mar. 30–Apr. 1, 1973, Chicago, Ill., p. 8.

21. See G. W. Choudhury, "Moscow's Influence in the Indian Subcontinent," *World Today,* July 1972, pp. 304–311.

22. William J. Barnds, "India, Pakistan and American Realpolitik," *Christianity and Crisis,* June 12, 1972.

23. Except where otherwise indicated, this section is based on my research and personal interviews in Pakistan, 1967–1971, and Choudhury, *Last Days, op. cit.*

24. *Dawn,* Dec. 7, 1971.

25. G. W. Choudhury, "Bangladesh: A Review Article," *Journal of International Affairs,* No. 2, 1973, pp. 282–286.

26. M. S. Rajan, "Bangladesh and After," *Pacific Affairs,* Summer 1972, pp. 191–206.

27. Nixon, *Emerging Structure, op. cit.*

28. Choudhury, "U.S. Policy," *op. cit.,* pp. 97–112.

29. See the June 29, 1971, statement by the U.S. Deputy Assistant Secretary of State for Near East and South Asian Affairs, in *United States Information Service Analysis* (London: American Embassy).

30. Choudhury, "U.S. Policy," *op. cit.*

31. William Millinship, "Has Nixon Paid a Smuggler's Debt to Pakistan?" *Observer Foreign News Service,* Dec. 10, 1971.

32. Cited in Barnds, *op. cit.*

33. See "Peking's Pakistan Dilemmas," *International Herald Tribune,* Apr. 13, 1971.

34. Except where otherwise indicated, this section is based on my research and personal interviews in Pakistan, 1967–1971.

35. *International Herald Tribune,* Apr. 13, 1971.

36. John Gittings, "How Many Wreaths for Bangladesh?" *The Guardian,* June 18, 1971.

37. *Christian Science Monitor,* Nov. 8, 1971 and *Financial Times,* Dec. 6, 1971.

38. *The Times* (London), Nov. 8, 1971.

39. Bhutto's failure to report accurately was noted by Yahya himself in his disposition before the Judicial Commission set up by Bhutto after he assumed power in December 1971. I received this account from a close associate of Bhutto who has now lost confidence in him.

40. *Dawn,* Nov. 9 and 10, 1971.

41. See Rajan, "Bangladesh and After," *op. cit.*

42. See G. W. Choudhury, "Dismemberment of Pakistan, 1971: Its International Implications," *Orbis,* Spring 1974, pp. 179–200.

43. Nixon, *Emerging Structure, op. cit.*

Chapter Eleven

THREE NATIONS
ON THE SUBCONTINENT

UNITED STATES SECRETARY OF STATE Rogers called the events on the Indian subcontinent "tragic" and "one of the major disappointments for U.S. foreign policy in 1971."[1] The Chinese could conceal their disappointment no better than the Americans; they denounced the government of Bangladesh as a "puppet regime" set up by India. Moscow viewed the Indian success as "a slap in the face for America and to a lesser extent, China," as Prime Minister Gandhi thanked the Soviet Union for its help during the war.

Since the Bangladesh crisis Soviet hopes have centered on India, but the Kremlin is mistaken if it imagines that Mrs. Gandhi would give up nonalignment as payment for the Soviet military and diplomatic support in the war. The most important fact of South Asian politics after the disintegration of Pakistan is the growth of India as a major regional force. At this hour of post-Bangladesh ascendancy India is not likely to do Moscow's bidding. "Indians," noted the *Christian Science Monitor* six days after Dacca's fall, "appeared to think more of their national pride, their history, their sense of destiny as a great nation than of the dictates of other powers, whether friendly or critical."[2]

This does not mean, of course, that friendship between Moscow and New Delhi has stopped growing. No other foreign power is more respected and influential in New Delhi than the Soviet Union. Soon to enter its third decade, the Indo–Soviet entente has proved profitable to both countries, with the U.S.S.R. capitalizing on the friendship in its approaches to nonaligned Afro–Asian countries and in its quarrel with China, and India benefiting through Soviet diplomatic, economic, and, eventually, military support. The events of 1971 strengthened enormously the ties between the two nations, and these will remain tight, barring a forceful new drive to make India a member of Brezhnev's "Socialist Commonwealth." Peace and stability in the subcontinent depend largely on Soviet moves, and these hinge on factors such as Sino–Soviet conflict, Indo–Soviet cooperation, and strategic and global rivalry or understanding between the two superpowers.

According to the Indian Bhabani Sen Gupta:

> Taking advantage of the U.S. predicament in Southeast Asia and on the domestic front, and of the leadership crisis in China, the USSR has succeeded in bringing South Asia within the expanding orbit of its Asian sphere of influence . . . the U.S. virtually recognized the subcontinent as a Soviet sphere of influence.[3]

This analysis is hard to accept. In his 1971 foreign policy report President Nixon said:

> We have a deep interest in insuring that the subcontinent does not become a focus of great power conflict. . . . We will try to keep our activities in balance with those of the other major powers concerned. . . . No outside power has a claim to a predominant influence. . . .[4]

Nixon reaffirmed these sentiments in his 1972 report. According to *The United States Interests in and Policies toward South Asia*, a 1973 report by the Subcommittee on the Near East and South Asia of the House Committee on Foreign Affairs:

> U.S. strategic interests in the area today relate primarily to regional stability and the avoidance of any situation or presence in South Asia or the adjoining Indian Ocean and Persian Gulf areas which attract a large scale presence, involvement, or intervention by any outside power.[5]

It is evident that South Asia under the Nixon–Kissinger regime, though not a priority area, was not to be forgotten.

Similarly, China will not abandon South Asia. Foreign Minister Chi Peng-fei was blunt during his visit to Pakistan and Iran in the summer of 1973. "Certain big powers have not abandoned their aggressive, subjugating and expansionist policy," he said, making it clear that China would be a factor in the subcontinent at least as long as would the Soviet Union.[6] Between Washington and Peking there seems to be a coincidence of purpose—one would hesitate to call it an identity—with regard to South Asia; both wish to restrict Soviet influence in the subcontinent and the adjourning Indian Ocean and Persian Gulf. Dr. William R. Kintner, currently head of a U.S. Department of State study group on Asian Affairs, formerly U.S. Ambassador to Thailand and formerly director of the Foreign Policy Research Institute, argued that American "support for China in this case would coincide with the classic balance of power strategy— that one supports the weaker power against the power threatening to become dominant."[7] On his part, Chou En-lai opposes complete U.S. withdrawal from South and Southeast Asia, according to Congressmen Hale Boggs (Democrat of Louisiana) and Gerald R. Ford (Republican of Michigan—and now, of course, President), who visited China in July 1972. "As they put it," Boggs recalled from his discussions with Chinese chiefs, "there are two superpowers—the United States and Russia—and if Russia becomes the greater superpower then much of the world is in difficulty." The Soviet press lambasted China on the basis of the American congressmen's report.[8]

The regional tensions among the three states of the subcontinent, the Sino–Soviet rivalry, the strategic and global competition between the two superpowers, the growing Soviet naval presence in, and the British withdrawal from, the Indian Ocean and Persian Gulf areas—all these indicate that after the Bangladesh crisis the subcontinent is likely to enjoy no greater stability than it did before.

AFTER BANGLADESH: THE SOVIET ROLE

What Price Friendship?

What dividends can the Kremlin extract from Mrs. Gandhi for its support in the 1971 crisis? After the war, the Prime Minister was reported to have said, "We are unable to display gratitude in any tangible sense for anything."[9] Yet the fact remains that India is securely knotted to the U.S.S.R.

The Soviets remain friends in what has become a rather unfriendly world. Partly as a result of its 1971 victory, India's diplomatic options today are not as wide as they were in the heyday of Nehru's nonalignment in the 1950s. Not only India's relations with the United States and China but even its image in the Third World soured as a result of the war—as demonstrated by the emerging nations' repudiation of India at the UN General Assembly in December 1971.[10] Moreover, India and the Soviet Union share such common objectives as containment of China and prevention of Pakistani-rearming. (This rearming might be achieved through the help of China, Iran, and others, perhaps including the United States —though Nixon told Bhutto in October 1973 that the United States would not supply weapons,[11] there is fear in New Delhi that Iran's vast acquisitions of U.S. arms might have a spillover effect for Pakistan.[12] Similarly, New Delhi quivers over the proposed plan for the oil-producing gulf states to finance the manufacture of French Mirage aircraft at plants located in Pakistan.[13]) A final reason for powerful Soviet leverage in New Delhi, of course, is the load of weapons supplied the Indian Army; after, as before the war, security and Moscow's contribution to it are paramount considerations.

With its long tradition of opposition to any form of military pact, India faces a dilemma in Brezhnev's plan for Asian collective security. As pointed out earlier, Brezhnev deliberately kept his plan vague for some time, but he and other Kremlin officials never missed an opportunity to harp on its virtues in their dialogues with Asian leaders. The Soviets tried to pass off the 1971 treaty of friendship, as well as the India–Bangladesh treaty of 1972, as preliminary steps toward the establishment of an Asian collective security system.[14] Eventually they changed tactics, announcing publicly details of the plan. Among the principles that, according to Brezhnev, "collective security in Asia must, in our view, be based on" were renunciation of the use of force in relations between states, respect for the sovereignty and inviolability of borders, noninterference in national affairs, and economic and other cooperation on the basis of full equality and mutual advantage.[15] The U.S.S.R.'s change in tactics probably resulted from the disappointing results of early attempts to win Asia over to the idea. Not only did Pakistan turn down Brezhnev, but Indian Foreign Minister Singh, having initially expressed interest in Brezhnev's proposal, soon declared that India did not believe in the notion of big powers as the guardian of security for India or its neighbors.

As part of the new public campaign pushing the proposed pact, a Radio Peace and Progress commentary on March 23, 1972, suggested that both Bangladesh and Pakistan should enter into agreements with the Soviet Union on the model of the Indo–Soviet treaty of 1971. Principles embodied in the Indo–Soviet treaty, the commentator claimed, were applicable to "any other people of the Asian Continent who want to live independently and freely."[16] Brezhnev, shrewd enough to emphasize that in Asia the security system would not be of "military blocs," but of "good-neighbourly cooperation by all interested states," claimed in his March 20, 1972, foreign policy speech to the Soviet Trade Union Congress that interest in his proposal was growing. Soviet press commentators repeatedly made the same claim,[17] despite the fact that most Asian governments balked at joining the Russian-sponsored scheme because, if for no other reason, they did not care to be sucked into the Sino–Soviet spat. Kosygin commended the plan during the Moscow welcome for the Afghan Prime Minister on March 16, 1972, and the Premier's speech was broadcast in eleven Asian languages as well as English. Visits to Moscow in October by Malaysian Prime Minister Tun Abdul Razak and the Shah of Iran gave the Soviets new opportunities to press their case.

In the face of the Soviets' mid-1972 propaganda offensive, Asian governments remained unconvinced, and the Kremlin switched tactics again, this time reverting to nongovernmental channels. They spread the Brezhnev plan gospel at a series of conferences, such as the Afro–Asian Peoples' Solidarity Organization (AAPSO) executive committee meeting in Aden in February 1973, the "peace" conventions in India and Nepal, and the Afro–Asian Women's Conference in Ulan Bator. A leading role in this new campaign was played by the World Peace Council (WPC), which held the Conference on Asian Security and Cooperation in Dacca May 23–26, 1973; this was a preliminary to the World Congress of Peace Forces, held in Moscow in October 1973, at which Brezhnev again spoke on his favorite idea for Asia.[18]

Meanwhile the Soviets were also "expanding economic ties in the name of establishing the 'material basis' of collective security."[19] Hoping that friendship treaties with developing countries might contribute to the construction of a wider economic network under its aegis, the U.S.S.R. in 1972–1973—in an apparent attempt to revive Kosygin's 1969 trade and transit plan—began to stress the importance of greater economic cooperation as the basis for regional security. Moscow Radio told Asia on September 30, 1972, that the three subcontinent countries, as well as Afghanistan and Nepal, were interested in "setting [in motion] regional cooperation with Soviet participation"—a contention that, at least insofar as Pakistan was concerned, was erroneous. On October 2, 1972, Moscow Radio lauded the Soviet Union's economic relations with India, Afghanistan, and Iraq "as an example to other Asian countries." The Soviets' technique was to stress first, through these radio commentaries and other media, "innocuous economic cooperation" and then to reveal their primary desire for the security plan.

India, in particular, has been subject to the Soviets' economic inducements with security pact implications. The Soviet Union and India signed an agreement on September 19, 1972, to set up a Commission "on economic, scientific and technical cooperation," presumably in accordance with article 6 of the 1971 friendship treaty. With the agreement stipulating that each country will take into account the needs of the other's economy when formulating national plans, one of the Commission's tasks is to supervise the implementation and operation of joint ventures.[20] In September 1972, when Planning Minister D. P. Dhar visited the U.S.S.R. to secure assistance for India's fifth five-year plan, due to start in 1974, the pro-Moscow Indian newspaper *Patriot* even recommended that India be linked with the Soviet bloc Council for Mutual Economic Assistance (CMEA). Mrs. Gandhi rejected the idea. But how well India fends off increasing Soviet pressure for 'economic cooperation'—and then for security system membership—is to be watched carefully. The South Asia Triangle will shake if the Soviets manage to induce India and, through India, Bangladesh to endorse their economic and military moves in South and Southeast Asia.

In response to Iran's U.S.-aided arms buildup—and the possible implications of that buildup for Pakistan—Indian Defense Minister Jagjivan Ram dashed to Moscow on a ten-day visit beginning July 7, 1973, with a long shopping list of Soviet weapons.[21] Indian defense policy makers, engaged in formulating a security plan for the next five years, had modified their earlier calculations as the Shah of Iran pledged to "protect the territorial integrity" of "New" Pakistan. New Delhi thought Washington had helped prompt that pledge. "In India's eyes," noted *The Guardian* on July 9, 1973, "American objectives are much wider and include—apart from building up an anti-Soviet bulwark . . . —a considered policy to build up a counterpoise to India, now that Pakistan can no longer play this role." Iran is constructing at Chah Bahar, on the Markan coast barely 50 miles from the Pakistani border, a naval and air base bigger than any other it has built in this region. Since Indian naval superiority in the Arabian Sea played a decisive role during the 1971 fighting, Indian admirals are worried at the prospect of a modern Iranian fleet coming to Pakistan's aid in any future Indo–Pakistan war.[22]

The arming of Iran, principally by the United States, is resulting in additional leverage for the Kremlin because of the alarms it sounds in New Delhi. India is still militarily superior to Iran and Pakistan combined, and it would be naïve to think that the Shah will open his new arsenal to Pakistan for any military adventure against India. Yet the Indians have. always been most sensitive to the slightest bulging of Pakistan's military potentialities, and Bhutto's recent boasts have not reassured them. In mid-1973 Bhutto told a Western correspondent that "the fall of Dacca was the beginning of the fall of India" and that "because they beat us once they cannot beat us always."[23] The Prime Minister's tone was "very different from [that of] the man who signed the Simla agreement with Mrs. Gandhi a year ago"—a difference, as *The Economist* pointed out, that may be explained partly by Bhutto's volatile personality; but Bhutto unquestionably has been reinforced in his new mood "by the thought of all these Iranian fighter-bombers at his rear."[24]

Hence, despite India's growing dependence on Moscow for military help, Jagjivan Ram scurried to Moscow for more help that could only yield more dependence. "Although most Indians regard India as an autonomous center of powers and Indo–Soviet alliance as a coalition of two co-equals," Bhabani Sen Gupta candidly observed, "the fact remains that much of the recent accretion to India's influence is the result of the powerful support it received from the U.S.S.R."[25] That a weakening of that support would cripple India is also a fact, and the Kremlin leaders are well aware of it.

Soviet fortunes in South Asia have waxed in intimate relation to Indo–Soviet ties. Departing from its initial period of indifference and hostility toward the subcontinent, the Soviet Union reexamined bourgeois nationalist movements and, by the mid-1950s, began courting New Delhi. The relationship became increasingly close as Moscow sided with India during the 1962 war with China and the 1965 and 1971 Pakistani wars, as it delivered huge arms orders, and as it concluded the 1971 treaty of friendship. Now the Soviets were pushing for open alliance.

Between the time of the announcement on October 3, 1973, and Brezhnev's visit to India the following month, hardly a day elapsed without the Soviet papers describing the Indians' anticipation of this "occurrence of tremendous importance," this "major, historic milestone"; "India hails Brezhnev's visit with its whole heart," claimed Moscow's press media.[26] One of Brezhnev's main objectives in going to India was to counteract Chinese efforts to discredit the U.S.S.R. among nonaligned nations; Moscow fretted when Middle East elder statesman President Habib Bourguiba of Tunisia echoed Peking's condemnation of "superpower hegemony." Peking's denial of great power status and its claim to champion "small and medium" countries unsettled Kremlin leaders, as did its support of the proposal put forward by Sri Lanka, Iran, and others for a "zone of peace" in the Indian Ocean; the proposal, according to China, furthered the "struggle against domination by some big powers and their efforts to create zones of influence."[27] In addition, Soviet propagandists pointed to alleged Chinese inspiration for Singapore Prime Minister Lee Kuan Yew's call, made at a Tokyo press conference on May 11, 1973, for the formation of an international naval task force to counter growing Soviet influence.[28]

If India no longer spoke with "the global voice" as in the heyday of Nehru, it remained "in the great game of Sino–Soviet rivalry a very substantial piece on the board."[29] Thus Brezhnev journeyed to India to squeeze out maximum political support and to check up on reports that New Delhi might begin to explore possibilities for improved relations with China—Moscow, of course, would regard such exploration as an unfriendly act.[30]

In regard to the Asian collective security plan, observers expected Brezhnev to carry with him to India one of two contrasting strategies. One was to drop the poorly received security plan altogether, inaugurating in its place a "peace offensive" in which India would be given the leading role. India would be praised as a stable and strong "bastion of anti-imperialism and peace," and its treaty of friendship with the U.S.S.R., augmented by additional fruitful aid and trade agreements, would serve as an example for others to follow; Bangladesh, Afghanistan, and even Pakistan would be among potential signatories to friendship treaties along the lines of the Indian treaty of 1971.[31] The other strategy that observers thought Brezhnev might pursue in India entailed not scrapping the collective security plan, but furthering it. The Soviet chief would pressure India to endorse his plan and thus not only cement the Soviet–Indian relationship but also render less likely Sino–Indian détente.

Brezhnev chose the latter strategy. "In a word, we are calling for an active, broad and constructive discussion," he told the Indian Parliament in forceful advocacy of a plan that Asia had already insisted it did not want. "The opportunity has arrived and the present situation in Asia has created prerequisites. Asia can and must become a continent of peace."[32] It is ironic that Brezhnev chose Parliament, where Nehru had denounced military pacts, to press the case for "the Russian version of SEATO." Mrs. Gandhi did not endorse Brezhnev's speech, but what went on behind the closed doors of the conference room is still debated. Some diplomats in New Delhi, mostly Europeans, gathered that Brezhnev gained major economic and political leverage and tacitly furthered the doctrine of Asian security. "I cannot help feeling that the Indians, in relations to the Soviet Union, take short-term steps to satisfy immediate needs," was the way one diplomat put it.[33] Other diplomats and most Indians, however, maintained that in signing various agreements Mrs. Gandhi strengthened economic ties while paying no price in political concessions. "We were not bullied," insisted one Indian government official, "and we are not toeing their line."[34]

Although details were not disclosed, it is known that a fifteen-year economic agreement signed during Brezhnev's visit provided Soviet assistance focusing on India's needs in steel, coal mining, oil exploration, and power generation. "There can be no doubt," wrote the *Times of India* on the agreement, "that Mr. Brezhnev's visit will open new vistas of Indo–Soviet economic cooperation in the next five years or more."[35] *Tass* Director General Leonid M. Zamyatin, who accompanied Brezhnev, said in New Delhi that "the exhaustive talks with Indian leaders have confirmed the extensive mutual understanding between the Soviet Union and India on major international problems. . . ."[36]

In a debate in Parliament on December 6, members of opposition parties voiced concern over the Soviet Union's growing influence, decrying alleged "secret agreements" that were said to include the grant of port facilities in India for Soviet naval vessels. In response, Foreign Minister Singh denied that India's ports had been opened to Soviet military use.[37]

It is likely that the U.S.S.R. secured some of the concessions that Mrs. Gandhi's government denied granting. While Brezhnev was in India, his hosts expressed interest in MIG 23 interceptors, fighter-bombers, mobile SAM-6 antiaircraft missiles, and assistance in plans for new naval vessels. I know from my experience in Pakistan from 1967 through 1970 that the Soviets provide arms, particularly of the most sophisticated variety, only in return for political as well as cash rewards.

Vexing the Pakistanis

The Pakistanis recollect with great bitterness the Soviet military and diplomatic support to India during the 1971 war, and it was out of fear and not love that Bhutto dashed to Moscow in March 1972. Reportedly, Bhutto had a rough time in Moscow: only if Pakistan followed the Indian and Bangladeshi precedent and signed a so-called treaty of friendship, warned the stern Soviet chiefs, could its territorial integrity be preserved. The March 18, 1972, joint communiqué issued at the end of Bhutto's visit contained, as expected, no cheerful words for the frustrated Pakistanis. Although the U.S.S.R. resumed economic aid in 1973 with the construction of a steel mill at Karachi, its attitude could hardly be described as cooperative, much less friendly.[38] The fragile honeymoon of the late 1960s had ended as the Soviets—who had always considered New Delhi before Islamabad—turned on the Pakistanis following Yahya's rejection of the Brezhnev and Kosygin plans for security and economic groupings and eventually, in contrast to their stand in 1965, came out fully against Pakistan in 1971. Certainly, Bhutto did not publicly reflect the Soviet hostility. "I am glad to say," he claimed in an April 1973 *Foreign Affairs* article, "that there has recently been a mental improvement in our relations with the Soviet Union";[39] but such improvement was surely not demonstrated at his Moscow talks. Noted the hosts, "If history were to repeat itself we would again take the same position [in the Bangladesh crisis] because we are convinced that it was correct."[40]

The implications of this Soviet statement on Bangladesh are profound when one considers the turbulence and rebellion in sections of Baluchistan and the Northwest Frontier. The Soviet role in current political unrest in Pakistan's "Wild West" was dramatized by the seizure of Russian arms smuggled through the Iraqi Embassy in Islamabad.[41] Baghdad Radio calls for a "greater Baluchistan" and Kabul Radio propagandizes for Pakhtoonistan, and Pakistan draws unpleasant, anti-Soviet conclusions. The 1973 Afghan coup, which was alleged to have Soviet blessing and established new rulers who threatened to press the old issue of Pakhtoonistan,[42] is regarded by Islamabad as a function of Soviet browbeating to induce Pakistan to accept the Brezhnev security system. Further fragmentation of Pakistan and the creation of Soviet client states of Baluchistan and Pakhtoonistan would fulfill the old czarist ambition of a

warm-water port in the south. Stability in the area would be threatened, and Iran as well as Pakistan might be endangered.

In Bengali Favor?

Of the great powers, the Soviet Union was the first to recognize
Bangladesh. After Mrs. Gandhi, Brezhnev, Podgorny, and Kosygin
were the first to send Prime Minister Mujib and President Abu
Sayeed Choudhury warm congratulations. Mujib, for his part, said
on his return home:

> While Bangladesh believes in the policy of friendship to all
> and malice toward none, she has special reasons to be grateful to
> the Soviet Union which had protested to the Pakistan authorities
> against the genocide of the Bengalis. We remember the Indian
> and Soviet roles; for that reason, I made my first visit to India;
> next I will visit the Soviet Union.[43]

The Soviet Union is attempting to please and, perhaps, penetrate
the new state through cooperation, exchange, and aid in such fields
as science, art, literature, education, public health, the media, and
sport. The Soviet aims are political, but Mujib seems to be unaware
of this. He also seems to overlook the fact that as late as 1967 the
U.S.S.R. disapproved of his Awami League, as demonstrated by a
March 16, 1967, Radio Peace and Progress broadcast: "The reactionaries from the Awami League," the broadcast ran in part, "have
exposed themselves for the whole country to see as American hire-
lings and traitors to the nation's unity." Not until August 14, 1970,
when all quarters considered sure Mujib's success in the upcoming
national elections, did the same station conclude that the Awami
League, headed by the "distinguished East Pakistani politician Mujibur Rahman," is to be found "standing in the vanguard of the
left-wing forces."

As regards Soviet aid to Bangladesh, the figure for fiscal 1972–
1973 was about $137 million, less than 11 percent of Bangladesh's
total foreign aid for the period and less than either the United
States or India contributed.[44] As part of its aid the Soviet Union
financed a much-publicized salvage operation at the seaports of
Chittagong and Chalna, and as a result the Soviet Navy seemed to
gain an opportunity to extend its influence in the waters surrounding the subcontinent;[45] the lengthy operation, however, created

misgivings in some quarters in Bangladesh.[46] What is more, Mujib criticized pro-Moscow political parties when violent demonstrations erupted in Dacca and elsewhere against U.S. bombing in North Vietnam. On the eve of the March 1973 elections, Soviet Ambassador Papov, suspected of encouraging National Awami party (NAP) pro-Moscow factions led by Professor Muzaffer Ahmed, was recalled from Dacca, presumably at the request of Mujib. With his recall, followers in Bangladesh lost their "viceroy," according to some observers.[47] The lessening of enthusiasm for Moscow was further demonstrated by the replacement after the elections of Foreign Minister Abdus Samed Azad, noted for his pro-Soviet views, with a well-known pro-Westerner, Dr. Kamal Hossain. Soviet-leaning Tajuddin Ahmed was deprived of the important portfolio of Planning, although he remained in the Cabinet as Minister of Finance until November 1974.[48]

But with the conclusion of the New Delhi–Dacca "treaty of friendship and cooperation," the Soviets believed their diplomatic objective, to draw Bangladesh under the umbrella of the Asian collective security scheme, had been achieved. Things became still brighter for the U.S.S.R. on September 3, 1973, when Mujib aligned with the pro-Moscow faction of the NAP and the Communist party of Bangladesh (CPB) to drive against dormant rightist as well as pro-China NAP elements.

AFTER BANGLADESH: THE AMERICAN ROLE

Gestures and Recriminations

"A great American love affair is over," said Henry Kissinger after the great events of 1971.[49] Henry Brandon, who quoted Kissinger's remarks, explained, "For a long time India could do no wrong and India could count on American Cornucopia";[50] Americans now knew better and would act differently. Despite the extreme, and largely unjustified, criticism of President Nixon's policy in the 1971 crisis, criticism that flourished with the natural upsurge of sympathy for the suffering humanity of Bangladesh, the truth about the roles of the three major powers and India has begun to come out. Newspapers such as the *New York Times* and writers such as Henry Brandon and Stanley Hoffmann now contend, for instance, that as early as April 1971 the Indian Cabinet reached a "secret decision" to resort to war against Pakistan,[51] and they point to "Moscow's successful exploitation of India's desire to dismantle Pakistan."[52]

Americans have vacillated in their feelings and actions toward India, with each administration in Washington following a policy slightly different than the one that preceded it. From President Truman's warm message of welcome through the present, however, the United States has always sought India's friendship. Even at those times when Washington seemed to favor the Pakistanis, it did not overlook the Indians—Dulles wanted the same anticommunist bulwark in India that he thought he molded in Pakistan, and even Pakistan's friend Nixon worked hard to patch up relations before and after the 1971 war. Indeed, there have been persistent calls in America to forget Pakistan in the pursuit of more sturdy ties with its neighbor.

In the post-1971 era some scholars, Professor Norman D. Palmer among them, urge the United States to "maintain friendly relations with what is left of Pakistan, which is an important member of the family of nations."[53] Others, however, suggest, as does John P. Lewis, that

> Surely no one in our [the U.S.] government can longer have any doubt about the fact of *Indian hegemony within the Subcontinent* [italics added] and therefore about the need for what Mr. Galbraith has called a "North American solution" (referring to the strategic accommodations between ourselves and the Canadians and Mexicans).[54]

This analysis is ill conceived. Indian hegemony is a pleasant notion to the Indians, who, in the wake of their victory, revived the old idea of confederation. Indian Foreign Secretary T. N. Kaul expressed the view that in the new era of peace a union among India, Pakistan, and Bangladesh could subsequently be expanded to include such other regional entities as Nepal, which badly needs improved transit facilities.[55] But Pakistan, truncated as it is, would fight against a North American solution, and even in Bangladesh such an idea is anathema. Today in "secular" Bangladesh the anti-Indian sentiments run strong and deep. Nirad Chaudhri proved correct in his prediction, made within five days of the creation of Bangladesh, that the "vicious spiral of Hindu–Muslim hatred" would not be eliminated in dealings between India and the new nation through the former's "thoughtless triumphing and gloating over humiliation inflicted on Pakistan."[56] Wrote *The Guardian* on August 22, 1972, "To be identified with India is about the last thing most Bangladeshis now want."

It is heartening to note that the U.S. government, at present, does not seem to accept Indian hegemony. In his 1973 foreign policy report President Nixon reaffirmed "our concern for the well-being and security of the people of Pakistan" and expressed interest in Bangladesh's "genuine non-alignment." The President also said that the United States respects India as a major country: "We are prepared to treat India in accordance with its new stature and responsibilities, on the basis of reciprocity. . . ."[57] But a January 1972 Indian interpretation of the Indo–American relationship contrasted with Nixon's:

> A strong India, *dominating its neighbours,* would definitely not suit U.S. global strategy. It would, therefore, be unrealistic to expect any improvement in Indo–American relations in the near future. In fact, with the Indian government also trying to work its way up towards a big-power status of sorts, the situation may be expected to deteriorate.[58]

Even if the United States were not interested in an Indo–Pakistani balance of power, it would take time to mend ties between New Delhi and Washington following Nixon's denunciation of India's role in the dismemberment of Pakistan. Mrs. Gandhi took revenge by assailing the U.S. bombing in Vietnam: "Would this sort of war or savage bombing which has taken place in the Vietnam war have been tolerated for so long had the people been European?"[59]

What are the prospects of ending what Norman Palmer has called "the 'cold war' between India and the United States?"[60] There are compelling reasons for improving relations between the world's largest democracy and its most powerful. First, India needs today as never before vast quantities of foreign aid. After twenty years of planned growth, concluded *The Observer* (London) on December 16, 1973, "India is effectively moving backwards . . . unprecedented inflation is believed to be adding thousands every month to the number—officially estimated at 250 million a year ago—of those who live below the poverty line." The cost of the "Bangladesh operation" and of the subsequent reconstruction of the new nation damaged India's already strained economy, as do continued huge expenditures on the military—New Delhi spends more than $2 billion annually for defense.[61] Then there is a problem crippling many developing (and developed) nations: "India is finding itself peculiarly vulnerable to the oil crisis," reported the *Washington Post* on January 30, 1974, "and the government, faced with the prospect of the economy grinding to a halt, appears to be stunned into ineffective fumbling." Since independence the Americans have been India's most generous benefactors in the economic sphere, and in the present conditions their continued help is all but indispensable.

At the October 1973 Conference on U.S.–South Asian Relations in the 1970s, convened by the Foreign Policy Research Institute, the consensus of the scholars in attendance was that America should increase the level of aid to India and the rest of South Asia. The trend does indeed appear to be toward more aid. Suspended during the 1971 war, U.S. economic assistance was resumed in 1972; the United States also participated in the World Bank's 1972 plan to reschedule the Indian foreign debt. The Aid to India Consortium met in early 1973 to consider India's request for $700 million of foreign aid, including $200 million from the United States, for its development projects under the fifth five-year plan.[62] Another recent Indo–American economic agreement stipulates that the United States will dispose of the equivalent of $2.2 billion in American "blocked rupee" holdings in India, which will then be used over the next five years for Indian development. Hailed as removing a key spoiler in American–Indian relations, this agreement opens the way to accelerated trade relations and further scientific and cultural exchanges.[63]

In the political and diplomatic spheres, we have already seen that in the 1970s South Asia constitutes a "low priority" area for the United States, in contrast to the Soviet Union and China. India should have no objections to the broad U.S. policy objectives of regional peace and stability and domination by no single major power. But the old issue of America's "help" to Pakistan is still an irritating factor. After the Nixon administration announced on March 14, 1973, resumption of some military shipments to Pakistan, amid the expected uproar in the Indian Parliament Foreign Minister Singh declared that the Americans, who claimed the arms to Pakistan would not hurt India, were given to prevarication.[64] Similarly, a statement by Assistant Secretary of State Joseph Sisco before the House Subcommittee on the Near East and South Asia—"We would regard any new threat to Pakistan's integrity as disruptive to the progress toward peace and stability in South Asia"[65]—was considered further evidence of "tilt toward Pakistan." Do not Indian objections to such a statement lend credence to Pakistan's fears of Indian imperialism and Indo–Soviet designs?

New Delhi cordially received new Ambassador Daniel P. Moynihan, a former aide of President Kennedy and an exponent of "a time for healing, a time for understanding, a time for sharing" between India and the United States.[66] In his 1973 foreign policy report, Nixon referred to Moynihan's reception as "a sign that passage of time and constructive attitudes on both sides have laid a foundation for a serious improvement in our relations."[67] But so far responses to the Nixon administration attempts to mend relations have been halfhearted or indefinite. In reply to Nixon's 1973 report, it was Foreign Minister Singh—not Prime Minister Gandhi—who spoke of the need for better bilateral understanding. India took exception to the Kashmir reference in the Shanghai communiqué issued at the end of Nixon's historic visit to China in 1972. Mrs. Gandhi also charged, without proper documentation, that the United States played a role in the 1973 Chilean coup and the death of President Salvadore Allende Gossens.[68]

Yet it is too pessimistic to say that there will be no good relations as long as Republicans occupy the White House. One should remember that Eisenhower was the target of violent criticism in 1954 for the same reason that Nixon was attacked in 1971—for allegedly favoring Pakistan. But this same Eisenhower was greeted as a "man of peace" when he visited India in 1959 in the midst of growing Sino–Indian tensions over the Himalayas. After all, India is a mature nation; Mrs. Gandhi knows how to further the interests of her country.

The Alliance Continues (More or Less)

After the Bangladeshi war, some looked upon Pakistan as a lost cause. These persons were mistaken. Within the short period of two years Pakistan has shown strategic and political as well as some economic strength. Even after its dismemberment, Pakistan retains strategic significance in Asia. "Throughout history," as Bhutto often remarks, "the part of the subcontinent now comprising Pakistan has been of vital importance as a gateway for trade and passage of people."[69] Politically, the more active role Pakistan has assumed of late in the affairs of the Middle East was dramatized by its February 1974 hosting of the Islamic Summit Conference on the Middle East. For their part, the Muslim countries of the Middle East have shown active interest in Pakistan's viability and territorial integrity. Thus, if the "new order" in the subcontinent does not favor Pakistan, at least it has not proved as bad as Pakistanis feared immediately after the catastrophes of December 1971.

President Nixon's role in 1971 pleased Pakistanis,[70] but there is fear that when a Democrat reaches the White House again U.S. policy may change adversely, as it did in the early 1960s. "Since its inception Pakistan has greatly benefited from the United States' development assistance," said Bhutto at an Islamabad reception marking the 196th anniversary of the signing of the Declaration of Independence. "Pakistan has had good relations with the United States. There were times when we experienced a few setbacks but now relations are again improving." Bhutto expressed the hope that the United States "can play a most beneficial role not only in helping our economic reconstruction and development but also in safeguarding our security."[71] The continuation of U.S. economic aid, American military aid shipments—resumed in October 1970 but suspended during the civil war in 1971—and the U.S. assurances vis-à-vis Pakistani territorial integrity[72] suggest a period of good bilateral relations for the foreseeable future. So, too, does the revived Pakistani interest in CENTO, an interest that reflects Islamabad's uneasiness over Soviet moves in the area. Pakistan participated fully in the June 1973 ministerial meeting in Tehran. This is ironic, since Bhutto once demanded that Pakistan withdraw from CENTO and SEATO. (On November 8, 1972, he did indeed drop out of SEATO, but this was because of the loss of East Pakistan and not because of policy differences with fellow members.)[73]

Despite all this, the U.S.–Pakistan special relationship of the mid-1950s is over for good, gone with the international environment in which it developed. The new, more pragmatic relationship is likely to be based on political dynamics in South Asia. In his 1973 foreign policy report Nixon spoke in friendly terms: "The United States has always had a close and warm relationship with Pakistan and we have a strong interest today in seeing it build a new future."[74] Although both Mrs. Gandhi and Mujib also visited North America in 1973, only Bhutto was greeted warmly in Washington (in September) by Nixon. Bhutto made a number of friendly speeches in the United States, and he tried his best to revive the old ties between the two countries.[75] Stated the joint communiqué issued at the end of Bhutto's visit, "President Nixon assured Prime Minister Bhutto of strong U.S. support for Pakistan's independence and territorial integrity which he considered a guiding principle of American foreign policy."[76] But the U.S. promised no arms supplies.[77] I learned from reliable sources, furthermore, that Washington has shown less concern in recent months over Soviet moves in Pakistan's turbulent North-West Frontier Province and Baluchistan than it did immediately after the 1971 crisis. Ambassador Moynihan's efforts to improve American ties with New Delhi are also being watched with concern in Pakistan.

A Relationship Begins

An initial period of coolness from both sides was to be expected, but the process of rapprochement came surprisingly quickly. Mujib, at least, knows that the United States did not oppose the legitimate aspirations of the Bengalis and that it helped to save his life. More important in the rapprochement has been the realization that U.S. economic aid is of great importance in alleviating the desperate economic conditions confronting Bangladesh. After some delay the United States recognized Bangladesh and the exchange of ambassadors was announced. In May 1972, less than two months after U.S. recognition, a bilateral agreement was signed under which the U.S. government made available $90 million.[78] This marked a watershed in Bangladesh–U.S. relations, which had been bogged down in Bengali resentment and frustration over American support to the Yahya regime in 1971. By the end of 1973 the United States had given about $347 million, amounting to over 27 percent of Bangladesh's total external aid and the largest single contribution.

As the need for economic development is a prime consideration in the formulation of foreign policy in Bangladesh, it will continue to seek U.S. friendship—and assistance—for at least the next five to seven years. But will America seek the friendship of Bangladesh —is it of strategic significance to U.S. policy in the Asia–Pacific system? A story circulated in Dacca following the civil war held that the United States wanted a base on Minipura Island in the Bay of Bengal; Bangladesh could be the Americans' last "Eastern staging post," it was said, after they pulled out of Southeast Asia. Americans in Dacca reportedly scoffed at the story: "This goddam place? You must be joking." A naval expert with experience in the Bay of Bengal confirmed that it would be a poor area in which to plant a base—channels do not permit very large ships, and channel course changes from one year to the next make access to the Indian Ocean problematic.[79] Still, Americans seem interested in making Bangladesh truly independent of both India and Moscow, and for this reason they are likely to work with Dacca in the years ahead.

AFTER BANGLADESH: THE CHINESE ROLE

Détente?

The year 1971 brought diplomatic success to China almost everywhere but in South Asia, where Peking, like Washington, suffered a setback and was unfairly maligned.

The 1971 crisis crippled the already stumbling Sino–Indian relationship, but it also proved that China was not prepared to assist Pakistan in any military confrontation with India, that New Delhi's fears of an "axis" against it were exaggerated. In the war's aftermath, Peking reportedly offered India the following: One decade after the India–China war it would renew full diplomatic relations with India if India released Pakistani prisoners of war and resolved such other outstanding issues over Bangladesh as the trial of 150 Pakistani prisoners. On India's side, on August 9, 1973, Deputy Foreign Minister S. P. Singh confirmed before Parliament that "there have been certain indications of a change on China's part,"[80] and even before that Foreign Minister Swaran Singh frankly told the same body that India, in a "mood of realism," wanted to make up with both Washington and Peking.[81] But no concrete improvement in relations between Peking and New Delhi has yet been effected. Peking still believes India to be the Soviet Union's "largest client" in its diplomatic and military moves against China, a belief reinforced by Brezhnev's November 1973 use of the Indian Parliament as a forum for extolling his collective security scheme. Similarly, China's continued military support of Pakistan is regarded as a hostile act by Indians, who are also unsettled by the current political unrest in Bangladesh. India is not likely to move toward

Peking if this would endanger its relationship with Moscow, and Peking will probably not seek New Delhi's friendship at the expense of Islamabad's.

Persisting, then, are the triangular relationships that complicated subcontinent affairs before the 1971 crisis. A few commentators, such as the Indian writer T. K. Hussain, have called for a reappraisal of these vicious triangles and the relationships they delimit:

> India, till now, missed the point that collusion between China and Pakistan may not be total though outwardly China might assure Pakistan of her support and sympathy. . . . There are also several stimulants on the Chinese side to normalize relations with India. In the Seventies, China does not consider India as a major competition in the international field. . . . It may be persuaded to ease tensions with India in view of its concentration on the Soviet problem.[82]

But since this assessment, published three months before the war, China has promised Pakistan continued support and no limit to its friendship for the sake of "bigger India." Furthermore, China has made clear that it expects Pakistan to shun any agreement with India that would jeopardize China's interests—this stern expectation was voiced (by Vice-Foreign Minister Chiao Kuan-hua during his sudden visit in August 1972) at a time when Prime Minister Bhutto was considering "a thousand years of peace" instead of "a thousand years of confrontation" with India.

The Bonds Remain Tight

Bhutto declared more than once that Peking's friendship, maintained with only slight interruption since the mid-1950s, would be cherished, and the first great power he visited as head of government was, of course, China. Although not happy with Pakistan's clumsy handling of the Bangladesh issue, Peking in the Bhutto visit's joint communiqué condemned "Indian naked aggression" and reiterated "firm support to the Pakistan Government and people in their just struggle to preserve their state sovereignty and territorial integrity against outside aggression." China also expressed its backing of Pakistan in the Nixon-Chou communiqué of February 27, 1972.[83] Declared Bhutto after his March 1972 Moscow visit: "Pakistan would always value the friendly help rendered by China. . . . We will never be a party to any conspiracy against China."[84]

Pakistan–China friendship was dramatized in 1973 by Army Chief of Staff General Tikka Khan's Peking trip, which was followed by fresh shipments to Pakistan of military equipment, including tanks and MIG 19 aircraft. With these shipments, according to reliable sources in Pakistan, China's total military aid equaled the sum of U.S. arms provided Pakistan during the period 1954–1965. On a twelve-day visit Chang Tsai-chien, Deputy Chief of Staff of the Chinese People's Liberation Army, and his military mission were welcomed by Bhutto for talks that "will contribute greatly to a far better understanding between our two countries." In reply, Chang said, "In recent years the friendly relations and cooperation between our two countries in economic, cultural and military [spheres] have attained a new dimension."[85] There were reports that Chang offered Chinese help in the production of ground-to-ground missiles. These reports were refuted by the Pakistani Ministry of Foreign Affairs, but that did not mean they were necessarily incorrect.

Showing considerable restraint, China has put little pressure on Pakistan for a *quid pro quo* for its valuable help. China does make a few demands, however. As we have seen, during the 1965 war Peking required only that Pakistan not reach with India any Kashmir settlement giving "undue advantages" to the other side and hurting Chinese security interests. It is significant that Vice-Foreign Minister Chiao made his 1972 visit to Pakistan—urging Islamabad away from rapprochement with India and perhaps embarrassing a Prime Minister contemplating an "era of peace"—at a time when Aziz Ahmad was in India following up the Simla agreement.[86] Chiao's visit demonstrated that Sino–Pakistani relations would suffer if Bhutto or Wali Khan (the leader of the National Awami party) leaned too far in the direction of Moscow or New Delhi. Such rapprochement remains only a remote possibility, in view of the internal determinants of Pakistani foreign policy. (Among other factors, the army strongly favors retaining close links with Peking.) Thus good relations and cooperation in various spheres, based on mutual advantage and identity of interest, are likely to continue through the 1970s.

A Nonrelationship

Mujib's Awami League, which now runs Bangladesh, has never smiled on the People's Republic, and—with the new nation's memories of 1971 still strong—Bangladeshi–Chinese relations remain far from satisfactory. China has made some gestures, but Bangladesh, presumably under pressure from New Delhi and perhaps also Moscow, has ignored them.[87] The relationship's major limiting factors include, first, Peking's August 26, 1972, veto of Bangladeshi membership in the UN and its continued support of Pakistan in the UN and elsewhere, and, second, Peking's conflict with Bangladesh's two closest friends, India and the Soviet Union. At least until New Delhi and Peking begin to make up, Dacca and Peking are likely to remain similarly estranged.

There has been little overt activity in Bangladesh on the part of the Maoist guerrillas, many of whom have been brutally killed by the Awami League for "collaboration"—the label applied to any political opponent whom one wishes to eliminate in Bangladesh today. Yet it would be naïve to think that Peking has no channel through which it can influence the Bengali state, though there is no direct contact at the governmental level.[88] There were strident protests over China's veto of Bangladesh's entry into the UN, but Mujib and his government have shown caution in referring to China. In November 1972 Mujib said that he would welcome friendship with China. Despite the fact that Peking had sought to thwart them, said Mujib, the people of Bangladesh were still prepared to "let bygones be bygones."[89]

THE SUBCONTINENT TO NOVEMBER 1974

The Internal Forces

The most spectacular development of the year 1974 took place May 18, with India's detonation of a nuclear device.[90] Claiming that the explosion was for peaceful purposes, Prime Minister Gandhi named the first Indian nuclear bomb after Lord Buddha, who is revered all over the world as a prophet of peace.[91] But this did not still the worldwide criticism. Only the Soviet government and press appeared willing to accept India's claim of "peaceful intentions."[92] The Western press protested that the costly dawning of India's nuclear age came at a time when the nation faced ghastly economic crisis and a famine threatening millions of lives.[93]

Of course, it was Pakistan that protested the loudest.[94] From various sources it sought protection against what it termed the danger of "nuclear blackmailing."[95] At the annual CENTO ministerial meeting, held in Washington May 21 and 22, it was turned down in its request for coverage under a "nuclear umbrella."[96] Pakistan looked to Peking, and China, according to Western press reports and my Pakistani sources, pledged protection against the Indian nuclear threat.[97] As Pakistani Foreign Secretary Aga Shahi journeyed to Peking in June, China announced "full and absolute support to Pakistan against foreign aggression and interference including nuclear blackmail."[98]

My reports from reliable Pakistani sources indicate that the country will desperately attempt to attain nuclear parity with India. Never satisfied with Indian assurances of peaceful intent, such as those India used to give Canada and other countries that aided its nuclear program, Pakistan initiated a nuclear contingency plan in 1964.[99] Pakistan, like India, refused to sign the Nuclear Non-Proliferation Treaty. Declared Bhutto on one occasion, "If India builds the bomb, we will eat leaves or grass, even go hungry but we will have to get one of our own."[100] Of course neither Bhutto nor his government will confirm the existence of the contingency plan, but the Indian subcontinent might well become in the near future a zone of small-scale nuclear war.

This development is not inevitable, however, and a step away from it was recently taken in the United Nations. Pakistan, despite its own plans for nuclearization, in September 1974 proposed in the General Assembly adoption of "a formal agreement to declare South Asia as a nuclear free zone,"[101] a proposal endorsed by the foreign ministers of thirty-seven Islamic states at their meeting in Kuala Lumpur on June 26, 1974.[102] The Chinese Vice-Minister for Foreign Affairs, Chiao Kuan-hua, gave full support to the proposal in his October 2 speech before the General Assembly,[103] but India and initially the Soviet Union stood opposed. India took exception to the idea when it was discussed in the Political Committee of the General Assembly on October 28, pointing out that it had been put forward without the prior approval of the countries involved; the implication here seemed to be that India should have veto power over the denuclearization of South Asia. Bhutto failed to secure Soviet support for his country's proposal during his October Moscow visit, and it seemed likely that the U.S.S.R. would vote with India on the issue. The United States said that it generally favored the Pakistani suggestion but stipulated that a "nuclear-free zone must be approved by all regional countries,"[104] this position was much closer to the Indian view than to the Pakistani. Australia, Canada, and Japan were reported by the Pakistani press to support the proposal.[105] All indications from the Political Committee of the General Assembly were that India's opposition would kill the Pakistani move,[106] but these were misleading: on November 20 the motion swept through the General Assembly by an astounding 82-to-2 vote; only India and Bhutan voted against it.[107]

It is heartening to note that offices of both the United Nations and the U.S. Congress have expressed concern over India's nuclear explosion.[108] Unfortunately, however, Nobel peace prize recipient Henry Kissinger, eager to heal Indo–American relations, has baptized India's status as a nuclear power and declared his faith in India's pledge of peaceful usage.[109]

In the summer of 1974 India annexed Sikkim,[110] having first fomented internal disorder and, on the excuse of this disorder, sent troops to occupy the Himalayan kingdom. To the point was the title of an article in an American newsmagazine: "While India preaches peace—the record shows something else."[111]

Earlier, in February 1974, Pakistan recognized Bangladesh as Mujib participated in the Islamic Summit Conference in Lahore; the Bangladeshi chief and Bhutto publicly and dramatically demonstrated affection.[112] But when Bhutto went to Dacca to heal the wounds of 1971, his experiences were mixed. Muslims of Bangladesh, already resentful of Indian domination, came out by the thousands to welcome the Pakistani leader and to shout "Long live Pakistan," but the Mujib government arranged other demonstrations, hostile demonstrations featuring slogans such as "Butcher Bhutto go back."[113] The Prime Minister's visit ended in fiasco. In the meantime, however, some of the harsh legacies of the Bangladesh war were fading. The Pakistani prisoners held in India since December 1971 were released,[114] and China allowed the September Bangladeshi entry to the UN by not repeating its 1972 veto.[115]

But Bangladesh's economic disaster deepens—this nation does not belong to the Third World of emerging nations, claims one Western writer, but to the "Fourth World" of destitute nations.[116] After visiting Bangladesh in 1972, an economic mission of the World Bank rendered a gloomy report, "Reconstruction and Economy of Bangladesh." It read in part, "Even under the best of circumstances Bangladesh constitutes a critical and complex development problem."[117] Not the best but nearly the worst of circumstances have obtained since this report was prepared. "Bangladesh," reported the *Financial Times* of June 18, 1974, "is losing its real battle—that of trying to conjure up some means of economic survival for the poorest and most over-crowded people in the world." Wrote Claire Sterling: "No country so far, however poor, has reached the point where millions of its citizens actually die because they have nothing to eat. If there is a place on the planet facing that nightmare, this [Bangladesh] is it."[118] Most recent press reports indicate widespread starvation and malnutrition deaths in Bangladesh; fears have been expressed that over 1 million people will die in the near future.[119] The calamity is hardly alleviated by the government's corruption, inefficiency, and failure to stop food smuggling across the Indian borders. If Bangladesh explodes as a result of its desperate situation, South Asia may be rocked by upheaval as serious as that of 1971, and outside intervention—Soviet, Indian, or Chinese—could ensue.

Together with new tensions arising from economic chaos and famine, old Indo–Pakistani and Afghan–Pakistani tensions persist, as evidenced by recent charges and countercharges of troop concentration along unfriendly borders. On July 11, 1974, Pakistan reported "unusual troop movements" on its borders with India and Afghanistan, and Bhutto suggested that the alleged deployment could be part of a "grand design" of the two countries to intimidate Pakistan.[120] Both India and Afghanistan denied Pakistan's charges. India termed them "part of the usual Pakistani line that is brought up from time to time"[121] and pointed to alleged Pakistani troop movements,[122] while Afghanistan not only denied such movements of its own but also contended that Pakistan "has bombed [Afghan] border districts."[123] Then came Afghanistan's September war warning. Afghan Deputy Foreign Minister Waheed Abdullah said on September 23, 1974, that the "long-smoldering border dispute with Pakistan [would] erupt into a full-scale war in less than a month." Abdullah also declared that the "outburst would swiftly involve other countries," notably India and the Soviet Union; both countries stepped up arms shipments to, and training of, the Afghan military forces. Abdullah compared Afghan's concern in Pakhtoonistan to that of Turkey in Cyprus: "If Turkey can take such great interest in one million Turkish Cypriots, how can we ignore the fate of ten million of our Pakhtun brothers?"[124] Earlier in the summer there were reports of Chinese military activities in Tibet. According to press reports, the Chinese buildup followed Vice-Premier Teng Hsiaoping's reaffirmation of support to the Kashmiri people's right to self-determination.[125]

The Outside Forces

Soviet expansionist designs in the subcontinent and the Indian Ocean persist, based on Indo–Soviet collaboration—which, as I have pointed out, is perhaps the dominant feature of the post-1971 subcontinent. Unequivocal Soviet support for India was expressed in an article by V. Pavloksky.[126] And the U.S.S.R. continues to promote its Asian collective security plan. Referring to the positive objectives cited in the joint communiqué issued at the end of Brezhnev's visit to India in November 1973, the Soviet Ambassador in New Delhi claimed in the following August, "The creation of a Collective Security System would substantially facilitate the achievement of these goals."[127]

The joint communiqué issued at the end of Foreign Minister Singh's September 8–10, 1974, visit to Moscow expressed "satisfaction at the strengthening of Indo–Soviet friendship."[128] Continued Soviet military shipments as well as the U.S.S.R.'s prompt acceptance of India's claim of benign intentions in exploding the atomic bomb and annexing Sikkim reflect still growing Indo–Soviet collaboration.

This collaboration is further demonstrated by the apparent Indian dual standard in regard to the presence of U.S. and Soviet navies in the Indian Ocean. India complained to other countries in the Indian Ocean region about "the increasing American presence in the Indian Ocean," and Foreign Minister Singh told Parliament on March 2 that "U.S. naval forces are intending to stay in the Indian Ocean for a considerable period of time."[129] Singh also expressed strong disapproval of the U.S. decision to improve facilities at the British base on Diego Garcia Island. By contrast, although Indian spokesmen often claim that they are opposed to the Soviet naval presence, former British Foreign Secretary Sir Alec Douglas-Home pointed out that New Delhi has issued no public protest. Indian officials even try to justify the Soviet naval presence by arguing that the Soviet Union is nearly a littoral state and that the Soviets have not sought naval parity with the Americans in the Pacific or the Atlantic.[130] In the meantime, the Indian representative to the UN's Ad Hoc Committee on the Indian Ocean pays lip service to the concept of a "zone of peace" in the area, and New Delhi denies (and is disbelieved by some Pakistanis, Chinese, and others) that it has granted Indian Ocean bases.[131] The Soviet Union asserted on May 8 its right to send ships into the Indian Ocean and bitterly attacked China. *Tass* accused China "of purposely misrepresenting the Soviet naval presence in an effort to whip up anti-Soviet sentiment in the region."[132]

In Bangladesh, throughout 1974 the U.S.S.R. continued to seek expanded influence. Moscow prolonged the presence of its 200-vessel salvage fleet at Bangladesh's main port of Chittagong, and it announced assistance in the transportation and oil-and gas-prospecting fields. The Soviet Union and Eastern Europe have given high priority to cultural contacts with Bangladesh. The number of Bengali students in communist countries rose considerably in 1973–1974, and in the same time period the Soviet Embassy in Dacca imported over 300,000 copies of sixteen magazines and produced locally four magazines with a combined circulation of more than 3 million. After two years, distribution of Soviet periodicals in Bangladesh reached a scale comparable to that achieved in India after twenty. At the first open Congress of the Communist Party of Bangladesh, held December 4–9, 1973, Indian delegation chief Bhupesh Gupta declared that "friendship and cooperation among Bangladesh, India and Soviet Union has emerged as a powerful force in the struggle for peace and security in the subcontinent."[133] Mujib, in pursuance of his shoot-on-sight policy in regard to the extreme leftist Naxalites, seems to have leaned heavily on pro-Moscow forces in Bangladesh, and they continue to support him today.[134]

The Soviets persist in their blackmail and blandishments of Pakistan. Pakistanis strongly believe President Daud's government in Kabul has the support of Kremlin leaders in its hardening toward Pakistan and troublemaking in Pakistani frontier provinces. In his desperate attempts to lessen the Kremlin's wrath against Pakistan, Bhutto planned his second Moscow trip, but this was abruptly postponed from June to October 1974 by the Soviets. Finally reaching Moscow at the same time Henry Kissinger was there, Bhutto sought help in the growing Pakistani–Afghan crisis. Brezhnev and Kosygin showed correct protocol and met Bhutto at the airport,[135] but in the lengthy joint communiqué issued at the end of the visit there were hardly any encouraging words for Pakistan.[136] Kosygin piously expressed hope that Pakistan's border dispute with "our friendly neighbor, Afghanistan" would be resolved speedily.[137] It is evident that Moscow refuses to restrain Afghanistan in the absence of a Pakistani signature to a so-called friendship treaty with the Soviet Union, a treaty similar to those concluded with Afghanistan and India. But if Bhutto were to sign such a treaty he would forfeit

China's friendship—which, even if he were willing to do so, would not be tolerated by the Pakistani Army. Within Pakistan, the most popular aspect of national foreign policy since 1965 has been close friendship with China.[138]

Bhutto went to China for a second time in May 1974 and during his four-day visit had dialogues with Mao, Chou En-lai (despite the Premier's ill health), and other top Chinese leaders.[139] The joint communiqué issued at the end of the visit asserted that the trip had "made a significant contribution to the further consolidation of close relations between two countries and to deepening the friendship between the Chinese and Pakistani peoples." Returning home, Bhutto claimed his trip had "opened a new vigorous phase" in bilateral ties.[140]

At the moment, Pakistan's diplomatic options are extremely limited: the Soviets are still wrathful, the Americans are still unwilling to provide arms, and the Iranians are growing cool. Pakistan expected to gain some U.S. military supplies indirectly through Iran, but the Shah is not happy with Bhutto's flirting with such Arab leaders as Libya's Colonel Mu'ammar el-Quadhafi and the sheiks of the oil-producing gulf states.[141] The Shah's displeasure with Pakistan was reflected in his refusal to attend the February 1974 Islamic summit meeting in Pakistan. Indeed, the Shah received Mrs. Gandhi in Tehran in the spring of 1974, and the two countries have since been developing closer ties.[142] An Indian–Iranian Joint Commission has already met four times to discuss new areas of trade and economic collaboration. Iran, from which India imports most of the oil it consumes, has extended long-term credits to India for oil purchases, while India has offered Iran technical collaboration in the field of nuclear energy. On October 2, 1974, the Shah received a grand welcome in New Delhi when he returned Mrs. Gandhi's visit.[143] Thus Bhutto's clumsy handling of the Iranian relationship has led Pakistan's best friend to smile at Pakistan's worst enemy.

With fewer options, Pakistan must now rely on China as never before. The Pakistan Army is particularly wedded to the Chinese because no one else will supply the arms, and enough of them, that the generals say they need.

Bhutto therefore never misses an opportunity to promote the Sino–Pakistani relationship. On September 23, before fixing the date for his second Moscow visit, he went to Danyore (Gilgit), dressed himself in Mao's style, and won a big ovation from the Chinese people on the border. He attended a reception at the headquarters of the

Pakistan–China Highway and spoke loudly of continued friendship. Chinese Vice-Foreign Minister Chiao traveled to Pakistan on September 25 and talked about the Sino–Pakistani relationship in warm terms.[144]

China has made no significant move toward either New Delhi or Dacca; both relationships remain frozen. A diplomat currently in New Delhi told me recently, however, that New Delhi is prompted to improve relations with Peking because of worries over increasing Maoist influence in Bangladesh as a result of near-anarchic conditions there; India is equally concerned over growing anti-India feelings in Bangladesh. If Bangladesh falls to Maoist forces, it will be most difficult for Mrs. Gandhi to maintain control in her part of Bengal—West Bengal and Assam. How far New Delhi can move toward Peking without endangering its more important links with Moscow and whether and to what degree Peking will respond are crucial questions of South Asian *realpolitik*.

China still does not recognize Bangladesh. The main obstacle to links between China and Bangladesh, according to a Bengali official in London, is New Delhi's reluctance "to allow a dangerous inroad into a turbulent region." Bangladesh's foreign policy and defense policy are, in the final analysis, decided in New Delhi. The China–Bangladesh relationship, then, is dependent upon the Sino–Indian one, which in turn largely, though not wholly, reflects Sino–Soviet relations. South Asian diplomacy's vicious circles live on.

So, too, does at least some American involvement in the subcontinent—despite Washington's low profile. "India's relations with the United States have become confused, reflecting a significant conflict in the New Delhi Government," wrote Bernard Weinraub of the *New York Times* on Sept. 27, 1974. "The Americans are not quite sure what is going to happen next."[145] Pakistan, for its part, is desperately calling for a lifting of the arms embargo following the Afghan war threat.[146] There were reports in both the American and Pakistani press about a "possible U.S. arms sale to Pakistan."[147] Bangladesh also is issuing frantic appeals to Washington, but for economic assistance and food rather than guns. Mujib met President Ford in Washington on October 1 and secured agreement for the shipment of 100,000 tons of wheat and 50,000 tons of rice.[148]

And then came Henry Kissinger's visit to the subcontinent. Engaged in such other diplomatic activities as pursuit of détente with the Soviet Union and China and peace in Vietnam and the Middle East, the National Security Adviser and Secretary of State had not devoted much time to the subcontinent prior to his October 1974 visit, part of a wide-ranging tour. Arriving in New Delhi on October 28 for a two-day visit, Kissinger suffered what was termed a snub from Mrs. Gandhi, who was at first absent from the capital as the American sought to bury the past and improve ties between Washington and New Delhi.[149] The same Kissinger who in 1971 compared the "Indian invasion of East Pakistan to Hitler's reoccupation of Rhineland"[150] went a long way to accept India's promise to make only peaceful use of the atom, and he urged India "to prevent the spread of nuclear technology."[151] According to Indian and U.S. press sources, Kissinger's visit to New Delhi and his talks with Mrs. Gandhi eased relations.[152] It is too early, however, to predict a new wave of amity: more difficult than inducing Egypt's President Anwar el-Sadat to call the Secretary "brother Henry" despite the U.S. arms supply to Israel will be making Indira Gandhi smile despite Kissinger's statements in Islamabad that Pakistan's request for arms "will be given consideration."[153] If the U.S. gives Pakistan more arms—no matter that India remains much stronger and the Russian arms still flow into India—any gains made by Kissinger in New Delhi will be negated.

In Pakistan on October 31, Kissinger got a grand reception from Bhutto, who apparently revealed no resentment at Kissinger's conciliatory speeches and gestures in New Delhi.[154] A careful reading of the communiqués issued after Kissinger's stops in New Delhi and Islamabad suggests that the United States, eager to improve ties with India, accepts India's new status as a nuclear power and a great regional power but will not forsake Pakistan. Kissinger reaffirmed U.S. interest in the territorial integrity of Pakistan and, as noted, assured Bhutto of consideration but not necessarily delivery of additional U.S. arms supplies.

In Dacca, where the Secretary landed October 30 in the midst of hungry crowds, Kissinger's discussion concerned only emergency U.S. food supply shipments to starving Bangladeshis.[155]

PEACE AND STABILITY?

It is easier to conclude this study with hope for than expectation of an end to the violent, destructive conflicts among the subcontinent's 700 million poverty-stricken people. As we have seen, external factors have often complicated the quest for regional peace and will continue to do so in the late 1970s and 1980s. Let us hope that India and Pakistan and even Bangladesh will learn from the past the evil of a major power's expansionist designs. Let us hope that the United States and China will restrain or counterbalance the Soviet Union and prevent it from drawing the subcontinent wholly into its sphere of influence. Let us hope that all parties—internal and external—someday will allow the subcontinent to live in peace.

NOTES

1. *International Herald Tribune,* Dec. 26, 1971.

2. *Christian Science Monitor,* Dec. 22, 1971.

3. Bhabani Sen Gupta, "The New Balance of Power in South Asia," *Pacific Community,* July 1972, pp. 698–713.

4. Richard M. Nixon, *United States Foreign Policy for the 1970s: Building for Peace* (Washington: Government Printing Office, 1971).

5. U.S. House of Representatives, Committee on Foreign Affairs, Subcommittee on the Near East and South Asia, *Hearings,* Mar. 12, 15, 20, and 27, 1973 (Washington: Government Printing Office, 1973).

6. Based on my research at the Royal Institute of International Affairs and at Columbia University's Research Institute on Communist Affairs, 1971–1974.

7. William R. Kintner, *The Impact of President Nixon's Visit to Peking on International Politics* (Philadelphia: Foreign Policy Research Institute, Research Monograph Series, no. 13, 1972), p. 13.

8. Donaldson, *op. cit.,* p. 22; "House Leaders Report on China Trip," *Facts on File,* Aug. 6–12, 1972, p. 508F1.

9. *New York Times,* Feb. 17, 1972.

10. Rajan, "Bangladesh and After," *op. cit.*

11. *New York Times* and *Washington Post,* Sept. 19–21, 1973.

12. See the report of the Indian Economic and Scientific Research Foundation on National Security in *Overseas Hindustan Times,* Jan. 25, 1973.

13. Based on my research at the Royal Institute of International Affairs and at Columbia University's Research Institute on Communist Affairs, 1971–1974.

14. See "Soviet–Indian Treaty in Action," *New Times,* no. 39, 1971, pp. 10–11.

15. *Pravda,* Mar. 21, 1972.

16. Donaldson, *op. cit.,* p. 6.

17. See, for example, *Tass,* Oct. 20, 1972.

18. Based on my research at the Royal Institute of International Affairs and Columbia University's Research Institute on Communist Affairs, 1971–1974.

19. Donaldson, *op. cit.,* p. 27.

20. *The Statesman,* Sept. 20, 1972.

21. *Daily Telegraph,* July 9, 1973.

22. *The Guardian,* July 9, 1973.

23. *The Economist,* July 14, 1973.

24. *Ibid.*

25. Sen Gupta, "New Balance of Power," *op. cit.*

26. See *The Times* (London), Nov. 23, 1973.

27. See the Chinese Foreign Minister's speech in Tehran, June 16, 1973, in *Dawn,* June 17, 1973.

28. *Pravda,* May 13, 1973.

29. See *The Times* (London), editorial, Nov. 26, 1973.

30. See *The Times* (London), Nov. 23, 1973.

31. See *The Observer,* Nov. 28, 1973.

32. *New York Times,* Nov. 29, 1973.

33. *Ibid.,* Dec. 12, 1973.

34. *Ibid.*

35. *Times of India,* Nov. 28, 1973.

36. *New York Times,* Nov. 30, 1973.

37. *Ibid.,* Dec. 7, 1973.

38. See Choudhury, "Moscow's Influence," *op. cit.,* pp. 304–311.

39. Z. A. Bhutto, "Pakistan Builds Anew," *Foreign Affairs,* April 1973, pp. 541–554.

40. *Pravda,* Mar. 18, 1972.

41. Salmat Ali, "An Embarrassment of Arms," *Far Eastern Economic Review,* Feb. 19, 1973; *New York Times,* Feb. 11, 1973.

42. See *The Times* (London), July 27, 1973, *The Guardian,* July 19, 1973, and *Daily Telegraph,* Aug. 19, 1973.

43. Mujib's interview with *Tass* and Radio Moscow on Feb. 23, 1972, published in *Bangladesh Observer* (Dacca), Feb. 24, 1972.

44. See G. W. Choudhury, *Foreign Policy of "New" Pakistan and of Bangladesh,* a report prepared for the Foreign Policy Research Institute (Philadelphia: 1973).

45. Based on my research at the Royal Institute of International Affairs and Columbia University's Research Institute on Communist Affairs, 1971–1974.

46. *The Guardian,* Jan. 9, 1973.

47. Wernem Adam, "Let Them Eat Love," *Far Eastern Economic Review,* Apr. 9, 1973.

48. S. Kamaluddin, "Fat Cabinet," *Far Eastern Economic Review,* Apr. 2, 1973.

49. Henry Brandon, *The Retreat of American Power* (Garden City, N.Y.: Doubleday & Company, Inc., 1973), p. 269.

50. *Ibid.,* p. 249.

51. *Ibid.*

52. Stanley Hoffmann, "Weighing the Balance of Power," *Foreign Affairs,* July 1972.

53. Norman D. Palmer, "The United States and the New Order in South Asia," *Current History,* November 1972.

54. Statement of John P. Lewis to the Subcommittee on The Near East and South Asia, *op. cit.,* p. 125.

55. T. J. S. George, "South Asian Confederation," *Far Eastern Economic Review,* Feb. 12, 1972, p. 19.

56. *The Times* (London), Dec. 21, 1972.

57. *U.S. Foreign Policy for the 1970's,* A Report to Congress by Richard Nixon, President of the United States, May 3, 1973 (Washington: Government Printing Office, 1973).

58. See "Indo–U.S. Relations: The War and After," *Economic and Political Weekly,* Jan. 15, 1972, pp. 99–100.

59. *New York Times,* Feb. 9, 1973.

60. Palmer, "The United States and the New Order," *op. cit.*

61. Subcommittee on the Near East and South Asia, *op. cit.,* p. 89.

62. Choudhury, "U.S. Policy," *op. cit.*

63. *New York Times,* Dec. 16, 1973.

64. A. Hariharan, "A Time for Healing," *Far Eastern Economic Review,* Mar. 26, 1973.

65. Subcommittee on the Near East and South Asia, *op. cit.,* p. 21.

66. Hariharan, *op. cit.*

67. Nixon, *U.S. Foreign Policy, op. cit.*

68. Choudhury, "U.S. Policy," *op. cit.*

69. Bhutto, "Pakistan Builds," *op. cit.*

70. *Ibid.*

71. *Ibid.*

72. Hariharan, *op. cit.*

73. See *Dawn,* Nov. 9, 1972; Choudhury, *"New" Pakistan, op. cit.*

74. Nixon, *U.S. Foreign Policy, op. cit.*

75. See *Prime Minister Zulfikar Ali Bhutto's Visit to the United States of America: Statements and Speeches, September 18–23* (Islamabad: Ministry of Foreign Affairs, Government of Pakistan, 1973).

76. *Ibid.*

77. *New York Times* and *Washington Post,* Sept. 19–21, 1973.

78. Choudhury, *"New" Pakistan, op. cit.*

79. *Financial Times,* supplement on Bangladesh, Dec. 14, 1972.

80. *The Guardian,* Aug. 10, 1973.

81. *Far Eastern Economic Review,* Dec. 16, 1972.

82. T. K. Hussain, "Sino–Indian Relations," *Economic and Political Weekly,* Sept. 18, 1971.

83. *New York Times,* Feb. 28, 1972.

84. *Pakistan New Digest* (Islamabad), April 7, 1972.

85. *Pakistan Affairs* (Washington: Pakistani Embassy), Feb. 1, 1974.

86. For the text of the Simla agreement, signed by India and Pakistan on July 2, 1972, see *Simla Agreement* (New Delhi: Ministry of External Affairs, Government of India, n.d.). Also see Choudhury, *"New" Pakistan, op. cit.*

87. Choudhury, "Pakistan and the Communist World," *op. cit.*

88. Based on my research at the Royal Institute of International Affairs and Columbia University's Research Institute on Communist Affairs, 1971–1974.

89. *Bangladesh Observer,* Nov. 20, 1972.

90. *Sunday Times,* May 19, 1974.

91. *The Times* (London), May 20, 1974, and *The Guardian,* June 17, 1974.

92. See *Pravda* and *Izvestia,* May 20–25, 1974.

93. See *The Times* (London), editorial, *The Guardian,* and *New York Times,* May 20, 1974.

94. *The Times* (London), May 20, 1974.

95. *Ibid.*

96. *The Guardian,* May 22, 1974.

97. See *The Times* (London), May 30, 1974.

98. *Ibid.,* May 30 and June 27, 1974.

99. Based on my research and personal interviews in Pakistan, 1967–1971.

100. *Sunday Times*, May 19, 1974.

101. *Pakistan Affairs*, Oct. 1, 1974.

102. *Ibid.*, Oct. 16, 1974.

103. *New York Times*, Oct. 3, 1974, and *Pakistan Affairs, op. cit.*, Oct. 16, 1974.

104. *New York Times*, Oct. 29, 1974.

105. *Pakistan Affairs*, Oct. 16, 1974.

106. *New York Times*, Oct. 29, 1974.

107. *Ibid.*, Nov. 21, 1974.

108. See the report of the Sept. 16 press conference of UN Secretary-General Kurt Waldheim in *Pakistan Affairs, op. cit.*, Oct. 1, and, for concern expressed on Oct. 29 in the U.S. House of Representatives Committee on Foreign Affairs, *New York Times*, Oct. 30, 1974.

109. *New York Times*, Oct. 29, 1974.

110. *The Observer*, June 23, 1974, and *The Times* (London), June 24, 1974.

111. *U.S. News & World Report*, Sept. 23, 1974, pp. 78–79.

112. See G. W. Choudhury, "Bangladesh Today," *South Atlantic Quarterly*, Summer 1974, pp. 283–293.

113. For accounts of Bhutto's strange reception in Dacca, see *The Times* (London), June 28, 1974, and *The Guardian*, June 27, 1974.

114. *The Times* (London), May 1, 1974.

115. *Financial Times*, June 18, 1974.

116. Elaine Sterling, "Bangladesh," *Atlantic*, September 1974, pp. 4–16.

117. "Reconstruction and Economy of Bangladesh," an unpublished World Bank report, submitted October 13, 1972.

118. Sterling, *op. cit.*

119. *Sunday Times*, Oct. 27, 1974.

120. *New York Times*, July 12, 1974.

121. *Ibid.*

122. *Ibid.*, July 13, 1974.

123. *Ibid.*, July 15, 1974.

124. *Washington Post*, Sept. 24, 1974.

125. *Daily Telegraph*, June 3, 1974.

126. Based on my research at the Royal Institute of International Affairs and Columbia University's Research Institute on Communist Affairs, 1971–1974.

127. *Ibid.*

128. *The Statesman*, Sept. 11, 1974.

129. *The Guardian,* Mar. 4, 1974.

130. *Ibid.*

131. *The Guardian,* March 4, 1974.

132. *New York Times,* May 9, 1974.

133. Based on my research at the Royal Institute of International Affairs and Columbia University's Research Institute on Communist Affairs, 1971–1974.

134. See Choudhury, "Bangladesh Today," *op. cit.*

135. *Dawn,* Oct. 25, 1974.

136. *Ibid.,* Oct. 27, 1974.

137. *New York Times,* Oct. 25, 1974.

138. See Choudhury, "Communist World," *op. cit.*

139. *Ibid.*

140. *Dawn,* May 18, 1974.

141. *New York Times,* Mar. 31, 1974.

142. *Ibid.,* Oct. 3, 1974.

143. *Ibid.*

144. *Pakistan News Digest* (Islamabad), Sept. 27, 1974.

145. *New York Times,* Sept. 28, 1974.

146. *Washington Post,* Sept. 25, 1974.

147. *Dawn,* Oct. 15, 1974, and *New York Times,* Oct. 17, 1974.

148. *Washington Post,* Oct. 2, 1974.

149. *New York Times,* Oct. 28, 1974.

150. *The Times* (London), Dec. 8, 1971.

151. *New York Times,* Oct. 29, 1974.

152. *Ibid.,* Oct. 30, 1974.

153. *Washington Post,* Nov. 1, 1974.

154. *Ibid.*

155. See *The Statesman,* Oct. 30, 1974, and *Dawn,* Nov. 1, 1974.

SELECTED BIBLIOGRAPHY

BOOKS AND REPORTS

BARNDS, WILLIAM J. *India, Pakistan and the Great Powers*. New York: Praeger for the Council on Foreign Relations, 1972.

BARNETT, A. DOAK. *Communist China and Asia: Challenges to American Policy*. New York: Harper for the Council on Foreign Relations, 1960.

————. *A New U.S. Policy toward China*. Washington: Brookings, 1971.

————, and EDWIN REISCHAUER. *The United States and China: The Next Decade*. New York: Praeger, 1970.

BAZAZ, PREMNATH. *The History of Struggle for Freedom in Kashmir*. New Delhi: Kashmir Publishing Co., 1954.

BELL, CAROL. *The Asian Balance of Power: A Comparison with European Precedents*. Adelphi Paper No. 44. London: Institute for Strategic Studies, February 1968.

BERKES, ROSE N., and MOHINDER S. BEDI. *The Diplomacy of India: Indian Foreign Policy in the United Nations*. Stanford, Calif.: Stanford, 1958.

BHUTTO, Z. A. *Foreign Policy of Pakistan: A Compendium of Speeches Made in the National Assembly, 1962–1964*. Karachi: Interservice Press for Pakistan Institute of International Affairs, 1964.

————. *The Myth of Independence*. London: Oxford University Press, 1969.

————. *Speeches and Statements of the President of Pakistan: December 20, 1971–March 31, 1972*. Karachi: Department of Films and Publications, Government of Pakistan, 1972.

————. *Speeches before the Security Council, 1964*. Karachi: Ministry of Foreign Affairs, Government of Pakistan, n.d.

BIRWOOD, LORD. *Two Nations and Kashmir*. London: Hale, Ltd., 1953. Published in the United States as *India and Pakistan*. New York: Praeger, 1954.

BOWLES, CHESTER. *Ambassador's Report*. New York: Harper, 1954.

BRAIBANTI, RALPH. *International Implications of the Manila Pact*. New York: American Institute of Pacific Relations, 1957.

BRECHER, MICHAEL. *Nehru: A Political Biography*. London: Oxford University Press, 1959.

———. *The Struggle for Kashmir*. London: Oxford University Press, 1952.

BRINES, R. *The Indo–Pakistan Conflicts*. London: Pall Mall Press, Ltd., 1968.

BROWN, W. NORMAN. *The United States and India, Pakistan and Bangladesh*. Cambridge, Mass.: Harvard, 1972.

BRZEZINSKI, ZBIGNIEW. *Between Two Ages: America's Role in the Technetronic Era*. New York: Viking, 1970.

BUDHRAJ, V. S. *Soviet Russia and the Hindustan Subcontinent*. Bombay: Somaiya Publications Ltd., 1973.

BURKE, S. M. *Pakistan's Foreign Policy: An Historical Analysis*. London: Oxford University Press, 1973.

CALLARD, KEITH. *Pakistan's Foreign Policy: An Interpretation*, 2d ed., revised and enlarged. New York: Institute of Pacific Relations, 1959.

CAMPBELL, JOHN C. *Defense of the Middle East: Problems of American Policy*, revised ed. New York: Praeger, 1960.

CHANKSHAW, EDWARD. *The New Cold War: Moscow vs. Peking*. Baltimore: Penguin, 1963.

CHAUDHURI, NIRAD C. *The Continent of Circe: Being an Essay on The Peoples of India*. New York: Oxford University Press, 1966.

CHOUDHURI, MOHAMMED AHSAN. *Pakistan and The Great Powers*. Karachi: Mirror Press for Council for Pakistan Studies in cooperation with the University of Karachi, 1970.

———. *Pakistan and the Regional Pacts*. Karachi: East Publications, 1958.

CHOUDHURY, G. W. *The Last Days of United Pakistan*. Bloomington: Indiana University Press, 1974.

———. *Pakistan's Relations with India*. New York: Praeger, 1968.

———, and PARVEZ HASAN. *Pakistan's External Relations*. Karachi: Din Mohammed Press for the Pakistan Institute of International Affairs, 1968.

DALLIN, DAVID J. *The Changing World of Soviet Russia*. New Haven, Conn.: Yale, 1956.

———. *Soviet Foreign Policy after Stalin*. Philadelphia: Lippincott, 1961.

DAS GUPTA, J. B. *Indo–Pakistan Relations 1947–1955*. Amsterdam: Djambatan, 1958.

DEUTSCHER, ISAAC. *Russia, China & the West, 1953–1966*. Harmonds-worth, Middlesex, England: Penguin Book Ltd., 1970.

DRUHE, DAVID N. *Soviet Russia & the Indian Communist*. New York: Brookman Associates, 1959.

DUTT, D. SAM. *The Defence of India's Northern Borders*. Adelphi Paper No. 25. London: Institute for Strategic Studies, January 1966.

DUTT, V. P. *China & the World: An Analysis of Communist China's For-eign Policy*. New York: Praeger, 1966.

FELDMAN, HERBERT. *From Crisis to Crisis: Pakistan 1962–1969*. London: Oxford University Press, 1972.

FISCHER, LOUIS. *Russia, America and the World*. New York: Harper & Row, 1961.

FISHER, MARGARET W. and LEO E. ROSE. *The North-East Frontier Agency of India*. Washington: Bureau of Intelligence Research, 1967.

————, and ROBERT A. HUTTENBACK. *Himalayan Battle Ground: Sino–Indian Rivalry in Ladakh*. New York: Praeger, 1963.

FITZGERALD, C. P. *The Chinese View of their Place in the World*. Lon-don: Oxford University Press for the Royal Institute of International Affairs, 1969.

GALBRAITH, JOHN KENNETH. *Ambassador's Journal: A Personal Account of the Kennedy Years*. Boston: Houghton Mifflin, 1969.

GANDHI, INDIRA. *India & Bangla Desh: Selected Speeches & Statements, March–December 1971*. New Delhi: Orient Longman Ltd., 1972.

GITTINGS, JOHN. *Survey of the Sino–Soviet Dispute 1963–1967*. London: Oxford University Press, 1968.

GREENE, FELIX. *The Wall Has Two Sides*. London: Jonathan Cape, Ltd., 1965.

GREENE, FRED. *U.S. Policy and Security of Asia*. New York: McGraw-Hill for the Council on Foreign Relations, 1968.

GRIFFITH, WILLIAM E. *The Sino–Soviet Rift*. Cambridge, Mass.: M.I.T., 1964.

GUPTA, SISIR. *Kashmir*. Bombay: Asia Publishing House, 1966.

HALPERIN, A., ed. *Policies towards China: Views from Six Continents*. New York: McGraw-Hill, 1965.

HARRISON, SELIG S. *India: The Most Dangerous Decades*. Princeton, N.J.: Princeton, 1960.

HINTON, HAROLD. *Communist China and World Politics*. Boston: Hough-ton Mifflin, 1966.

HODSON, H. V. *The Great Divide: Britain–India–Pakistan*. London: Hutchinson, 1969.

HUTHEESINGH, KRISHNA, ed. *Nehru's Letters to His Sister*. London: Faber & Faber, Ltd., 1963.

Issacs, Harold. *Scratches on Our Minds: American Images of China & India*. New York: John Day, 1958.

Jinnah, Mohammed Ali. *Speeches as Governor-General of Pakistan, 1947–1948*. Karachi: Pakistan Publications, 1970.

Karuna-Karan, K. P. *India in World Affairs: August 1947–January 1950*. Bombay: Oxford University Press, 1958.

––––––. *India in World Affairs: February 1950–December 1955*. Bombay: Oxford University Press, 1952.

Kavic, Lorne J. *India's Quest for Security: Defense Policies, 1947–1955*. Berkeley: University of California Press, 1967.

Kennedy, D. E. *The Security of Southern Asia*. New York: Praeger, 1965.

Khan, Mohammed Ayub. *Friends Not Masters*. London: Oxford University Press, 1967.

––––––. *Speeches and Statements*. Six volumes. Karachi: Pakistan Publications, n.d.

Khan, Mohammed Zafrullah. *Pakistan's Foreign Policy*. Karachi: Pakistan Institute of International Affairs, 1951.

––––––. "Reminiscenses," unpublished manuscript. New York: History Research Office, Columbia University, 1962.

Kintner, William R. *The Impact of President Nixon's Visit to Peking on International Politics*. Research Monograph Series, No. 13. Philadelphia: Foreign Policy Research Institute, 1972.

Korbel, Josef. *Danger in Kashmir*, 2d ed. London: Oxford University Press, 1966.

Lamb, Alastair. *Asian Frontiers: Studies in a Continuing Problem*. London: Pall Mall Press, Ltd., 1968.

––––––. *The China–India Border*. London: Oxford University Press for the Royal Institute of International Affairs, 1964.

––––––. *Crisis in Kashmir: 1947–1966*. London: Routledge & Kegan Paul, Ltd., 1966.

Lamb, Beatrice P. *India: A World in Transition*. London: Pall Mall Press, Ltd., 1963.

Laqueur, Walter Z. *The Soviet Union & the Middle East*. New York: Praeger, 1959.

Lewis, John P. *Quiet Crisis in India: Economic Development & American Policy*. Washington: Brookings, 1962.

Lyon, Peter. "Foreign Policy of India." Chapter 8 of F. S. Northedge, ed., *The Foreign Policies of the Powers*. London: Faber & Faber, Ltd., 1968.

––––––. *India & Pakistan*. London: Routledge & Kegan Paul, Ltd., forthcoming.

––––––. *Neutralism*. Leicester, England: Leicester University Press, 1963.

Macridis, Roy C., ed. *Foreign Policies in World Politics*, 4th ed. Englewood Cliffs, N.J.: Prentice-Hall, 1972.

Mansergh, Nicholas, ed. *Documents and Speeches on Commonwealth Affairs 1931–1952*. London: Oxford University Press for the Royal Institute of International Affairs, 1953.

Maxwell, Neville. *India's China War*. London: Jonathan Cape, Ltd., 1970.

Millar, T. B. *The Indian and Pacific Oceans: Some Strategic Considerations*. Adelphi Paper No. 57. London: Institute for Strategic Studies, May 1969.

Miller, Bruce J. D. *The Politics of the Third World*. London: Oxford University Press for the Royal Institute of International Affairs, 1966.

Moorsteen, R., and Morton Abramowitz. *Remaking China Policy: U.S. China Relations and Governmental Decision-Making*. Cambridge, Mass.: Harvard, 1971.

Mosely, Philip E. *The Kremlin and World Politics*. New York: Vintage Books, 1960.

————, ed. *New Trends in Kremlin Policy*. Special Report Series, No. 11. Washington: The Center for Strategic and International Studies, Georgetown University, August, 1970.

Mustag, Ahmad. *Foreign Policy of Pakistan*. Karachi: Space Publishers, 1968.

————. *The United Nations and Pakistan*. Karachi: The Time Press for Pakistan Institute of International Affairs, 1955.

Myrdal, Gunnar. *Asian Drama: An Inquiry into the Poverty of Nations*. New York: Pantheon, 1968.

Naik, J. A. *India, Russia, China and Bangladesh*. New. Delhi: S. Chand and Co. Ltd., 1972.

————. *Soviet Policy towards India, from Stalin to Brezhnev*. New Delhi: Vikas Publications, 1971.

Neelhant, K. *Partners in Peace: A Study in Indo–Soviet Relations*. New Delhi: Vikas Publications, 1972.

Nehru, J. *The Discovery of India*. New York: John Day, 1946.

————. *India's Foreign Policy: Selected Speeches, September 1946–April 1961*. New Delhi: Ministry of Information and Broadcasting, Government of India, 1961.

Northedge, F. S. *The Foreign Policies of the Powers*. London: Faber & Faber, Ltd., 1968.

Palmer, Norman D. *Recent Soviet and Chinese Penetration in India and Pakistan: Guidelines for Political-Military Policy*. McLean, Va.: Research Analysis Corporation, 1970.

————. *South Asia and United States Policy.* Boston: Houghton Mifflin, 1966.

PANIKKAR, K. M. *In Two Chinas: Memoirs of a Diplomat.* London: George Allen & Unwin, Ltd., 1955.

PAPANEK, GUSTAV F. *Pakistan's Development: Social Goals and Private Incentives.* Cambridge, Mass.: Harvard, 1967.

RAHMAN, MUJIB. *Bangladesh, My Bangladesh: Selected Speeches and Statements.* Edited by Ramendu Majumder. New Delhi: Orient Longman, Ltd., 1972.

RAJAN, M. S. *India in World Affairs: 1954–1956.* Bombay: Asia Publishing House, 1964.

RAZI, M. *The Frontiers of Pakistan: A Study of Frontier Problem in Pakistan's Foreign Policy.* Karachi: National Publishing House, 1971.

REISCHAUER, EDWIN O. *Beyond Vietnam: The United States and Asia.* New York: Vintage Books, 1967.

SAGER, PETER. *Moscow's Hand in India: An Analysis of Soviet Propaganda.* Bombay: Lalvani Publishing, 1967.

SEN GUPTA, BHABANI. *Communism in Indian Politics.* New York: Columbia, 1972.

————. *Fulcrum of Asia: Relations among China, India, Pakistan and the USSR.* New York: Pegasus, 1970.

SETON-WATSON, HUGH. *From Lenin to Malenkov: The History of World Communism.* New York: Praeger, 1953.

SHARMA, B. L. *The Pakistan–China Axis.* Bombay: Asia Publishing House, 1968.

SHERWANI, LATIF AHMED. *India, China and Pakistan.* Karachi: Feroz Sons for the Council for Pakistan Studies, 1967.

————, et al. *Foreign Policy of Pakistan.* Karachi: Allies Book Corporation, 1964.

SIDDIQI, ASLAM. *Pakistan Seeks Security.* Lahore: Longmans, 1960.

SINGH, PATWANT. *India and the Future of Asia.* New York: Knopf, 1966.

SPANIER, JOHN. *American Foreign Policy since World War II,* 2d ed. New York: Praeger, 1965.

STEIN, ARTHUR. *India and the Soviet Union.* Chicago: The University of Chicago Press, 1969.

STEPHENS, IAN. *Pakistan.* New York: Praeger, 1963.

STOCKHOLM INTERNATIONAL PEACE RESEARCH INSTITUTE. *The Arms Trade with the Third World.* London: Paul Elek, Ltd., 1971.

SUBRAHMANYAM, K. *The Asian Balance of Power in the Seventies: An Indian View.* New Delhi: The Institute for Defence Studies and Analysis, 1968.

SUHRAWARDY, H. S. *Statements on Foreign Policy.* Karachi: Government of Pakistan, 1956.

TALBOT, PHILIPS, and S. L. POPLAI. *India and America: A Study of Their Relations.* New York: Harper & Row, 1958.

TAUSKY, LEO. *U.S. and USSR Aid to Developing Countries: A Comparative Study of India, Turkey and the UAR.* New York: Praeger, 1967.

VAN NESS, PETER. *Revolution and Chinese Foreign Policy: Peking's Support for Wars of National Liberation.* Berkeley: University of California Press, 1971.

VARMA, S. N. *Trends in India's Foreign Policy 1954–1957.* New Delhi: Indian Council of World Affairs, 1957.

WILCOX, WAYNE A. *Asia and United States Policy.* Englewood Cliffs, N.J.: Prentice-Hall, 1967.

————. "China's Strategic Alternatives in South Asia." In Tang Tsou, ed., *China's Policies in Asia and American Alternatives,* vol. II. Chicago: The University of Chicago Press, 1968.

————, et al. *Asia and the International System.* Cambridge, Mass.: Winthrop Publishers, Inc., 1972.

————. *India, Pakistan and the Rise of China.* New York: Walker, 1964.

WRIGGINS, HOWARD. *South and Southeast Asia in the Asian State System.* New York: Southern Asian Institute, Columbia University, 1971.

ZAGORIA, DONALD S. *The Sino–Soviet Conflict, 1956–1961.* Princeton, N.J.: Princeton, 1961.

PERIODICALS

Asian Survey (Berkeley, Calif.)

Central Asian Review (London)

China Quarterly (London)

Foreign Affairs (New York)

International Affairs (London)

International Affairs (Moscow)

India Quarterly (New Delhi)

International Studies (New Delhi)

Orbis (Philadelphia)

Pacific Affairs (Vancouver)

Pacific Community (Tokyo)

Round Table (London)

INDEX